I Heard You Singing

I Heard You Singing

My Life with Ramon Opie

Corinne Bridge-Opie

Foreword by Donald Munro

BRIDGEPRESS

Foreword

I am delighted to have been asked to write this Foreword. Corinne Opie has been a loyal friend down the years and a faithful servant of music in New Zealand.

I first met Corinne Bridge, as she was in those days, in Wellington when she was aged twenty. She was a promising young mezzo-soprano, fresh faced and eager and I was in the throes of consolidating the New Zealand Opera Company after a successful enough first season. I offered Corinne a role in *The Medium* which she declined, telling me she was not ready for such a step in the world. Corinne remembers I was slightly disappointed with her decision, feeling that she was not making the most of her opportunities. I seem to remember my reaction was somewhat stronger, but I'll defer to Corinne's memory on this one. Two years later, I offered her the role of Vera Boronel in *The Consul* (also by Menotti) and this time she didn't let anyone down, including herself.

Even in those days – which take me back further than I care to remember at my age – she had a lovely voice with a rich, full tone, and it is not surprising that she was recognised with the award of a NZ Government Bursary to study overseas. However, the big OE is not always what it's cracked up to be, and she had the misfortune to be assigned to the wrong teacher at the Guildhall School of Music. When I arrived in England in 1959 to study opera production at Glyndebourne, Corinne's voice was at the point of disintegration. I directed her to Clive Carey for advice. Corinne's force of character – never to be trifled with – enabled her to prevail upon the resentful Guildhall authorities to accept that she simply must have a new teacher.

Returning to New Zealand, Corinne became the New Zealand

Opera Company's leading mezzo, performing many memorable roles and finding the love of her life, that marvellous tenor, Ramon Opie. I have always maintained that New Zealand has the home-grown singing talent to stage almost any opera in the classical repertoire. This was amply demonstrated by the production of Wagner's *Parsifal* at the 2006 New Zealand International Arts Festival. Every role was filled by a New Zealander and they gave superlative performances at Wellington's Michael Fowler Centre with an ease that disguised effort. The fact remains that such levels of accomplishment do not spring from nowhere but are the result of a long tradition of carefully nurtured excellence. Corinne Bridge-Opie's single-minded commitment to her art and craft exemplifies why New Zealand opera is in such good health.

Donald Munro
Founder of the New Zealand Opera Company (1954–1971)

Acknowledgements

Several chapters of this book had been written before I realised that it might be wise to study the skills of writing – rather like being able to sing but needing to know how to use the voice correctly. The Centre for Continuing Education Faculty of Arts at the University of Auckland offers Life Writing courses, tutored by Dr Deborah Shepard, and I attended three of these. Deborah was most helpful and encouraging, as was another tutor, Jocelyn Watkin. Deborah and Jocelyn provided the necessary assurance that completing a book and getting it into print was do-able and I thank them both.

Deborah suggested that I join the New Zealand Society of Authors, which proved a source of valuable assistance. I submitted the first 6000 words of my manuscript to the NZSA for appraisal and they wisely selected Wellington author Julia Millen to do this. Julia has also written the libretti for two New Zealand operas, so who better to consider my literary efforts. She kindly agreed to let me quote her words on the cover, for which I am most appreciative.

A long-standing associate, Max Cryer, had no hesitation in agreeing to help as well. Max's association with Ray goes back a long way to when, as a young man, he was one of Ray's accompanists. Thank you, Max, for your kindness and support, both now and over the years.

Of the many students who attended Deborah's courses, sixteen of us still get together each month to share our latest writing endeavours and make suggestions that will improve them. This has been invaluable, and I thank my wonderful writing buddies, particularly Colin Radford who also makes sure I have transport to our meetings.

While I had dozens of cartons of programmes, press reviews, letters, diaries, and all manner of other material covering Ray's later career and my own, it was still necessary to carry out research. Various libraries and individuals assisted in this regard, and I can thoroughly recommend the National Library of New Zealand's website *Papers Past*. To find a review there of my mother's first 1927 recital in New Zealand, more than eighty years after the event, was hugely exciting. Particular thanks go to Cathy Bentley, Music Archivist, Archive of New Zealand Music at the Alexander Turnbull Library (now part of the National Library), and other staff there who pointed me in the right direction. An amazing find in their records was four huge files containing press reviews, interviews and photographs of the New Zealand Opera Quartet, most of which I had never seen before. While mentioning the Quartet, a special thank you goes to Kathleen Johnson who searched out an original photograph of the four of us that I very much wanted.

Marilyn Portman, Music Librarian at the Auckland Public Library, was exceptionally helpful. Although much of the Library's reference material is now on-line, I still needed her help to locate early newspaper articles. Nothing was too much trouble for Marilyn and I am most grateful to her.

Long-standing friend and music associate, Les Andrews, introduced me to his sister-in-law, Anne Rennie (née Campbell), who studied with Ray's first singing teacher, Lilian McDonald, in Timaru. Anne kindly sent photographs and an obituary notice for Lilian, as well as her own personal recollections of Lilian's singing career. My thanks go to Les and Anne.

Other friends whose help, advice and assistance have been much appreciated are Olwyn Keymer, Jill Roberts, Simon Grant, Susannah MacDonald and Allison Elliott. Olwyn checked the entire manuscript for errors and Jill, who lived in the UK during World War Two, also helped with checking and clarified my recollections of the war years. Simon allowed me to include the verses written by his mother, Lee Dowrick-Grant, and Susannah agreed to the inclusion of her wonderful cartoon. Allison was the first person just to read the book and give me feedback from a reader's point of view.

The old adage about not judging a book by its cover is only partly true. An arresting cover will certainly inspire interest as to what lies within, and I am deeply appreciative of the excellent work done by award-winning graphic design artist, Katy Yiakmis.

To anyone I have missed, my apologies. The greatest vote of thanks, however, goes to Ian Watt who, as well as editing the manuscript, has patiently guided me through the process of publication and put up with my constant emails. Nothing is too much trouble for Ian and without his assistance, this book, while probably still getting to print, would certainly not have reached the standard I so much wanted it to have. I am forever in your debt, Ian.

Prologue

A glib expression constantly heard these days worries me. It's just two words: *move on.* It is used to cover everything from avoiding responsibility for wrongdoing or social embarrassment, to being offered as a somewhat ironical form of condolence during a time of deep unhappiness. In my experience, it is not so easy to resolve life's difficulties by simply moving on. I am grateful nobody tried to console me with this advice when, after our 31 years of music, love and laughter together, my beloved husband Ramon passed away four months before my 61st birthday. The devastating challenge for me at that point was how to move on.

I did all the things one is supposed to avoid during the grieving process. In an attempt to start life anew, I sold our Auckland home and returned to Wellington, the city of my birth. Friends there, with a large garden they wished to sub-divide, were delighted when I expressed interest in buying the land and before long my new residence, with views to the sea, was being built behind theirs. I became deeply engrossed in trying to decipher architectural plans and make appropriate decisions about everything from joinery, roof and exterior colours to such mundane things as where the power points, television aerial sockets and telephone jack-points would be best situated in each room. Once the shell of the house was completed, the interior fittings, colours, floor and window coverings and so on had to be chosen. When I moved in, the external landscaping had to be resolved, taking Wellington's famous wind and my garden's proximity to sand and surf into consideration. I was immersed in a whole new world of experiences, trying desperately hard to *move on.* But it didn't work. Deep down the pain and loneliness remained, as did the lack of any real purpose in a life without Ray.

I continued to sing occasionally through my involvement with two very different musical groups. The lighter one entertained at various Wellington community gatherings such as support group functions, social clubs, rest homes, retirement villages, or in fact wherever we were wanted. The other was entirely made up of professional singers who presented occasional classical music concerts or unstaged versions of opera. When it first became known that I might be returning to Wellington, I was engaged to sing a very familiar role for me, the Mother Abbess in a short season of *The Sound of Music* at the St James Theatre. But singing wasn't the same pleasure now without Ray either performing beside me or giving backstage support.

I noticed an article in a suburban newspaper which invited the submission of entries into a smart animal story competition. The article stated the publisher's objective was to produce 'entertaining, reader-contributed books that give something back to society. Profit from sales would go to the SPCA.' The publisher's email address was supplied so, having recently bought a computer, I nonchalantly decided to try my luck. For some strange reason, sending a story by email didn't seem quite so daunting as writing or typing it on a piece of paper, enclosing it an envelope and mailing it, and it was certainly much easier. I typed a tale about a childhood pet and blithely clicked the 'send' button, assuring myself that if there was no reply, or I received the typical theatrical response ('don't call us, we'll call you'), it wouldn't matter.

But there was an immediate answer advising that the publisher liked the story and it would be considered with other submissions at the end of a three-month deadline period. This was encouraging, but an even more exciting letter came later to confirm that my story was definitely to be included in the initial book of what would become an ongoing series. For the first time since Ray died, I felt happy about something. This small attempt at writing anything other than work-related reports, newsletters, programme notes or introductions to concerts had been successful. Was writing the key to *moving on*? I desperately wanted to tell Ray my good news but perhaps, somehow, he already knew.

If writing was the panacea, what should I write about? That

decision was easy. While a limited number of books have been written covering prominent New Zealand musicians, composers, opera companies, choral societies and orchestras, these tend to be mainly academic records covering their history and achievements. I wanted to relate the day-to-day experiences of two singers, Ray and me, trying to forge professional careers in a country which generally respects its sports stars far more than anyone involved in the arts. Soon after I started writing the book, a friend asked me what it was about. I tried to explain that it wasn't just a list of what and where we sang and with whom, but more a 'behind the scenes' account of our musical lives. 'Sounds good,' he said. 'The other side of singing.'

At the same time, I began to realise that it had been a mistake to leave the city where Ray and I had spent most of our time together, so I sold my new house and returned to Auckland. I needed the warmth and comfort it gave me whenever our friends there talked about him, recalling his outrageous sense of humour and irresistible joy of living. I wanted to keep experiencing that inner glow of pride when people told me how much they admired and now missed his magnificent voice. While it's pointless to dwell too much in the past, there is wonderful healing in sharing memories of the person you have most treasured.

The book has taken over six years to complete, largely because I've found myself almost loath to finish it. There's probably some deep psychological significance in this: perhaps I'm avoiding *closure,* another word so often inappropriately used. But time is marching on and the final chapter had to be written. And somewhere, behind the scenes, an insistent and much-loved voice was urging me to 'Get on with it, darling. Tell our story.'

Chapter 1

Songs, ships and wartime

'If you don't go out there and sing for the soldiers, I'll never ask you to sing with us again.' It is wartime Britain, I am eight years old, dressed in my Sunday best, and my mother is desperately trying to persuade me to walk on to the largest stage I have ever seen. The venue is an Odeon Cinema in Brighton, where my father has arranged a concert for the Allied Forces servicemen on leave there. The cinema seats at least a thousand and the 'House Full' signs are out. A massive grand piano, lit by a long row of footlights and resembling a huge, black, one-winged monster with masses of teeth, lurks centre-stage, while a hovering spotlight menacingly chases every movement. I am absolutely petrified. Perhaps I should explain how a 'Kiwi kid' came to be here in the first place.

My parents, Nora Evelyn Greene (born on 13 April 1904 in London) and William Arthur Bridge (born on 7 December 1899 in London), married on 3 February 1927 and immigrated to New Zealand soon after their wedding. Both were singers, Mum a contralto, Dad a tenor. My mother came from an exceedingly musical family. Her parents, all six brothers and one sister were able to sing or play an instrument, often both. As a young man her father, Harold Greene, had been a tenor in the choir of the Chapel Royal, Sandringham, but became better known to the general public during the First World War when he toured the Music Halls in an act called The Four Tommies. Grandma Greene was a contralto, singing under the professional name of Isabel Wallace Wilson. She played the piano and also hand-bells on which, she told me proudly, she had once performed for Queen Victoria. Her bells fascinated me from the moment I saw them, as they did my mother when she was a child. Made of brightly polished brass and topped with a thick, brown leather handle, each differently sized bell nestled snugly in its own special compartment of a worn leather case lined with faded red velvet. Mum and I longed to possess those bells, but we never found out what happened to them after Grandma died.

My mother, her brother Eric (tenor) and sister Dorothy (soprano) each won scholarships to study singing and piano at the Royal Academy of Music, London, and all three went on to have professional vocal careers. It was Uncle Eric who introduced his youngest sister to another handsome young tenor and would later be best man at their wedding.

After a leisurely honeymoon on their long voyage to New Zealand, my parents arrived in Wellington and eventually settled in the windswept seaside suburb of Island Bay. They found a large community of Italian migrants in this rugged coastal area, many of them fishermen like their fathers back home in Naples. The opera-loving Neapolitans were delighted to discover that these English newcomers were classically trained singers, and welcomed them with great enthusiasm. Mum's only experience with the Italian language at this stage was from the operatic arias and romantic *Arie Antiche* (ancient arias) which she sang, but when she decided to study it in more depth to improve her pronunciation and make it easier to communicate with her new friends, they were willing helpers.

Singing under her maiden name, Nora Greene, my mother gave her first New Zealand recital on the 14 May 1927 in the Wellington Town Hall's Concert Chamber. *The Evening Post* reviewer commented: 'Miss Greene has a warm, beautiful voice, not as full as usual in the lower register but marked by characteristics of the best contraltos we have heard here.'[1]

My father sang under the professional name of William

Renshaw, Renshaw being a family name, and he and Mum soon became busily involved in the New Zealand music scene over the next twelve years. Their engagements included performing as oratorio soloists with various choral and orchestral societies, not only in Wellington and nearby Lower Hutt, but further afield in Levin, Shannon, Napier, New Plymouth, Hawera and Nelson as well. Familiar works in their repertoire were Handel's *The Messiah,* Mendelssohn's *St Paul* and *Elijah,* and Stainer's *The Crucifixion,* and a popular light opera, Edward German's *Merrie England.* (Family history would be repeated when I performed this last work for my professional debut some 27 years later.) They were also frequent guest artists at the many variety concerts so fashionable during that era. These included band concerts in Wellington presented by the Port Nicholson Band and the Wellington Municipal Tramways Band, at such venues as the De Luxe Theatre (currently the Embassy Cinema,) His Majesty's Theatre (now demolished) and the Town Hall.

Besides their individual singing careers, Dad formed a vocal quartet in which he and Mum were joined by soprano Amy Dunn and baritone Tom Wood. The William Renshaw Quartet's versatile mix of solos, duets, trios and quartets proved highly acceptable to its audiences and the four singers were in constant demand for concert and later radio programmes. Tom Wood's career included writing music reviews for *The Evening Post,* choral conducting and twenty years as a singing teacher. His most outstanding pupil, tenor Ramon Opie, would many years later become my husband.

On 16 July 1927, the New Zealand Prime Minister, the Rt. Hon J. Gordon Coates, launched the Wellington radio station 2YA, 'before a gathering of state and civic dignitaries, invited guests and broadcasting staff.'[2] Mum and Dad were two of the artists engaged for this historic ceremony, which began with the 8 o'clock chimes from the Wellington General Post Office clock. The venue was Studio B of the new broadcasting premises on the corner of Waring Taylor and Featherston Streets. The premises were 'new' 'only in the sense that broadcasting was occupying them for the first time. As the Wellesley Club, the building had already seen a good many years service. 2YA would be the most powerful radio station in the Southern Hemisphere at that time and the second most powerful in the British Empire.'[3] I still have the original programme for this event and my mother sang four songs, one of which was the perennial favourite 'My Ain Folk', while Dad sang 'The Old Spinet' and 'Passing By'. Other artists taking part were violin and flute soloists, instrumental trios, the Salvation Army Citadel Silver Band and the Wellington Municipal Tramways Band, as well as three other singers, one of whom – the bass Lucien Cesaroni – was another prominent vocal teacher in Wellington. The musical director was H. Temple White, who continued to be musically involved with my parents over the next few years.

One interesting item in Mum's scrapbook concerning the early days of broadcasting in Wellington is a letter from a listener in Eketahuna, Miss Constance M. Wilson, who says:

> Congratulations on last night's solos, per medium 2YA. On hearing you and Mr Renshaw sing, I was carried back to the evening last May, the night of your recital in Wellington. Hoping you can favour us again, as wireless takes the place of recitals in this small town.

The address is District High School, Eketahuna and the letter is dated 17 July 1927.

Another item in the scrapbook is a newspaper cutting headed '2YA Heard in Iowa – Record Long-Distance Reception':

> The latest mail from America and Canada brings reports of the far range of the New Zealand stations. The change to the shorter days in the Northern Hemisphere is no doubt greatly responsible for the improved reception. The reports show that an increasing number of people in the Eastern States of America and in Canada are sitting up till the early hours of the morning to listen-in to New Zealand.
>
> The record long-distance report comes from Iowa, where Mr F.W. Work of Tiffin reports having heard 2YA and specially mentions the singing of Miss Nora Greene. He remarks on the

> reception by his seven-valve set, 'Sometimes the programme came in so loud on the speaker that it could easily be heard all over a large nine-roomed house and then would completely fade away.'

Mum and Dad became regular broadcasters, either as soloists or with the quartet, and in a manner that would be considered most eccentric these days, they and 2YA's chief announcer during the 1920s and 30s, Clive Drummond, who usually introduced their programmes, were always immaculately attired in evening dress when 'On Air'.

I was born on 8 January 1935. My parents' hopes that I might have inherited some musical ability were immediately realised when a nurse at the maternity hospital where I made my first appearance told my mother: 'This one is certainly going to be a singer; she has the loudest bawl of any baby here.'

Following in the family footsteps, I was soon performing my 'party pieces' with great aplomb. Whether this was because I really wanted to sing or that Mum and Dad were simply encouraging me to do so, I've never decided: the attention my efforts received was probably the attraction. Whatever the reason, I won my first singing competition at the age of four and this was recorded in *The Evening Post* under a section headed 'Vocal – clever little winners'.[4] Besides receiving a prize, I had to perform my winning song, 'Smilin' Through', on the 2YA Children's Hour programme. This is the first time I can remember being a 'prima donna' and refusing to sing unless Daddy was in the broadcasting studio as well. He obliged, so with my mother playing the piano accompaniment and me standing on a chair because I was too small to reach the microphone, he held my hand while I sang.

Ignoring the rumours of a possible war in Europe and perhaps homesick to be nearer their loved ones in England, my parents decided to return to Britain that same year, 1939. By early July we were aboard the Orient Line's Steam Ship *Oronsay*, and I was on my first big journey to the other side of the world. The ship called at several ports including Naples, where we were generously entertained by some of our Island Bay friends' relatives. All I can remember about this visit is that while I loved the delicious spaghetti we were served, Mum hated the fact that everything seemed to be 'swimming in olive oil'. Naples was the first port I had been allowed ashore after we left the Australian ports, as I had been taken ill with impetigo and immediately quarantined. This highly contagious disease spread quickly among the younger children on board, so when the ship docked at some exotic port and our parents went ashore to see the sights, all we young ones could do was gaze wistfully from the deck, our faces and bodies copiously splotched with gentian violet. We reached the port of Southampton only a few days before the Prime Minister, Neville Chamberlain, announced through the static of a radio broadcast from 10 Downing Street that 'Britain is now at war with Germany'. Three years later we would hear that the *Oronsay* had been torpedoed and sunk off Liberia while operating as a troop ship.

We initially stayed with my maternal grandparents in Leytonstone, London, and an entire family get-together was arranged to welcome us soon after we arrived. With so many musicians in the family, this inevitably turned into an impromptu concert. Seated on my mother's lap in the front parlour, I listened wide-eyed and attentive to the items enthusiastically performed by my newly met relatives. First Uncle Les, Mum's best-loved brother, sang about the 'Fisherman of England' going down to the sea in ships; I knew all about ships now so I enjoyed this one. Auntie Dorrie then blithely chirped about her heart being 'like a singing bird' because it's her birthday. I couldn't make much sense of that and asked Mum if it was really Auntie Dorrie's birthday; she whispered back 'No, darling. That's just what the song is called.' Grandpa's contribution was very sad and romantic, all about someone he once loved called his beautiful 'Annabelle Lee', but she died. I wondered if he was really singing this for Grandma as he always spoke of her as 'my darling Bella'. I looked after Mummy's chair while she and Dad sang a duet, harmoniously lamenting that 'Life's long dream is o'er, farewell', which of course I'd heard them sing before, and then Uncle Cyril entertained with a violin solo. At last it was my turn. I shyly sang that I was 'Daddy's sweetheart', but wouldn't be able to marry him when I grew up because he's 'already married to

Mummy'. This went down well, so I was encouraged to give an encore. Feeling more confident this time, I decided to show off a little by performing my favourite song 'Christopher Robin is saying his prayers' with plenty of actions, just to add a touch of drama. Mum played the piano for my songs but everyone else was accompanied by either Uncle Eric or Grandma and, joy of joys because I'd been really good, Grandma brought out her bells and let me strap one on and give it a resounding clang whenever she gave me the nod. Finally, Uncle Eric sang 'The faery song' just for me. I was very much in awe of Uncle Eric; he was the really famous singer in the family.[5]

Soon after war was declared, my father enlisted with the First Echelon of the New Zealand Forces and transferred to the Military Training Camp at Aldershot. Dad had also served in the First World War, joining up as a Probationary Flight Officer with the Royal Naval Air Service on becoming eligible in 1917; by Christmas of that year he was stationed in France. To enlist in 1939 he had to be a little 'creative' about his age, but the army still accepted him when the truth was revealed. Dad gained an immediate commission and served with the 34th Anti-Tank Battery. It wouldn't be long before this group of gunners, or the Hollywood Battery, as they called themselves, left for the Western Desert. His luck held throughout both world wars for, despite being shot down while flying over France in World War One and torpedoed on the *Empress of Japan* in World War Two, he survived to tell the tale.

In the early months of the war, children up to the age of 11 and other vulnerable citizens living in the larger British cities were being evacuated to more remote and hopefully safer parts of the country. The anticipation was that densely populated areas would be targeted for massive enemy attack and relocation of those least able to protect themselves would help make the inevitable rescue work easier. With Dad due to go overseas and the expectation that I could be sent miles away to some isolated spot in Britain, it became obvious that Mum, Dad and I were about to be completely separated. I guess it was this, together with the sight of miserable young children labelled like parcels and clutching little gas-masks as they waited forlornly on railway or bus station platforms to be collected by strangers, which convinced my mother to move us both out of London. Why she chose to live in Bognor Regis on the south-east coast of England is one of the many questions I wish I could still ask her. She obviously thought we'd be safer in this popular holiday resort and couldn't have anticipated that it would be constantly battered by bombs throughout the war. Could it have been the fact that one of her brothers, my Uncle Reg, was living there with his family, or did its seaside location vaguely remind her of more peaceful times in Wellington's Island Bay?

As soon as I turned five it was time to start school. I lasted just two days at the first one, through being teased about my New Zealand accent. Still the budding 'prima donna', I refused to go back there and after checking the other options, Mum found a place for me at the local convent. Villa Maria was normally a boarding school but for understandable reasons took only day students during the war years. Four other Protestant children attended Villa Maria when I was there, but the daily teaching routine remained the same for everyone, apart from one period when we did Bible studies while the Catholic students studied catechism. I loved my five years at the convent and the nuns who taught us. I particularly enjoyed being taken to the Catholic Church to admire the decorations for special saints' days and festivals, especially at Christmas when a life-size nativity tableau almost filled the nave, complete with the Virgin Mary, Joseph, three kings, shepherds, lambs, straw, donkey and a manger containing a 'real' baby Jesus, as I told my mother. The only thing I loathed at the convent was the Friday midday meal. It consisted of a small piece of smelly fish covered in thin white sauce with a few rounds of limp orange carrot floating in it; I had to eat it, but have not willingly eaten fish in white sauce again.

Besides studying all the usual subjects at Villa Maria, we were taught the ladylike assets of good posture, fine handwriting, delicate hand-embroidery and an appreciation of the arts. I continued to be a 'prima donna' and was often in trouble throughout my school years for talking when I should be listening and generally being disruptive. But the nuns had taken a great liking to my mother and her musical abilities, so whenever I got into trouble and had to report to the Mother Superior, I was gently advised to 'learn to behave like a good girl and grow up to be a gracious lady like your mother'.

Bognor Regis, situated in West Sussex, received more than its fair share of bombing during World War Two. In the earlier years there were regular attacks by small groups of German aircraft, particularly during daylight hours. Arriving too quickly for an air raid warning siren to be sounded, the fighter-bombers flew in from the coast, dropped their 500 or 1000 lb bombs on a school or public building, machine-gunned people in the main streets and then made a run for it. These raids earned the appropriate title of 'tip and run' raids and were largely carried out by inexperienced young airmen. They managed to do a great deal of damage in the brief time they flew over the town, but many were shot down before they could get away out to sea again. Ironically, the remains of German pilots killed in this way would sometimes be buried in the same cemeteries as their victims.

Hitler's next menace was a pilotless plane, known as the V-1 or flying bomb. These bombs, or 'doodlebugs', to use the nickname they were given in Britain, made a loud throbbing noise as they chugged overhead. We eventually became somewhat blasé about the need to take shelter while that chilling sound could still be heard. They were usually destined for London and not expected to fall before reaching the metropolis; while this made us slightly less fearful for our own fate, we realised sadly that the beleaguered capital was 'for it' again. If the sound stopped, however, the doodlebugs simply dropped from the sky and we made a beeline for safety. Hitler later found another weapon to torment us, the V-2, shaped like a rocket and silent in its approach. These were far more frightening as there was no indication of where they would fall, and they had to be visible before the alarm could be given. As a result, there was often insufficient time to seek shelter. The V-2s triggered loud explosions and caused devastating damage when they fell, and the toll from their attacks was considerable.

One pleasant spring morning in May 1941, my mother caught an early morning train to London where she had an engagement to sing at the Queen's Hall later that day. This famous concert venue was much renowned both for its perfect acoustics and for being the place where Promenade Concerts first began in 1895. She arrived safely at London's Victoria Station, only to be met by the concert organisers and advised to catch the next train back to Bognor. During the night, a major incendiary bomb attack had completely destroyed the 3000-seat hall; it was still on fire, and other prominent buildings including the Houses of Parliament and the British Museum had also been damaged during the attack. Photographs of the Queen's Hall taken a few days after the fires were finally extinguished showed that little remained of it other than fractured and uneven sections of the walls. Originally a circular building, it now resembled a small, rubble-filled Roman arena. The loss of the hall caused such distress that a suggestion was made to leave it permanently in this state of ruin as a memorial.

One school in the Bognor region was totally wiped out by a doodlebug, resulting in the deaths of at least 300 children. Mine had a lucky escape when a bomb dropped during a 'tip and run' raid landed in the Villa Maria grounds, missing the assembly hall where we were gathered for prayers by a few yards. As soon as the nuns became aware that an air raid was in progress, they told us to lie face down on the floor and did what they could to protect us. When the bomb fell, it shattered every window in the hall and we were peppered with splinters of broken glass. Our prayers must have been heard, as I don't recall anyone being too badly hurt. But while the school buildings also remained standing, the playground was one huge crater.

When this German aircraft had completed its attack and the 'All Clear' siren sounded, we were instructed to make our way carefully back to the classrooms, where any cuts or other problems could be attended to while we waited for our families to collect us. That took some time, as many parts of Bognor were badly damaged and several streets completely cut off, making it difficult to reach the school. Very few people owned cars in those days, or if they did, there was little petrol for private use. We either rode bicycles or walked. I was among the last in my class to be collected and was desperately upset by the time my mother arrived, terrified she might have been injured, or worse, during the raid.

We gingerly started for home, being diverted several times by members of the Home Guard or Police where there were road blocks or injured people receiving treatment. As we passed the local Boots chemist shop Mum suddenly spun me around, pressing me against her coat to prevent me seeing what was about to happen. The shop's plate-glass window had been shattered, and a young female assistant was trying to retrieve undamaged stock from the window display when a jagged piece of glass above her dislodged and fell on her bending head. Thanks to my mother's quick action I didn't see the horrific result of this, but it must have tormented her dreams, as she cried out in the night for many weeks afterwards.

Children are amazingly resilient, however, and my young friends and I were delighted to be given an extra-long holiday from school while the bomb damage was being repaired. The fact that we found ways to entertain ourselves despite the dangers of wartime astonishes me when I think of it now. Our gas-masks were a great source of fun. We put them on and pretended we were underwater explorers weaving our way through faraway tropical reefs, or alien creatures stomping around some distant planet. Even the air-raid shelters provided us with amusement.

Most homes in England had some form of shelter. Houses with a sufficiently large garden had a 'dug-out' containing a corrugated-iron Anderson shelter that could accommodate up to six people. Probably more common was the inside Morrison or table-shelter, which occupied a great deal of space in either the dining room or parlour. While it doubled as a table, the Morrison was actually a large steel cage with heavy wire-mesh sides, one of which could be raised to allow two or three adults to crawl in and sleep on a mattress that was permanently kept there. We had a Morrison and if we were at home during an air-raid, we quickly huddled together inside our 'cage', making sure the adjustable side was securely fastened behind us. The theory was that if the house were bombed we might be buried under the rubble for some time, but could hopefully survive until we were rescued. Had there been a fire, however, I guess we'd have been well and truly roasted when our cage became a red-hot oven.

Emergency items were kept in the shelters, including First Aid boxes and bottles of water. But the Morrison made an excellent playhouse for children and our favourite game was to play 'zoos' there, prowling around on all fours and roaring like lions and tigers. When that got boring, we tried being monkeys or King Kong gorillas, with much chest-pounding, teeth-gnashing and under-arm scratching, and giggled while we carefully inspected each other's 'fur' for fleas which we then pretended to eat. Mum sang a silly song to us when we played 'zoos'. It went something like this:

> That's the way to the Zoo, that's the way to the Zoo;
> The monkey house is nearly full, but there's room enough
> for you.
> Take a bus to Regent's Park, make haste before it shuts;
> Next Sunday I will come and bring you such a bunch of nuts!

Mothers with only one child got together at night to share a shelter, and as two other such families lived in our street, we took turns at spending alternate weeks together in one of our homes. In the event of an air raid, our mothers were on a roster to carry out street warden duties. Immediately the warning siren sounded, two of them put on metal safety hats and white armbands, slung gas-masks over their shoulders and went out to make sure every house in the street was obeying the black-out rules, with no chinks of light or other identity signs showing. The third mother stayed to look after the children, hastily tucking us up together inside the Morrison shelter. This worked well and allowed the women to get on with their duties without worrying too much about the care of their young ones.

Besides being heavily rationed, food was in short supply and there were no treats like lollies, ice cream or chocolate. However, the chemist shops sold little tins of Ovaltine tablets which I loved. I can't remember if these tablets were covered by our ration book coupon allowance, but I do recall being given pocket money to buy them when they were in stock. A little song about Ovaltine played on the radio during the BBC's Children's Hour programmes and I merrily joined in. The words were as follows:

> We are the Ovalteenies, little girls and boys,
> Make your request we'll not refuse you,
> We are here just to amuse you.
> Would you like a song or story,
> Will you share our joys?
> Because we all drink Ovaltine
> We're happy girls and boys.

It was splendid when the Americans joined the battle and were on leave in Britain, as they seemed to have an endless supply of restricted or unavailable luxuries to give away. These included silk stockings for the young women and all kinds of mouth-watering candies, chewing gum and chocolate for the children. These were like manna from heaven.

Mum's records of the war years contain many examples of the severe food rationing we experienced from 1940 until our return to New Zealand in 1946. She details the monotony of our diet, listing the allowable quantities of foods and the number of coupon points needed for each item before we could purchase it. All clothing and household linen was covered by points as well and, Mum writes, 'even though we were shabbily dressed and often hungry, our spirits remained undaunted and we found ever-ingenious ways of coping.' The occasional 'red-letter day' occurred when we received a food parcel from New Zealand. This caused great excitement and its contents were shared with our friends.[6]

From time to time, a limited quantity of some particular food became available, such as a small allowance of fresh fish or meat, an ounce of butter or another egg. With only one egg allowable per month, an extra one was always welcome. The news spread quickly and before long, dozens of people had formed a queue in the hope of getting whatever was on offer before it ran out. On one occasion Mum found such a queue and eagerly joined it, without knowing what it was for. After waiting for more than half an hour, during which the line of people hardly moved, she asked someone to save her place while she went to find out. My mother was hopeless when it came to medical matters and practically fainted at the sight of blood, so it is hardly surprising that she beat a hasty retreat when she discovered the queue was not for food but for blood donors. After that, she became extremely wary of queues.

It is easy to overlook the fact that while we were enduring the fear and misery of air-raids, food shortages, curfews and all the other dangers and restrictions, the enemy was suffering in much the same way. One event from those years continues to haunt me. On a soft summer's day I was playing in the garden when I heard a distant rumbling noise, like thunder, coming nearer and nearer. Looking up I saw dozens of aircraft flying towards me, seemingly wing to wing, and the sky turned menacingly black as they passed overhead. I was just five at the time and for me, those noisy planes were terrifying. It would be many years before I understood that these were in fact 'our boys', a British fighter patrol under the command of a New Zealander, Air Vice-Marshal Keith Park, who were flying towards the south-east coast of England to take part in what later became known as the Battle of Britain campaign. Their success in helping to defeat the German Luftwaffe saved England from being invaded by the enemy forces that were ready and waiting in France; it also led to Winston Churchill's famous utterance, 'Never in the field of human conflict was so much owed by so many to so few.' However, the eventual overnight obliteration of historic cities in Germany by the RAF Bomber Command would have created much the same fear and distress among its victims as we in Britain suffered during similar Luftwaffe raids. It is also a fact that by the end of the war, the devastation and loss of life was even greater in Germany.

When I visited that country for the first time some sixty years later, my childhood memories of World War Two came flooding back so vividly that it was strangely difficult to dissociate myself from the feeling I was in enemy territory – 'where the bad people come from'. Despite the magnificent architecture, art and music in the cities I visited, there were still reminders of Hitler's evil influence, especially in Berlin. One memorial there that particularly disturbed me acknowledged the Nazi 'Burning of the books' episode in 1933, on the site where it actually occurred. In the middle of a cobblestone square, the Bebelplatz, there is a translucent glass panel at ground level through which one can see a large underground room full of empty white bookshelves, dramatically lit like a stage-set with eerie yellow lighting. A nearby plaque is inscribed with the words of the German-Jewish poet and playwright, Heinrich Heine: 'Where they burn books, in the end they will burn people.' Overlooking the square is the Humboldt University, from whose library many of those books were taken and where Heine himself was a student in the early 1800s. This seat of learning seems so incongruous besides a place that records the destruction of scholarship.

Life throughout the war years wasn't all wretched, however, and there were many ways to have fun and be distracted. One of my favourite things happened nearly every Saturday when Mum took me to the 'pictures'. Even though I was allowed to stay up later on these evenings, we usually went to the cinema about 3 pm so my bedtime wouldn't be too late and we'd be home before dark. The movie sessions were continuous and normally included a morale-boosting British Paramount newsreel, several 'shorts', a promotional trailer for the following week's film and, if we children were really lucky, a Mickey Mouse or Donald Duck cartoon. After a brief interval which allowed people to come and go before the main feature, and little girls to use the toilet, the film luring me into a safe new world of fantasy and excitement began. Within minutes I was a glamorous dancer with long blond hair and perfectly shaped legs, just like Betty Grable, whirling around in the arms of Fred Astaire, or a 12-year-old Elizabeth Taylor with lustrous black tresses and soulful, violet-coloured eyes, urging my beloved piebald horse to victory in *National Velvet*. Each week I became another star, silently singing my heart out and clanging the trolley bell with Judy Garland in *Meet Me in St Louis*, or being ill-treated at a desolate Yorkshire school, like poor Margaret O'Brien in *Jane Eyre,* but growing up to find happiness with the mysterious Mr Rochester. I even managed to 'take the veil', and tried hard to look devout and beautiful like Ingrid Bergman in *The Bells of St Mary's.*

When the movie finished and it was time to leave the cinema, I remained in my fantasy world for the rest of the evening. As soon as we arrived home, Mum helped me find something appropriate to dress up in that vaguely resembled my new identity, and left me to get ready while she prepared supper. She then pretended to be enormously honoured at seeing that evening's 'star' clambering down from the upstairs bedroom, as elegantly as possible in a pair of her high heels, to join her for a sumptuous meal of powdered egg on dry toast and watery cocoa.

One movie star I always wanted to impersonate, whether having just seen her on the silver screen or not, was the exotically titled 'Brazilian Bombshell', Carmen Miranda. Mum helped me make a flamboyant headdress similar to those that became a trademark wardrobe item in all the star's films. Using as many unusual and garishly coloured fabrics as we could find, we fashioned a huge turban-like creation and decorated it with a lavish array of imitation fruit including bananas, cherries and grapes. Whenever we had visitors, I slipped into one of Mum's slinkier evening dresses, hitching it well up around the waist so as not to trip over when I made my grand entrance, and donned the fruity turban. Making sure the audience was keenly awaiting my performance, I assumed my best *femme fatale* pose, flung the front room door open with a dramatic flourish, and launched into Carmen Miranda's sexiest torch song, 'O wenn I lurve, I lurve!' This was my favourite 'party piece' and it became a regular feature during an evening's entertainment at home.

When we moved to Bognor, my mother established herself as a piano and singing teacher and took over the leadership of the Bognor Ladies Choir. They presented fund-raising concerts throughout Sussex in various towns and villages including Chichester, Selsey, Portsmouth, Felpham, Littlehampton, Worthing and Hove, with the proceeds going to the Red Cross, Merchant Navy League and St John organisation. The programmes consisted of choral items and a mixture of instrumental and vocal solos performed by members of the choir, together with the occasional guest artist. Mum wrote short sketches or plays that were included in the programmes and I often sang two or three songs as well. We usually entertained in small halls for audiences of approximately 100 to 300 people at most. To avoid the curfews and evening black-outs the concerts were mainly daytime affairs, on Wednesday afternoons when the shops had half-day closing, and Saturdays or Sundays.

In 1942, my father was invalided out of military service in Egypt and returned to live with us in Bognor. He took a job at New Zealand House in the Strand, staying in London during the week but coming home at weekends and joining Mum in the performances. As the war progressed, large numbers of servicemen began arriving on leave in Britain and my parents organised variety shows especially for them. The initial venues for these troop concerts were canteens and church halls but as they became more popular, Dad decided to try them out in larger theatres and cinemas which could accommodate more 'bums on seats'. The first of these was the Brighton Odeon event mentioned at the beginning of this chapter, which almost led to the end of my singing career.

Magic acts, comedians and tap-dancers were now added to the programmes, together with the much-loved Music Hall recitations of the day, such as 'The lion and Albert', 'The eye of the little yellow god', 'Sam, pick oop tha' musket' and 'With 'er 'ead tucked underneath 'er arm'. Mum and Dad sang solos and duets and, until this concert, I had sung as well.

After much cajoling and promises of a special treat if I 'do my stuff', I hesitantly venture onstage, and am so blinded by the brilliant follow-spot and glaring footlights that it's impossible to see the thousand or more people in the cinema. As my mother seats herself at the piano, I stand shyly centre-stage, surrounded by a huge pool of light, and prepare to sing in this sunny little world of my own. Enthusiastic applause bursts out at the end of my performance and I find I have stolen the show. As the saying goes, 'If you don't want to be upstaged, never perform with children or animals'. Best of all, when we get home I'm allowed to join Mummy and Daddy for a really late supper, and play dress-ups in one of her glamorous gowns.

Chapter 2

A 'Sallie' lass

When they first lived in New Zealand during the 1930s, my parents joined the Salvation Army and attended the Wellington Citadel Corps. Both sang in the choir, or Songsters, as the 'Sallies' call their choral groups, and Dad played in the band. There was no Salvation Army Corps in Bognor Regis when we moved there, so Mum became a member of the Waterloo Square Methodist Church and I attended their Sunday school. She sang in the choir and I was occasionally asked to sing a solo at various young people's gatherings. Dad also joined this church when he returned from Egypt, and began conducting services as a lay preacher in the Methodist and other Protestant churches in Bognor and throughout the neighbouring areas. These became real family affairs with Mum and me reading the Bible lessons, Dad giving the sermon and the three of us singing – a solo from me and duets from my parents. Towards the end of the war Dad felt he had a vocation to enter the ministry and spent a year studying at Cliff College, the Methodist Theological Training Centre. But my parents were also keen to return to New Zealand, so in 1946, with the war over and Dad having completed his theological studies, we left England aboard the troop ship Stirling Castle to come back home. Shortly after we arrived, Dad was ordained into the Methodist ministry.

During his time as a parson, my father had three parishes: two in the North Island and one in the South. His first church was at Grey Lynn in Auckland, where I became a pupil at the Pasadena Intermediate School in Westmere. The teasing from classmates this time was again because of my accent, but now it was the posh English one which they thought gave me 'airs and graces'. I had no choice but to stay at Pasadena, however, and eventually my tormentors either found someone else to bully or my English twang disappeared. We spent one year in Grey Lynn before Dad was transferred to the Island Bay Methodist Church in Wellington. I spent my second year of intermediate study at South Wellington Intermediate School and then went to Wellington East Girls' College for two years in the third and fourth forms. Dad became the school padre at the college while I was there, and this provided the opportunity for further taunts whenever he led the prayers or gave a talk at important assemblies, such as end-of-term functions. But there was one major bonus. Besides singing in the Junior School Choir, I was one of five third-formers chosen to sing in the Senior Choir. After my father's next appointment to a South Island parish, the only things I missed at Wellington East were the choirs and two of our teachers – Miss Ellis, the music-mistress and Miss Bycroft, who taught English.

Dad's transfers around the country and the inevitable changes of school for me didn't do a lot for my education. However, each place we lived in enabled me to learn more about my homeland. I don't remember being particularly bright at school, even though I'd been assessed as capable of taking the Professional Course when enrolled at Wellington East. This included French, Latin, Mathematics, English, Science, Biology, History and Geography. Being an awkward and rather fat teenager led to further teasing and even humiliation from some of my fellow-students and one of our teachers as well, the physical education and dancing instructor, Miss Dixon. This woman took a fiendish delight in insisting I perform activities that were beyond me, like hand-stands, cartwheels and vaulting the gymnasium 'horse', and mocked me when I failed. Her classes were a nightmare. We wore hideous black Italian-cloth bloomers for Phys. Ed., and these added to my discomfort by making me look even more enormous. It's sad that the memories of my WEGC days are not happier, but this was somewhat remedied when I attended the school's 75th Jubilee celebrations in 2000. I was warmly welcomed by many of my classmates who had apparently taken an interest in my singing career over the years and were complimentary about what I had managed to achieve.

I joined a Girls Life Brigade group at the Island Bay church and worked hard to earn the great array of badges that eventually decorated my uniform by successfully completing all kinds of domestic tasks. The GLB met once a week, but we were more than willing to spend extra time participating in any big local event. Perhaps because of my father's involvement in both World Wars, our parish made a highlight of the Anzac Day commemorations and the church pews were filled to overflowing for the service on 25 April. The GLB members teamed up with the local Cubs, Boy Scouts and Girl Guides to practise marching in the weeks beforehand, so we could proudly join the war veterans and army, navy and air-force personnel in the grand parade to the church. On one memorable day in the late 1940s, the Governor-General, Sir Bernard Freyberg (under whom my father had served during World War Two), came to take the salute at our spick and span march-past, and attended the service to read the lesson. This caused tremendous excitement in our little seaside suburb. Shoes were shined, buttons polished and hair well-brushed, or slicked down with handfuls of Brylcreem to make sure we all looked our best.

Dad's South Island transfer took us to the small rural township of Cromwell in Central Otago. The move proved challenging for various reasons. His circuit spread over an area of approximately 78 miles, and initially his only form of transport around the mountainous region was a bicycle. With a little ingenuity and some vigorous fund-raising, he eventually managed to obtain a car, which made his work a little easier.

The parsonage in Cromwell, situated beside the church, was a typical New Zealand colonial-style wooden villa with a wide veranda stretching across its entire frontage. The main entrance in the middle of the veranda led to a hallway running the length of the house, off which there were two bedrooms to the left, the lounge and kitchen/dining room to the right and a tiny bathroom at the end. The toilet and wash-house, or laundry, were outside at the back of the property. Cooking was done on a coal range, which also provided hot water. Its continuous warmth kept the house wonderfully cosy during the bitterly cold Central Otago winters, but we sweltered in the long, hot summers when the range had to be lit if we wanted to cook a meal or have a bath. The house was sparsely furnished with items donated by the church's congregation, as our previous church houses had been.

Recalling sparse furnishings brings back images of the many ugly, mismatched and uncomfortable pieces that 'graced' our three parsonages. One of the most hideous was a heavy, brass-studded, brown-leatherette and wooden-sided couch, which occupied almost an entire wall of the Wellington property's dining room. I was a sleepwalker during my childhood and teenage years, and often woke up in some strange part of the house, cold and bemused at why I was there instead of being snugly tucked up in bed. The most miserable place of all to find myself was on that hard couch in the Island Bay Methodist parsonage. After years of wondering how to cure me of the habit, Mum finally tried placing a large oven-dish full of water beside the bed, in the hope that the shock of landing my feet in something cold and wet might wake me before I got any further. The floors in the parsonages were usually covered with linoleum rather than carpet, so the water was easily mopped up if I managed to tip the pan over. The remedy seemed to work, except when my mind was under some sort of stress, like taking examinations or learning a difficult piece of music. I would then wake up seated forlornly at the piano, not only cold but with wet feet as well. The most unlikely time to go sleepwalking was on my honeymoon, which could have easily ended in disaster, but more of that later.

One of the events the Cromwell church folk delighted in celebrating was Harvest Festival. Central Otago is New Zealand's 'fruit bowl' and particularly famous for its excellent apricots, peaches, cherries and walnuts. Today it is also one of the country's best grape-growing and wine-making regions. When autumn came and it was time to take in the harvest, our little wooden church creaked under the weight of fruit, vegetables, flowers, homemade preserves and baking, liberally donated by the congregation for the special Sunday service. The Saturday before the service was spent decorating the choir stalls and altar with the goods received, and by the end of that day not an inch of space remained. With everything suitably arranged, the traditional Lammas, or loaf mass, baked in the shape of a wheat sheaf, took pride of place as the centrepiece of the display.

The Harvest morning service was longer than usual to allow the younger children to add their contributions. After a lively rendition of 'All things bright and beautiful', each little one walked shyly up the aisle bearing his or her gift as if it were a pot of gold. They had carefully selected the best things they could find in their Dads' gardens, including big red tomatoes, bunches of carrots, radishes or silver beet, brown paper bags of potatoes, marrows, pumpkins and cabbages almost as big as themselves, and apples they'd polished to make them bright and shiny. They also brought flowers, sometimes pinched on the way to church from somebody else's garden, with a few weeds as well for good measure. When the parade was over, the children went to the Church hall for their Sunday school lessons while the grown-ups continued the Harvest service. Now it was their turn to sing the favourite hymns, 'We plough the fields and scatter', 'Come ye thankful people, come' and 'Now the year is crowned with blessing'. The produce remained in the church for the later service, but its appetising aroma lingered to the following Sunday.

The next day, the Festival contributions were transferred to the hall and made ready for an auction that took place in the evening to raise funds for some particular project. This was supported by the whole congregation, including the children, and the bidding got very animated when their Mum's delicious blackberry-and-apple pie or her lighter-than-light, thickly creamed and jammy sponge went up for sale. Little hands shot up to make sure the bid went as high as the product deserved, and amid all the fun a great deal of money was raised. The women organising supper in the kitchen made sure some of the home-baking stayed out of the auctioneer's sight so we could all enjoy it later. Anything unsold or donated back again was to be distributed to needy families, but I don't remember many of those in Cromwell. The local people's generosity, which knew no limits at harvest time, was well practised throughout the year and the excess bounty from their gardens and orchards liberally shared with others.

I spent my final year of secondary education at the Cromwell District High School, where there were only ten students in what was then the 5th form, now Year 11. Several of the subjects I'd been studying at Wellington East were not included in the District High School curriculum, and taking these through the Correspondence School system didn't work for me. It came as a great relief to leave school at the end of 1950. Sporting and social opportunities were more productive, however, and although I wasn't much interested in or any good at sport, the lack of numbers made it compulsory for me to be included in the tennis team and the basketball (now netball) side, where, despite not being very tall, I was a reasonably accurate 'goalie'. The most enjoyable part of these activities was competing against other co-educational schools' sporting teams from the neighbouring townships of Roxburgh, Alexandra, Wanaka and Queenstown, because it provided the chance to meet more boys.

Originally a gold-mining town, 1950s Cromwell lay nestled between two major rivers, the Clutha and the Kawerau. The ruggedly beautiful landscape of bare brown hills, tussock and gorse-covered plateaux, fertile valleys and nearby lakes that surrounded the small town provided a wonderful playground for adventurous young adolescents. In winter, when the distant mountain range, The Remarkables, was covered with dense, glistening snow, and visiting skiers flocked to Queenstown to display their prowess on the slopes, we honed our ice-skating skills on a little frozen pond in the centre of Cromwell. At night, the temperature fell well below zero, but the days dawned bright and clear and it was almost summery by noon.

Living in a teenager's paradise would not be complete without falling in love and I did this madly, deeply and everlastingly, at least once a month. One of my many boyfriends was the local stationmaster's son and on a never-to-be-forgotten occasion, we got into really serious trouble by hopping on a manual railway jigger and ferrying it all the way down to Clyde and back, a total distance of about 40 miles. The journey to Clyde was easy because it's downhill, but pushing the jigger back up the Gorge to the Cromwell railway station was an entirely different matter. We knew only one train a day used the single track and made sure we weren't there at the same time, but this didn't prevent us from being severely reprimanded for our escapade. A large part of that rail track, which once continued all the way to Dunedin, is now under water. The Cromwell Gorge was eventually flooded to create the Clyde Dam, and further areas along the route currently form a widely used cycle track for both locals and tourists.

Sadly, as with my academic difficulties at the District High School, the Cromwell church circuit proved too much for my father. He eventually left both the township and the ministry and we returned to live in Wellington.

One of Dad's friends in Wellington was Len Malaghan, the founder of New Zealand's Tip Top Ice Cream Company. Dad suggested I apply for a job at Tip Top and I was taken on as the office junior in their Waterloo Quay factory office. Len Malaghan and the company secretary, Miss Treloar, were extraordinarily good to me and made sure I received a thorough grounding in all aspects of clerical work. During my employment with Tip Top a new factory was built at Johnsonville, some distance out of Wellington, and the firm's entire activities moved there. I was granted additional travelling time to remain with the company and even encouraged to complete my School Certificate and University Entrance examinations at night school and then work towards an accountancy degree, for which the company would allow me study leave. I can't imagine what life would have been like had I followed that path. My heart was set on music and the possibility of a singing career.

One of my duties at Tip Top included acting as a relief telephone operator. After leaving that company, I briefly worked for Dunlop NZ in their Taranaki Street offices in Wellington. On one occasion when I was on telephone duties there, I stunned a caller by greeting him with a cheery, 'Good afternoon, Dunlop Ice Cream'. Miss Treloar's determined tuition had left its mark. Some years later, for my 21st birthday party, Len Malaghan provided 21 of the company's highly popular ice cream cakes.

Soon after returning to Wellington, Dad rejoined the Salvation Army. Before leaving for the UK, and during his and Mum's Salvation Army membership in the 1930s, Dad had spent several years working for their trade section and still had a number of friends in the organisation. Mum and I continued to attend the Methodist Church for about a year longer, where we both sang in the choir and I taught the 'littlies' at Sunday school.

My mother must have found it difficult worshipping at one church while Dad was at another, and eventually all three of us became uniformed Salvation Army 'soldiers'. When Mum and I left the Methodist church, the choir members presented me with my first oratorio score, Handel's *The Messiah*. They would be pleased to know this has been well used over the more than fifty years since.

The Salvation Army made full use of Mum and Dad's previous experience in the Methodist ministry by promoting them to the position of Envoys. This led to them conducting services throughout the Wellington district and the lower North Island, at both Salvation Army Corps and other churches; I had some involvement with this when singing for special occasions. In 1956, I was invited to sing at the annual Salvation Army Congress in Wellington's Town Hall where General Wilfred Kitching, the Musician-General from America, was the guest preacher at all the meetings. This resulted in the General and his wife suggesting that I travel with them as their gospel soloist throughout his worldwide ministry. Such a prospect held no appeal for me. My firm focus was on making singing my career, but in a classical sphere which included opera.

While my parents remained in the Salvation Army for the rest of their lives, and are well remembered for their musical abilities and Christian service throughout New Zealand, my days as a 'Sallie lass' came to an end soon after the 1956 Congress. My desire for an operatic career was not looked on favourably by some of the Salvation Army officers who knew me at the time, and there was even a hint of my 'going to the Devil' if I pursued a theatrical profession. There were repeated warnings about 'life upon the wicked stage' which I found confusing, as my few experiences in musical shows up to that time had been most enjoyable, and in no way did I feel compromised. In fact, the other cast members seemed intrigued to have an innocent, non-smoking, teetotal young Salvationist working with them; there were always soft drinks provided for me at parties and the more colourful language and jokes were toned down when I was around. It was the beginning of a huge learning curve for me, but my parents were totally supportive of whatever road I might choose to follow. Many years later, it would be pleasing to meet people throughout New Zealand who had heard my parents sing, and be told, 'We know where your singing talent comes from.' There was a great deal of pride in this as well – if that's not too big a sin.

Chapter 3

Competitions, concerts and counterpoint

As I neared my seventeenth birthday, Mum suggested that if my mind was set on a singing career, I should look for a suitable teacher and start formal lessons. Up to this time she had simply taught me how to breathe properly, from the diaphragm, and assisted in the choosing, phrasing and interpretation of songs to sing. My mother didn't believe in full vocal training for singers under the age of seventeen, owing to the physical changes which take place during puberty and the possibility of doing more harm than good if the voice is forced too early. While Mum was still teaching singing and could easily have started my training, she probably considered that I'd work harder for someone else.

Annual Performing Arts Festivals were held by the Competition Societies in both Wellington and the nearby Hutt Valley. One prize (for the winner of a class they both included) was sponsored by a prominent Wellington singing teacher, Hamilton Dickson, and offered a year's free tuition with him. To be eligible for this, contestants should have received no previous professional tuition and if my memory is correct, be aged between 16 and 18 years. When I entered the class at the Hutt Valley Competition Society festival in May 1952, Mr Dickson was the adjudicator, and he placed me second. At the end of his written report on my performance he wrote: 'I hope you are not too disappointed. You have a voice of decided promise and I suggest you enter my scholarship at the Wellington Festival in August.' I duly did so and this time was awarded the scholarship by the adjudicator at that festival, Will Hutchins. My studies with Hamilton Dickson began immediately and I remained with him for the next five years.

Hammy, as his students affectionately called him, had a city studio in Lambton Quay, above the Dunbar Sloane Auction Rooms and next to the Midland Hotel. The end of my lesson coincided with the pubs' early closing time, or 'six o'clock swill', as it was popularly known. Waiting for the bus home at the stop outside the Midland, while inebriated patrons poured out of the public bar, was quite an experience and offers were made that I was more than happy to refuse.

Hammy taught some fine young singers, a few of whom went on to have impressive vocal careers both in New Zealand and overseas. Foremost among these is the bass-baritone Grant Dickson, who has achieved wide international success. There were other students who, while they had very promising voices, succeeded in completely different fields, and their vocal skills would have no doubt surprised their employers and work colleagues. One of these was Alex Veysey, a very fine baritone singer but who became well known as a prominent journalist, sports writer and author. Alex was at various times sports editor, features editor and political writer for The Dominion newspaper in Wellington and the author of several books about prominent All Black rugby players, including Colin Meads. A comment made in an obituary after Alex's death in 2002 described his trained singing voice as 'a largely undiscovered delight'.

As well as teaching singing, Hammy composed songs, light operas and works for piano, cello and string orchestra. In 1953, his first light opera, *The Gypsies*, was premiered and performed by his pupils at the Wellington Town Hall Concert Chamber. Singing with me in the chorus of that production was Michael Lancaster, who, many years later, would become my boss in his position as the District Commissioner for Works in Auckland.

From time to time Hammy was contacted by various organisations to recommend suitable concert soloists or entertainers from among his pupils. In August 1954, he was approached by the Royal Wellington Choral Union, who needed a contralto soloist for their forthcoming October performance of Edward German's *Merrie England.* I had a contralto or low voice at that time, although my vocal range would ultimately settle in the middle as a mezzo-soprano. Hammy sent me along to audition for the RWCU with the result that they engaged me to sing the dual contralto roles of Jill and Queen Elizabeth in the light opera. Their letter offering me this work stated: '... the hope was expressed that your appearance on the 2nd October may lead to further engagements not only with the RWCU but with Societies outside of Wellington.'

It is to be hoped that most young singers can look back on their professional debut with pleasure, but while the outcome of mine was personally successful, the event was an anxious one for all concerned. The choir's conductor had recently arrived from Britain and, although he was possibly good with choirs, he apparently had little experience in conducting an orchestra. We started the first full rehearsal, with soloists, choir and orchestra, at 7.30 pm on the Friday evening before the Saturday concert, but by 8.30 pm the orchestra had packed up their instruments and walked out, refusing to continue so long as he remained in charge. Everyone else was sent home, but told to come back for a further rehearsal at 10 am the following day, by which time a replacement conductor would perhaps have been found. When we arrived for that session, the orchestra was there and seemed happy with the person now wielding the baton, one of their own double-bass players, Harry Botham. However, I became more and more anxious during this rehearsal as Mr Botham appeared to be focusing most of his attention on the orchestra and choir. Added to that, two of the other soloists were widely experienced opera stars from Australia, soprano Linda Parker and the eminently successful international tenor, Ronald Dowd. At the end of the rehearsal, and possibly aware of my anxiety, Ron and Linda graciously suggested that the baritone soloist, Raymond Windsor, and I join them at their hotel for a private run-through of our concerted work there. My 'prima donna' attitude came to the fore again and I said that although their offer was appreciated, I would prefer to practise at home and try to relax a little before the evening performance.

That afternoon I came very close to going the same way as the first unfortunate conductor and suggesting they find someone to replace me; this would have been quite simple as my mother had often sung the work in her younger days. But Mum and Dad kept up the encouragement, and at 8 pm I walked on to the Wellington Town Hall stage determined to sing as well as I possibly could, despite being terribly nervous. Before going on stage, Harry Botham gave me a hug and said, 'You're going to be fine. Just keep an eye on me and I'll be with you all the way.' He was as good as his word: the concert went well and the newspaper reviews were favourable. *The Dominion* music critic, Russell Bond, wrote a review that included the following paragraph under the heading 'Impressive debut':

> Miss Bridge made an impressive debut. A 19 year old appearing in such company could have been expected to be somewhat out of her class. Not so Miss Bridge. She has a voice of quite exceptional quality and she uses it well. There was not much in what she had to sing to test her interpretative powers, but once she had overcome a slight lack of control in her first number, she sang with assurance and evident musicianship. With the greater authority that will come, Miss Bridge should occupy a high place among New Zealand's singers.

Even the *Evening Post*'s critic, Owen Jensen, whose review of the performance bore the headline 'Not So *Merrie England*', wrote:

> This makes even more noteworthy the achievements of the young Wellington contralto, Corinne Bridge, who matched her more experienced associates note for note, except once when a tickling throat caught her out for a moment. What is more, her singing had an engaging freshness as if she was singing the music for the very first time which, very likely, she was.

This was high praise from a reviewer who could be a bit caustic at times.

The dress I wore for the concert was my first formal, full-length evening dress, made of pale blue net over slightly deeper blue taffeta with an off-the-shoulder neckline, close-fitting bodice and a very full skirt. Due to my nervousness, the perspiration that continuously dripped from my armpits during the performance had completely frayed both sides of the bodice's net fabric by the end of the performance. To wear that dress again, I had to find some matching net and carefully patch the damaged areas.

Having now broken the professional ice, engagements for me to sing as a principal soloist came fairly regularly. I sang my first paid *Messiah* the following December when the bass soloist, Charles Naylor, who would become one of New Zealand's leading oratorio singers, was making his debut. This time, Owen Jensen took me to task over my diction, saying: 'Miss Bridge should tidy up her vowels and not sing 'Then shall the oyes of the bloynd be opened.' Shades of an accent problem again?

Wanting to learn more about stagecraft, I joined a Wellington Technical College night-school class that concentrated on opera performance. This was in the safe hands of the *Merrie England* saviour, the multi-talented Harry Botham, and its success led to the formation of an amateur opera company called Opera-Technique, of which we students were the foundation members. Over fifty years later, this little company still exists in Wellington. Our first fully staged production in 1955 was Smetana's opera *The Bartered Bride*, in which I sang the role of Hata. Another young singer in that cast was Grant Tilly, who went on to become one of New Zealand's finest actors, as well as a skilled illustrative artist and woodwork craftsman.

Hammy continued to organise musical seasons to showcase his students, including the premiere of another of his own light-opera compositions, *General Gore*. Alex Veysey was brilliant in his comedy role of Major Algernon Murgatroyd-Jones and I played the role of Madam Gore. Alex and the rest of the cast had great delight in kidding me about one of the newspaper reviews for this show which stated: '[Corinne Bridge] both sang and moved with assurance, showed real evidence of dramatic ability and, unlike so many other people on the stage, knew how to control her hands.'

This review was put up on the Green Room notice board, with

various rude comments added as to what the rest of the cast were doing with their hands while I exercised self-control.

By now I was entering as many classes as possible in local Competition Festivals, and had set myself a specific goal. Besides the usual silver cups for individual classes and a gold medal for winning the Vocal Championship, the Wellington Competition Society offered the prize of a diamond ring, donated by a local jeweller, L. J. Brabin, which would be awarded to the female singer gaining the highest aggregate marks in seven classes: British Art Song, Test Song, Operatic Aria, Lieder, National Song, Continental Art Song and Song by a New Zealand Composer. By winning most of these classes in 1956, I managed to accumulate the qualifying marks.

A demonstration concert was held at the end of each Festival during which the winners of all sections – Vocal, Instrumental, Dance and Speech – performed and were then presented with their awards. The great night came with Mum, Dad, my godmother and her husband and other friends in the audience, all of us keenly looking forward to the moment when I would receive the diamond ring. After I had sung my winning aria, the vocal championship gold medal and various other cups and prizes, including a little white plastic jewellery box, were presented to me. I quickly left the stage and eagerly opened the box to admire the ring. All the excitement and pleasure at winning this award and achieving my goal were instantly shattered: the box contained a ring set with a pretty, pale blue stone, but it was most certainly not a diamond. Joining my parents and friends in the audience, I fought back tears while they passed the jewellery box around, all just as puzzled and upset as I was. At the end of the concert we asked for an explanation, and were told that the sponsor had died before the Festival commenced, but after the syllabus advertising the classes and detailing the awards had been circulated and the entries received. His family, who were now operating the jewellery business, had agreed to make one last donation of a ring, but without a diamond.

About three months later my godmother, who should perhaps

be named my fairy godmother, gave me a little parcel and said she hoped it would make up for all the disappointment at the end of the Wellington Competition Festival. Inside the parcel was a purple velvet-covered jewellery box containing a small solitaire diamond ring. An insurance policy had matured and she used most of the proceeds to buy me this gift. Needless to say, I was elated and all the previous disappointment was swept away by her loving gesture.

The publicity that followed these competition successes led to more professional engagements, including a considerable amount of broadcasting work. Brian Salkeld, who worked for the New Zealand Broadcasting Service, presented a nationally networked radio programme on the ZB stations entitled Sunday Showcase, which included New Zealand-produced plays, documentaries and musical works. I sang two roles in opera recordings for that series, Olga in Tchaikovsky's *Eugene Onegin* and Sandman in Humperdinck's *Hansel and Gretel.* The operas were accompanied by what was then known as the National Orchestra of New Zealand, under its musical director/conductor, James Robertson – my first experience of working with a major orchestra. A singer in another opera broadcast at that time, Puccini's opera *Il Tabarro*, was Ramon Opie, whom I had yet to meet. Further unusual but interesting radio assignments involved providing the singing voice for two well-loved actors who were taking parts in plays with a musical content, Davina Whitehouse and Jessica Weddell.

I was engaged to sing at a number of noteworthy concerts as well, including the official openings of the Lower Hutt War Memorial Library and Cultural Centre in 1956, and later the Lower Hutt Town Hall in 1957. Private guest artist engagements included two memorable events: first on 15 June 1956 for the Hutt Labour Party Golden Jubilee celebration in honour of the Rt. Hon Walter Nash and Mrs Nash's Golden Wedding, and secondly a banquet given by the Mayor and Councillors of Lower Hutt to honour the same anniversary on 25 June 1956. I also passed my Associate Trinity College of Music singing examination, and was again awarded a gold medal for being the diploma candidate gaining the highest marks in New Zealand in 1957.

My day job was now with the New Zealand Broadcasting Service as a clerk in their Accounts office, but because of my singing ability, I was 'borrowed' from time to time to assist in the training of young technicians who were learning the techniques of recording music programmes, both at live concerts and in the studio. Once fully trained, they would be able to control the balance, volume and sound of the artists involved. As a singer, my accompaniment is normally provided by either a piano or an orchestra and the microphone balance between us obviously has to be right. Even in today's digital age, radio recording techniques are apparently still much the same.

Working with the current intake of twelve technical trainees was both interesting and fun. Each trainee had to arrange two microphones, one for me and the other for the piano, in the positions and at the height they thought most suitable and where they could control and adjust the balance between us and the sound we produced. As soon as the trainee had everything, including me, where he thought it should be, he disappeared behind the glass window of the studio's control room, and when he was ready, switched on the red 'On Air' recording light which was our indication to start. He then continued to twiddle various levers and check dials while we performed. This was repeated twelve times so that each aspiring technician could test his skill.

At the end of the session everyone involved listened to the playbacks and made their comments regarding the quality of the individual recordings. The instructor dealt with the more technical aspects of the trainees' endeavours, while the pianist and I were asked whether we liked what we heard, if we thought it was a fair representation of our performance and if the balance between piano and voice was suitable. It quickly became apparent to me how easy it is for technicians to alter what one thinks is the actual sound one makes. In my case, if too much treble was added, my voice lost its depth and sounded like a high soprano, while too much bass made me sound very masculine. The sound colour can also be altered and the voice becomes completely different from what one expects to hear 'in the flesh'. My parents told me that in the early days of broadcasting, recording technicians kept card-index file records of the most suitable microphone placements and other factors covering regular broadcasting artists, so these could be referred to when that particular person was recording a programme. I found the whole business fascinating and thoroughly enjoyed being the trainee technicians' guinea pig. It also allowed me to increase my musical experience and prepare for the career I really wanted.

During this same period the Wellington Gilbert and Sullivan Society, which had been in abeyance for several years, was re-established, and before long I was on their committee and singing in the full-scale productions of Gilbert and Sullivan operas which the Society presented, as well as their smaller concerts. Most importantly, however, one of their members, John Malcolm, worked for the Department of Internal Affairs which annually awarded five New Zealand Government bursaries to enable successful musical applicants to live and study overseas. John took an interest in my singing, and in 1956 suggested I apply for a bursary.

My initial reaction was that I wouldn't have much chance of being considered because, although my voice might be suitable, the rest of my musical education was somewhat limited. Like many children who are sent off to music lessons at an early age but hate practising, I only completed two terms of piano tuition before my parents decided it was a waste of time and money and the lessons were stopped. To gain a Government bursary, the selection process included not only a vocal audition and an interview, where the candidate was expected to detail his or her proposed course of studies, but also aural and sight-reading tests. John Malcolm advised that the only way to become a serious competitor was to recognise my limitations and do something about them.

Thus began an intensive year of harmony and counterpoint studies, aural training and general musical knowledge, with a remarkably helpful teacher and musicologist, Paul Magill.

This had to be done in whatever spare time I had, as I still worked a normal eight-hour day and fulfilled concert and other engagements in the evening. But the hard work paid off and the following year, 1957, I was awarded a Government bursary valued at £800 for a two-year study period overseas, plus £50 towards sea passages. Other bursary winners that year were bass-baritone Donald McIntyre, (now Sir Donald and one of New Zealand's most successful international singing stars,) pianist Joan Havill, Ralph Aldrich (who played both violin and viola) and violinist Barbara Chipper.

Winning the bursary was a thrill I had dared not anticipate. The next major task was to raise enough money to cover the overseas travel costs. To help boost my finances, I added a part-time evening job, as an usher at the Wellington Opera House, to my other activities. This proved both enjoyable and useful, as it gave me the opportunity to see local and visiting performers at work, and absorb a little more of my craft in the process.

I worked onstage at the Opera House during this period as well, singing for the first time with the recently established New Zealand Opera Company in two operas, Menotti's *The Consul* and Mozart's *The Marriage of Figaro*. Unbeknown to me, Donald Munro, who launched the New Zealand Opera Company in 1954 and is considered the 'father' of opera in New Zealand, had been watching my progress, and in 1955 offered me the role of Mrs Nolan in Menotti's *The Medium*. Mrs Nolan is a middle-aged, grieving mother who wants to regain contact with her deceased daughter through the spirit world during one of the medium's séances. This would have been my first engagement as a professional opera singer and I certainly didn't want to make a mess of it. I was 20 years old, had no formal stage training other than the experience gained when working with Opera-Technique, the Wellington Gilbert and Sullivan Society and in Hammy's productions, and I felt daunted by both the music of this modern opera and the character I would have to play. I refused the offer, hoping Donald would reconsider me for something more suitable in the future. He told me that I was very foolish to miss the opportunity, but thankfully didn't let it deter him from offering me the role of Vera Boronel in Menotti's *The Consul* two years later.

The story of *The Consul* concerns a number of people suffering persecution under an Iron Curtain regime, each trying to obtain a visa to escape the country. Vera Boronel succeeds, so she at least has a happy ending. Feeling better equipped to cope with both the role and the music, I accepted my first professional opera engagement with the New Zealand Opera Company. There couldn't have been better role models to inspire me during this production as the cast included the company's founder himself, baritone Donald Munro, together with soprano Vincente Major and mezzo-soprano Mona Ross, all very fine singers and actors. Many years later, I sang the larger role of Secretary with great success, which I attribute to that first opportunity of working with Mona Ross, who was wonderful in the part.

Richard Campion, who, together with his actor wife Edith, formed a national theatre company known as The New Zealand Players, was the director for *The Consul*. Rehearsals were held at the Players' rooms in John Street, Wellington. I now learned that you wrote pencil notes detailing the stage movements into your vocal score, pencil being the operative word as the moves have to be constantly erased and rewritten when the director changes his mind. It was all terribly confusing, but the expertise of other members of the cast helped me enormously. One of these was a delightful Irish tenor, Terence Finnegan, who played the role of the Magician. Terry was a typical Irishman, who greatly enjoyed his tipple, had an irrepressible sense of humour and was thoroughly roguish, but charming with it.

In his role as the Magician, Terry had to master several conjuring tricks in order to give a credible performance. Terry's magic tricks occasionally led to some precarious moments, especially during one scene, when he produced the inevitable doves from his top-hat. Once released, the doves flew up into the flies above the stage, doing what doves do when they're a bit nervous, and we spent the rest of the Act avoiding their little 'messages'. Thank goodness my costume included a hat! When I later sang the Secretary role, the Magician was in fact the real thing, Auckland's popular Jon Zealando, who creditably sang this difficult part and mystified the audience with his trickery.

Terry took me under his own 'wing' during that NZOC season, teaching me a little more about stagecraft and making my first professional opera a valuable exercise. Whenever we had day-into-evening rehearsals, which made it necessary to have a dinner break, Terry liked to eat at a little Italian restaurant in Adelaide Road, not far from the Players' rehearsal rooms, and he sometimes took me with him. In typical tenor fashion he was happy to sing at the drop of a hat, and naturally the Italian staff enthusiastically encouraged him. Tears of happiness poured down their faces when he sang such favourites as 'Torna a Surriento' and 'O sole mio' in their own language, as well as the sentimental songs of his own country like 'Danny Boy' and 'Mother McCree'. I was far too shy to join in, but delighted in Terry's uninhibited behaviour.

Some of the New Zealand Players' actors assisted in this production, and I had a crush on a talented young man who acted as our stage manager for that season, Bryon O'Leary. Bryon later married New Zealand beauty queen and actor Ngaire Porter who went on to have a highly successful acting career in Britain, where she was known as Nyree Dawn Porter. She is probably best remembered for her role as Irene in the acclaimed BBC television production of *The Forsyte Saga*. Another actor I met at this time was a rising young star with the Players, Patricia Dallas, who remains a good friend to this day. Trish was also awarded a Government Bursary, in her case for drama, and we eventually studied together at the same institution in London, sharing a flat just around the corner from Ngaire and Bryon.

Looking back, I am staggered at the number of tasks I managed to fit in during that period: a full-time day job and a part-time evening one, several concert, opera and lighter show engagements with all the necessary rehearsals involved, plus singing and music theory lessons. I still managed to find time for an active social life with various boyfriends as well, and even the possibility of marriage to one of them. But that's another story.

One real life-saver, which I used regularly, was the Ladies' Rest Room at the Wellington Railway Station. In those days the Rest Rooms included a bathroom facility, mainly for travellers but available to anyone who wanted to hire it. If I was singing in an evening concert during the week, I'd pack a small case with my evening wear, makeup, sparkly jewellery, toiletries, plus music of course, and take this to my day job in the morning. After work,

I had a quick meal in town and then headed for the station to bathe, change into my finery, do my makeup and hair and proceed to my evening engagement. The attendants became accustomed to my visits, even showing an interest in where I was going and what I'd be singing. However, I spared them the agony of hearing me practise my scales in the bath.

Another refuge was the Wellington Public Library, now the City Art Gallery, where one could hire small private rooms by the hour and play gramophone records. Taking some sandwiches and a soft drink with me (strictly forbidden by the library, of course), I consumed these while listening to and learning new music. Even if I could have afforded a car, I didn't drive (and still don't), so there was insufficient time to slip home for a wash and brush-up and a quick meal between my day job and the evening engagement, rehearsal or part-time work at the Opera House. Thus the railway station and the library became my homes away from home.

Nearly a year after the award of the Government bursary, I had saved enough money to cover the cost of travel to the United Kingdom. With the help of my uncle, Eric Greene, I'd been accepted as a student at the Guildhall School of Music and Drama in London. My last performances before leaving New Zealand were with the New Zealand Opera Company as Marcellina in Mozart's *The Marriage of Figaro*. The cast again included the wild Irishman Terence Finnegan, Donald Munro, Geoffrey de Latour, Beryl Dalley, Marie Robinson, Honor McKellar and a soprano who would later become a very good friend and musical colleague, Kathleen Johnson.

Chapter 4

Guildhall School of Opera and the National

I left New Zealand on 1 November 1958, spending six weeks travelling by sea to England aboard RMS *Ruahine*. After taking the tropical route through the Panama Canal, the ship finally docked at Southampton on a miserable, dark and cold winter's day. I was grateful that relatives were there to meet me and take me to stay at their home in Bexhill-on-Sea over the Christmas period. But the Guildhall's first term in the New Year commenced early in January, so accommodation in London needed to be organised quickly. During the voyage I'd become friendly with three other young travellers who suggested there might be a vacancy at the Shepherds Bush boarding house where they had already arranged to live. I followed this up and was offered a tiny third-floor room, where one could sit on the bed and practically touch all four walls. Kitchen and bathroom facilities were shared. While this really wasn't suitable, and practising there would have been impossible, it was at least a start. I was hopeful that once my studies at the Guildhall began, it might be possible to find a flat with some of the other students. Luck was with me, and within a few weeks two pianists and I were sharing a large, two-bedroom apartment in a lovely old three-storey house in Notting Hill Gate. The house backed on to a small private park which we were allowed to use, so this made our new home particularly pleasant.

My Guildhall flatmates were from South Africa and, true to form in those days they were completely undomesticated, having had native staff do that sort of work for them in their own country. Sharing accommodation turned out to be educational for all of us. I'd never flatted before, but at least I was house-trained, so I proceeded to show the South Africans how to do the usual chores of bed-making, cleaning, shopping and cooking. They preferred to take their washing to the laundromat, so that got rid of one job, but buying the weekly provisions with them proved to be quite an experience. We lived midway between two good shopping areas: Notting Hill Gate, where we used the underground rail system to travel to and from our studies and shopped on the way home, and the Portobello Road Market. But the South Africans had much more money than I did, and I had to curb their extravagant expenditure in order to afford my share of the costs. This applied to the telephone and gas bills as well, for both local and toll calls carried charges, and heating was the usual shilling-in-the-slot meter system. Being used to the high temperatures of their homeland, they were always cold in England and couldn't believe how quickly a shilling's worth of gas ran out.

At the end of their study period the South Africans returned home, and my New Zealand friend from Gisborne, Patricia Dallas, moved in, together with an English friend, Jane Trigger. During the cold winter evenings, we saved expenditure on gas by either going to bed early or sitting wrapped up in blankets and hugging hot-water bottles. Mention of blankets reminds me that while the various London flats I lived in were furnished, linen was not supplied and only a few items of crockery, cutlery, cooking pots and so on were provided. My first few weeks in London were spent scouring the Shepherds Bush Market for cheap supplies. Purchases included Army Surplus sheets, grey blankets, pillowcases and towels, plus the all important 'hottie bottle'. An urgent SOS was sent home to Mum and Dad for more supplies.

The New Zealand Department of Internal Affairs administered the bursary through New Zealand House, and after they paid the Guildhall fees at the beginning of each school term, the remaining funds were lodged into my bank account on a monthly basis. These funds, approximately £5 per week, had to cover the shared costs of rent, food and running the flat, plus travel to and from my studies and personal living expenses, including the purchase of music. When Trish Dallas (now Campbell) arrived to share the flat, her bursary funding was similar to mine and no matter how careful we were, we struggled to make ends meet. While it may sound dramatic, it is true that towards the end of each month we were usually running out of money and had to decide which had the greater priority, food or travel to the Guildhall. Because Internal Affairs considered there was adequate provision for living expenses within the grant, we were instructed not to take part-time employment, other than during the school holidays. Had we done so, it could have jeopardised our continuing bursary payments.

The ever-resourceful Trish discovered that if we went down to the Portobello Market immediately after it closed in the late afternoon on a Saturday, we could get all manner of 'freebies', including various kinds of vegetables, fruit, bread and buns which hadn't been sold or were too damaged to sell. For some ghastly reason, she also decided that as we were eating hardly any meat and fish, we must buy a roll of black pudding and have a slice of that each day at breakfast or dinner in order to keep healthy. Black pudding was not one of my favourites, but I went along with it for the sake of my health. Like the smelly fish in white sauce during my Villa Maria school days, black pudding is definitely not on the menu now. Saturdays would therefore see us scavenging down at the market, and coming home with a variety of goodies to keep us going until the next month's allowance went into the bank. Needs must, as the saying goes, and we were both forced to become efficient at making ends meet. Trish actually credits me with teaching her how to economise and live fairly healthily, if frugally, on a tight budget.

From time to time, other New Zealand friends joined us briefly and shared expenses. We ate a lot better on these occasions. One friend, Jeanette Trenwith (now Mackinnon), sometimes came to stay from the USA, where she was working for the New Zealand Embassy in Washington. Jeanette's mother, Jean, also spent time at the flat when she came on holiday from New Zealand, and instantly treated us all as her children, spoiling us with mouth-watering home-baking and roast dinners. Like Trish, who remains in London, Jeanette is still a valued friend, in spite of the fact that she lives in the USA.

Soon after my bursary award in 1957, Mum wrote to inform her brother, Eric, of my desire for an operatic career and asked him to recommend a suitable teacher. Eric Greene won a choral scholarship at the age of ten to Winchester Cathedral where he was solo boy (the main boy soloist) for the greater part of his five-and-a-half years as a chorister. While there, he was also accepted as an organ pupil and eventually allowed to take choir practices and even play the cathedral organ for some of the less important services. This included playing at Sunday evensong for members of the armed forces during World War One. Family history was therefore repeated when my parents and I became involved in music-making for servicemen some 25 years later. The prospects for earning a living in music were not particularly bright when Uncle Eric left school, so at the age of 17 he began a banking career in the Head Office of the Westminster Bank in Lothbury, London. At the same time, he was also lucky enough to be awarded a scholarship to study singing, piano and organ at the Royal Academy of Music, and special arrangements were made for him to begin his studies at 4 pm each afternoon so that he could continue working at the bank.

Eric Greene's first opportunity to shine as a singer came in 1926, when Sir Henry Wood chose him for the Evangelist's part in Bach's *St Matthew Passion* at a performance given in the Queen's Hall by students from the Academy. His vocal success eventually encouraged him to abandon banking for music, and he went on to become one of England's foremost oratorio tenors, performing all the major works including Elgar's *Dream of Gerontius*, and sometimes even playing the continuo as well as singing the Evangelist in the *St Matthew Passion* and the *St John Passion*. He regularly performed both as a recitalist and oratorio singer at concerts on the Continent and in America and Canada, and had the honour of being personally chosen to sing in the choir for the coronation of King George VI and Queen Elizabeth by the Master of the King's Music, Sir Walford Davies. During World War Two, he acted as regional officer for the CEMA (Council for the Encouragement of Music and the Arts) in the East and West Ridings of Yorkshire, and in later years returned to the Royal Academy of Music as a Professor of Singing.[1] Uncle Eric met my father while they were both working at the same bank and became matchmaker when he introduced his new friend to his youngest sister, Nora, my mother.

My uncle was still active with his international concert work when Mum contacted him, as well as teaching singing at the Royal Academy of Music. He suggested that because my main interest was opera, which was not his sphere of music, it might be better for me to study at the Guildhall under one of his friends, Parry Jones. Mr Jones, a noted Welsh tenor, had worked with all the major opera companies in the UK and at the Metropolitan Opera in New York, and still had useful connections with The Royal Opera House, Covent Garden. Not knowing of any other appropriate teacher at this stage, and obviously willing to trust my uncle's superior knowledge, I took his advice.

Without becoming too technical about the finer points of voice production, it was Parry Jones' approach to vocal technique that almost ruined my voice. I am quite prepared to accept part of the blame, as I came to dislike the man intensely. In my opinion, a student needs to respect his or her teacher and have complete trust in the instruction being given. I dreaded going to my singing lessons with Mr Jones; my throat would constrict and I could barely get through a simple scale, let alone sing a complete song or aria. Besides vocal tuition, my studies at Guildhall included theory and counterpoint, languages (Italian and German), drama, mime and movement, fencing, and coaching with various repetiteurs. While these subjects gave me few problems, the singing lessons were a nightmare.

Towards the end of my first term at Guildhall I met up with Donald Munro, who was on a short visit to London. He asked how my studies were going, and I poured out my worries about my singing teacher and the fear that my voice was being irreparably harmed. I begged for his help, and Donald immediately arranged an audition for me with his friend, Clive Carey, a noted singer, director, teacher and one-time administrator of the Sadler's

Wells Opera Company. Without mentioning my current singing teacher's name, I simply requested an opinion as to the state of my voice, and whether too much damage had been done to allow me to consider singing as a future career. After hearing me, he advised that the voice was still promising but there were problems and my vocal cords needed to be rested as much as possible. He recommended that I find a new teacher who he was sure would go back to basics and attempt to nurture my voice back to good health.

Happily a singing career was at least still an option, but my next task was to inform the Guildhall hierarchy that I wanted a different teacher. This proved difficult, especially as Uncle Eric had 'pulled strings' to get me under Parry Jones in the first place. The Guildhall management made various comments about overseas bursary arrangements, that students didn't always know best, and so on. My feisty 'prima donna' attitude came to the fore once again; I insisted I was the best judge of how my throat felt and the damage being done. If they refused to let me work with a new singing teacher, I would not attend vocal lessons for the remainder of the year and simply concentrate on the other subjects I was studying. In the second year of the bursary I would resume the vocal studies, as long as it was under a different tutor. To their credit, they finally agreed to the change and asked whether I had a preference among their other singing teachers.

Throughout the first term I had listened carefully to all the female singing students, particularly noting their vocal techniques. Those I preferred were the students of Joyce Newton who, before teaching, not only had an extensive career as a mezzo-soprano in opera, but also specialised in lieder recital work. Agreement was reached that I could study with her, and we started working together in the second term. Joyce immediately restricted my vocal use, only gradually allowing me to actually sing in the third term. She worked on my breathing and on what she called my 'tight colonial jaw', that is, my mouth shape and movement when I sang. She gave me many exercises to help with these problems and extensive repertoire to learn mentally but not vocalise. As a result of her care, my voice responded well by the end of the third term and the future began to look brighter again.

However, there was a downside to my change of teacher. Uncle Eric was unimpressed by my actions, and left me in no doubt that this was the end of any assistance that might be forthcoming from him. It was a considerable blow, as his wife happened to be a director in one of the largest concert agencies in London at that time, Ibbs and Tillett. This sort of contact would have been extremely useful in any future singing career.

During 1960, I was awarded several more monetary scholarships which would allow me to continue my studies when the New Zealand Government Bursary finished at the end of that year. These included grants to cover singing tuition at the Guildhall, and a Benjamin Britten Scholarship to cover fees for one year at the National School of Opera, now the London School of Opera. Other awards followed, including the Guildhall School Mezzo-Soprano/ Contralto prize in 1962 and the Schubert Lieder Prize in 1963. Funds to cover living expenses were not included however, and it was necessary to find a number of part-time and casual jobs.

Each term, both at the Guildhall and the National School of Opera, students who were considered vocally ready to do so took part in opera productions, either a complete opera or just one act. I sang several roles in these productions, including Orfeo in Gluck's *Orfeo ed Euridice*, Third Lady in Mozart's *The Magic Flute*, Marthe in Gounod's *Faust*, and Aunt Jane in Vaughan Williams' *Hugh the Drover*. The most memorable for me was a six-night season of Offenbach's *The Tales of Hoffmann* at the National School of Opera. Colin Graham directed the opera, with sets by Ralph Koltai and costumes on loan from The Royal Opera House, Covent Garden. The director and set designer were at the start of their outstandingly successful careers in opera and, even at this stage, had both worked in some of the major European opera houses. The Opera School students chosen to sing in *Hoffmann* were therefore thrilled to have the opportunity to work under such experienced guidance. Another New Zealander, not a student at Opera School but especially engaged for this production, was Dunedin-born bass-baritone Bryan Drake. Bryan was excellent in the 'evil genius' roles of Lindorf, Coppelius, Dapertutto and Dr Miracle, and equally impressive was another guest artist singing the role of Antonia, Pauline Tinsley, an up-and-coming English soprano who later became one of Britain's most important opera stars. In my small role as Antonia's Mother, I joined these two singers in the magnificent Act 3 trio, and was thrilled to be noticed and given a favourable mention in Harold Rosenthal's review of the season for *Opera* magazine.

In March 1961, the Henry Wood Concert Society organised a performance at the Royal Albert Hall to commemorate Sir Henry Wood's birthday. Soloists, combined choirs and orchestras from the four music schools in London (Royal Academy, Royal College, Guildhall School and Trinity College) took part in this concert under the baton of Sir Malcolm Sargent. Included in the programme was Vaughan Williams' *Serenade to Music*, a work for sixteen vocal soloists and orchestra. This piece had originally been written as a tribute to Sir Henry, to mark the fiftieth anniversary of his first Promenade concert. Four singers were selected from each music school to make up the required number, and an Australian baritone, Russell Smith, and I were among the four representing the Guildhall. The concert was held in the presence of Her Majesty, Queen Elizabeth the Queen Mother, and one singer from each school was to be presented to her at the end of the performance. The 'Aussie' was the lucky one chosen from Guildhall. But this concert stands out for another reason.

The preliminary rehearsals for the soloists were held at Sir Malcolm Sargent's private apartment in the Albert Hall Mansions. The many autographed photographs of famous musicians and members of the royal family which adorned the walls of his music room and stood on the grand piano were so fascinating that I almost forgot to sing. Sir Malcolm's personal secretary constantly hovered around in the background, obeying her master's every whim and ensuring we behaved ourselves respectfully.

The female soloists were asked to wear full-length white

evening dresses for the concert, so with the help of an urgent money order from home, I managed to buy a fairly inexpensive but very attractive gown. It was made of white nylon chiffon with one completely bare shoulder and a long piece of the same fabric, which could be used as a stole if needed, attached to a thin strap on the other. A white flower, also made of chiffon, concealed the stitching securing the stole to the shoulder strap. Because my hair was long, black and straight I rarely went to a hairdresser, either tying it back in a pony-tail or styling it into a chignon for more formal occasions. However, I decided this event warranted something special, and found enough money to have my hair professionally styled in the heavily back-combed, high bouffant, French-pleated style that was so popular during the 1960s.

On the night of the concert, we arrived at the Royal Albert Hall's stage door and were shown to our dressing rooms where we changed into our finery. As we waited in the wings to be called on stage, Sir Malcolm's secretary suddenly darted towards me with a little pair of nail scissors in her hand, snipped the stitches attaching the white flower to my dress and removed it. Completely stunned, I asked her what on earth she thought she was doing. She replied brusquely, 'Only Sir Malcolm wears a flower.' Malcolm Sargent had been the chief conductor of London's Promenade Concerts since 1948 and continued in this capacity until his death in 1967. Early in his career, he gained the nickname 'Flash Harry' both for his reputation as a 'ladies' man' and for always wearing immaculately tailored suits, with either a white or red carnation as a buttonhole. However, I found it hard to believe that my nylon chiffon flower was about to upstage him.

The previous year, our Drama Professor at Guildhall was asked to recommend one of his singing students for the role of Dido in an outdoor presentation of Purcell's opera Dido and Aeneas, and he chose me. The opera was performed during the summer break at St John's College in Cambridge, and was set in the grounds of the College, 'the Backs' as they are known, looking towards the river Cam. During performances we could see elegantly blazered young college men in the distance, rhythmically punting their boats through the water and having to duck every now and then under the enchanting little bridges that criss-cross the river. The opera was played on a temporarily erected stage built at the base of three wide stone steps which led up to a beautiful, ivy-covered stone archway. It was here, on the top step and in front of this impressive backdrop, that poor Dido had to 'take her leave of life' towards the end of the opera. Having done the suicidal deed, poison in this case, I was placed on a stone slab bier in the centre of the archway and covered with a black cloak, while little cupids and angels decorated me with garlands of flowers and scattered petals around. The lighting gradually dimmed as I breathed my last, and two heavy velvet curtains slowly closed in front of me. It was very atmospheric.

Due to the vagaries of the English weather, our *Dido and Aeneas* cast were constantly in a state of suspense during that season. Performances started at 7.30 pm while it was still daylight and, because this is a short piece, darkness was only just setting in as the show finished. But we were never quite sure if the entire opera would continue to its end or if it would have to be curtailed at some stage, for neither the stage nor the orchestra pit had any overhead cover. The musicians would have made a swift exit at the merest hint of a heavy dew or rain, as their instruments could be adversely affected and some even go out of tune. I wasn't too thrilled about singing in the open air either, for cold air hitting the back of your throat when you take a quick breath can make you cough. This is not one of those operas in which the heroine dies of consumption, so coughing would have been most inappropriate.

That summer in Cambridge was just magical. I relished the beauty and lifestyle of the place and the chance to work with so many clever and talented people. Each day I attended evensong at either King's or St John's College chapel, not, I must admit for religious reasons, but simply to delight in the magnificent organ playing and peerless choral work. On one occasion at King's the sheer perfection of the music, together with the chapel's majestic Gothic architecture and glorious windows, were all so overwhelming that I thought, 'if I have to die sometime, it might as well be now for I'm already in heaven.'

During the August and September holidays, people from many different countries came to participate in short courses at the various Cambridge colleges. A gentleman from Wolfsburg, Germany was a course student while I was there and attended one of the *Dido* performances. He waited backstage to see me afterwards and requested I meet him the following day to discuss the possibility of my singing the same role in a concert version of the opera which he planned to present in his home town. His English wasn't very good but he gave me his card which simply stated his name, Heinz Meyer-Kundt, and his Wolfsburg address and telephone number. Herr Meyer-Kundt was a very intense, rather overpowering man with brooding eyes, and I felt somewhat intimidated by him, finding it difficult to believe this offer was authentic. I told him it would be impossible to meet him as I was returning to London immediately after the next performance, which was the final one. I gave him my home telephone number and suggested that he put something in writing for my agent to consider. I had no agent at that stage of course, but it sounded impressive and if his offer wasn't genuine I hoped it might put him off. However, he came to London on his way back to Germany and rang me to organise a meeting.

Now I had a problem. If the offer was the real thing, it could be good for my career and lead to more opportunities in Europe, so it needed to be given consideration. However, without an agent to check the legitimacy of the offer and do the bargaining, I felt ill-equipped to handle the whole business. Herr Meyer-Kundt asked me to meet him at an address in Earls Court Road so, to avoid being on my own, I quickly telephoned my current boyfriend, a chartered accountant, gave him the address and asked him to meet me there, in lieu of an agent. When I arrived at the meeting place Herr Meyer-Kundt, and another gentleman with him, suggested we go a little further along the road for a coffee, and I began to worry about whether my boyfriend would find us. They gave me a brochure which contained the conductor's photograph and a history of the choir he directed, the Wolfsburger Chorgemeinschaft von 1869. There were details covering the places throughout Europe where they had performed, with related press reviews, but everything was written in German. If only we had had the internet in those days; while writing this I checked online and discovered that the choir is still in existence and that Herr Meyer-Kundt had been one of its most celebrated conductors. After a quick search of possible coffee places, my boyfriend found us and proceeded to be very businesslike. He insisted that some official form of contract covering the engagement, with details of the fee, travel and accommodation arrangements be forwarded to him as soon as possible, when it would be given due consideration.

The written offer came, but now the travel and accommodation details worried me. The choir was, and still is, sponsored by the Volkswagen Motor Company, with many of their employees as choristers. To help reduce expenses, it was suggested that I travel by sea on one of the ferries used to transport the company's cars. These left from the port of Harwich, some 70 miles north-east of London, and docked at the Hook of Holland. From there I was to be driven by car to Wolfsburg, a distance of approximately 300 miles, and billeted privately. These arrangements made me nervous; I wouldn't be travelling on normal passenger ferries or road transport services either way between England and Germany, nor did I speak conversational German, which would make it difficult to communicate with my hosts, and moreover I would be entirely on my own. There was another consideration that worried me. During the 1960s in London, there were many instances of young women being lured both ways across the channel with enticing promises of job opportunities, only to be forced into prostitution once they reached their destination. Perhaps I was being a bit paranoid, but this prospect lurked uncomfortably at the back of my mind as well. I therefore replied that, because it would not be appropriate to take too much time away from my studies, travel should be by air, hotel accommodation provided, and my stay be only as long as necessary for rehearsals and the performance. This was not agreed to, so perhaps it was a valuable opportunity lost.

The New Zealand Music Society was very active in London at that time and I sang at several of their concerts, including a particularly important one at Wigmore Hall to celebrate the society's 10th anniversary. Other artists on the programme, who were all of course New Zealanders, included clarinettist Murray Khouri and conductor Ashley Lawrence. The concert went well, with Ashley being engaged soon afterwards to become one of the permanent conductors for the Royal Ballet at Covent Garden. He went on to have a distinguished conducting career in the United Kingdom before his untimely death during an overseas tour with the ballet company some years later. Ashley helped me considerably during my student days in London, and often played for me at the New Zealand Music Society's concerts.

There were many other performances, including student recitals, choral society and church choir concerts, which helped to broaden my repertoire and experience. The venues continued to fascinate me, for example St Clement's near Eastcheap, famous from the nursery rhyme 'Oranges and Lemons'. I sang at a concert there with two other New Zealanders: violinists Barbara Chipper, a bursary winner with me in 1957, and Vincent Aspey jnr, whose father led the National Orchestra of New Zealand from its inception and for 27 years afterwards. I was also the mezzo soloist in a performance of Verdi's *Requiem* conducted by Sir David Willcocks at the Guildhall of London, where the huge statues of the giants Gog and Magog, the traditional guardians of the City of London, glowered over us and kept a wary eye on proceedings.

Another famous venue was the Tower of London, where Gilbert and Sullivan's opera *The Yeomen of the Guard* was staged by the D'Oyly Carte Opera Company during the inaugural City of London Festival in 1962. Directed by Antony Besch, this production was performed in the open, on a stage erected beside one of the Tower walls and in what had originally been the moat, no longer filled with water but grassed over. Several notable Gilbert and Sullivan singers were in that production including tenor Thomas Round singing Colonel Fairfax and baritone John Reed as Jack Point. I understudied the role of Dame Carruthers, but never actually sang a performance. This is probably just as well because the singer I covered, Johanna Peters, was extremely tall and I am not, so it would have been a matter of trying not to trip over her costumes had I been required on stage. During the performances I spent most of my time watching the show from the lighting box, which was perched high up on scaffolding behind the audience.

There were many clever staging ideas for this production, made possible because the opera was being performed in its true setting. The Tower's ramparts and lofty grey stone buildings created a natural backdrop and provided excellent options for entries and exits. Even the arquebus, or rifle, mentioned by one of the characters, could be fired appropriately from the Tower's turrets. The resident ravens weren't too impressed about this and raucously expressed their disapproval. At the end-of-show party after a completely booked-out season, there was much amusement when someone suggested that the moat be flooded the following year, and we do *The Gondoliers*.

During our time at the Opera School, students were encouraged to audition for anyone and anything that might further our careers, including agents who could find us work and deal with the negotiations. I kept away from Uncle Eric's wife, Kathleen Chiseldon, at Ibbs and Tillett, but auditioned for and was accepted by the concert agency, Norman McCann Ltd. Several engagements followed, including broadcasting work with the BBC. A long-running and popular hour-long radio programme called *Variety Playhouse* went to air live every Saturday evening at 7.30 pm in front of a studio audience, and the artists included many well-known entertainers from the worlds of theatre, opera and comedy. Versatile comedian, actor and musician, Vic Oliver, hosted these programmes, conducted the BBC Revue Orchestra and occasionally played solo violin. Each programme included a segment entitled 'First Broadcast', and my agent organised an engagement for me to sing on this show as a new broadcaster (at least in the UK).

If I remember correctly, I sang one of the *Carmen* arias, but what I clearly remember are the people I worked with. On that particular programme I shared a dressing room with the very much larger-than-life Hattie Jacques. She was part of a comedy trio which included a comedian with the *Black and White Minstrel Show*, Leslie Crowther, and the man with limitless talents, Ronnie

Barker, who would go on to become so internationally known and loved in such shows as *The Two Ronnies*, *Open all Hours* and many other television comedy series. I was engaged to sing on another *Variety Playhouse* programme at a later date, this time as Maddalena in the quartet from Verdi's *Rigoletto* with soprano Ava June, tenor Edward Byles, and baritone Peter Glossop. On this occasion, the comedy trio included June Whitfield, familiar from such films as the *Carry On* series and the radio and television shows *Take it from Here* and *Terry and June*, right up to more recent programmes like *Last of the Summer Wine* and *Absolutely Fabulous*. As had been the case with the photographs on Sir Malcolm Sargent's piano and walls, these widely experienced artists were fascinating and I had the added advantage of working with and indeed learning much from them during rehearsal time.

The fees received for these various engagements were useful, but certainly not enough to live on. The scholarships awarded after the New Zealand Government bursary finished were for tuition only at the Guildhall and the National School of Opera, so it was necessary to find numerous part-time and one-off jobs to cover all other expenses. An obvious option was to get on the books of a 'temping' agency, and I was also advised to check a 'frightfully upper-class' magazine called *The Lady*, much favoured by the rich and famous and still in existence today. As well as private advertisements requiring nannies, cooks, nursing care, home help and so on, the magazine contained details of a very refined Knightsbridge employment agency, appropriately named *Universal Aunts*. They engaged temporary staff to undertake all sorts of casual and unusual jobs that could be completed within two or three hours, over a weekend or during the school holidays. This timing was perfect for me, so I contacted them and after the usual interviews, became a part-time 'Auntie'.

One of my jobs was remarkably simple. All I had to do was to meet young children who were travelling by train via London on their holidays from some posh boarding school in the country and were on their way home to another part of the United Kingdom, and make sure they made the right transfer connections and didn't get lost. I met them at Paddington, Waterloo, Victoria or whichever station they came into and, if there was time before their next train left, found something to amuse them. The most popular pastime proved to be a visit to Madame Tussaud's Waxworks, especially the grisly dungeon area known as the Chamber of Horrors. We caught an underground train to Baker Street, raced up to the Waxworks and bought our tickets, giggling with embarrassment when we handed them to a wax ticket collector by mistake, and then scurried around the dark and gloomy Chamber, where torturers and murderers lurked at every turn scaring us half to death, until it was time to hurry the children back to catch their next train.

Other jobs included 'charring' for people who were visiting London for short periods to work on various projects, usually films. They rented luxury apartments in Kensington or Knightsbridge, and I was required to go in for a couple of hours a day to do the usual cleaning chores while they were out. This suited me well, as I could organise the work around my study times, coming and going as convenient. There are many stories to be told about these jobs, both good and bad, but the favourite has to be working for an American actor and comedian, Ernie Kovacs. We never actually met, but corresponded with each other by handwritten notes. I kept a few that he wrote, one of which advised me that his bathroom had a plumbing problem: 'The W.C. is so upset that it is choked with emotion; anyway it's choked up so I think before it is flushed, could you please ask the housekeeper to get a plumber.'

Ernie Kovacs loved flowers. He requested I buy fresh ones regularly and arrange them around the apartment, to give it a more homely touch. Those flowers could have ruined my part-time employment opportunities, as well as my bank balance, for many years to come had Mr Kovacs not been such a kind and understanding man. While the apartment was well-furnished with all the necessities, there didn't seem to be anything to arrange flowers in. With hindsight, I should have asked the housekeeper for something suitable, but it didn't occur to me at the time. There were, however, two large, identical and very ornate porcelain vases adorning either end of a marble mantelpiece above the fireplace in the lounge, so I decided to use these. The vases had delicate little gold handles on each side of the neck which I ought to have realised were purely decorative. I carefully placed one of the vases under the taps in the kitchen sink, filled it with water and then made the disastrous mistake of trying to lift it out by the handles. There was a resounding crash and I was left with the handles in my hands, while the rest of the vase fell back into the sink and smashed into dozens of pieces. I was distraught as I thought the matching pair might be genuine antiques, and now one of them was broken. I wrote a desperate note of apology saying I'd pay for the damage, although how this was going to be possible I had no idea. Mr Kovacs' note back to me the next day was a huge relief. He told me not to worry, as he felt sure any breakages would be covered by insurance, but if not, he'd meet the cost himself. How I loved that man.

During his last week of filming, Ernie Kovacs asked me to purchase gifts for some of the other stars he was working with, as well as his wife back in the States. He gave me a long list of items he'd already chosen, where these could be obtained and the messages he wanted engraved on a few of them, requesting also that each be attractively gift-wrapped. He left large sums of cash for me to buy the goods, and in return I left the receipts and any change so that he knew what I'd been up to with his money. When I made my final visit to clean the apartment after he left, there was a large tip and a note suggesting I take all the remaining food and liquor from a farewell party he had given the previous night, as well as the flowers if these were of any use. My flatmates and I dined rather well for the next few days, with flowers on the table as well.

In addition to the temporary work, I had two regular jobs. Every Sunday I was one of four singers who performed as a professional quartet at the morning service of a Unitarian Church. We were under an annual contract to sing 50 days in the year. We arrived at the church for a rehearsal at 8.30 am to practise the hymns, anthem or solo to be performed that day, and after a short break at 9.30 we donned our choir gowns and promenaded into the church at 10 am. By the end of the first year's contract I decided more money was needed than the church job offered, and took a sole-charge position in a small kiosk which sold cigarettes, magazines, sweets and chocolate on one of the platforms at Paddington Station. I worked a 12-hour shift from 6.30 am to 6.30 pm on a Sunday, closing the kiosk only 'when nature called'. It was extremely boring but the longer hours brought in more money.

There were also casual, but rather more lucrative church jobs that involved singing in choirs on an 'as required' basis for society weddings, funerals and other occasions. One of the churches was St Margaret's, a beautiful and historic old building situated in the grounds of Westminster Abbey. St Margaret's has been the venue for many famous society weddings, including that of Sir Winston Churchill. Other part-time jobs included typing and filling envelopes at the Spanish Embassy for a large promotional mail-out, then being wined and dined at an exotic Knightsbridge restaurant by the handsome Spanish press attaché at the end of the assignment. A stint as a barmaid in a lovely old Hampstead pub didn't last long because the patrons' continual smoking so affected my voice that it descended into basso profundo when I tried to sing at opera school the following morning.

A somewhat hectic job, which ran for about four weeks over a Christmas/New Year holiday period, was at the BBC television studios in Alexandra Palace, working on an early-evening programme called *Town and Around*. This programme was the BBC's first regional news programme for the south-east of England and its presenters included Michael Aspel, later to become familiar as a presenter of *Antiques Roadshow*. Other presenters were Richard Baker, the well-loved newsreader and host of *The Last Night at the Proms* television specials for many years, and Corbett Woodhall, who fronted the programmes I worked on. Being a reasonably accurate typist, I had to type the news items direct from the dictation of the journalists who prepared the material for the 15-minute programme. Again I had a twelve-hour working day, 8 am to 8 pm, three days on and one day off, but we were allowed adequate tea and meal breaks during these hours. The scripts were constantly altered as the news changed or was updated. These were the days of old-fashioned typewriters and carbon paper, so it wasn't as easy as it would be today with computers. When the programme went out live to the viewers at around 6.30 pm, I had to be careful to check for any mistakes or word-changes made by the presenter and alter the master script accordingly, in order that an entirely accurate record was kept of what had actually been said on the programme. The hourly rate was good, as were the excellent meals served in the staff cafeteria at the Ally Pally, as Alexandra Palace was nicknamed. The meals were especially enjoyable over the festive period.

While finding my way around London by public transport sometimes proved difficult, each assignment offered a new adventure and provided the opportunity to meet unusual and intriguing people. Even though I was there to study and further my career as a professional singer, I was just like any other Kiwi on their grand OE, eager to try new things, travel to exciting places and enjoy life to the full.

In addition to the excellent tuition we received at the National School of Opera, there were many new experiences to be enjoyed there. We attended dress rehearsals at The Royal Opera House and Glyndebourne Festival Opera theatres, so I heard and saw many of the greatest singers of the 1960s era. On one occasion, we were invited to sell programmes for a Royal Gala performance of Verdi's *Otello* at Covent Garden – as long as we wore something suitable and didn't turn up in our usual scruffy student gear. The Queen Mother and Princess Margaret were in attendance on this occasion and we 'rubbernecked' from the stairs above the Crush Bar while they were being escorted to the Royal Box. After completing our programme selling, we were allowed to watch the performance from one of the more humble boxes.

I heard and partly saw my first Wagner operas at the Garden. Seated in the view-obstructed area known as the 'slips' way up at the top and sides of the theatre, I had my first experience of Wagner's fifteen-hour *Ring* cycle. Only half the stage is visible from up there, so a small lectern with a well-shaded light was provided in front of the seat to allow one to take the vocal score and follow this when it was impossible to see the action on stage. I spent four nights on those hard, narrow seats in the 'slips' enjoying

Wagner's masterpiece and will never forget the wonder and excitement of hearing some of the greatest Wagnerian singers of all time. They included the bass Hans Hotter as Wotan, soprano Birgit Nielsen as Brünnhilde and tenor Wolfgang Windgassen as Siegfried, who were all at the peak of their singing careers. My co-bursary winner and fellow New Zealander, bass-baritone Donald McIntyre, eventually joined this illustrious list and became a notable Wotan in his own right.

It is said that your student days are the most enjoyable time of your life; I certainly enjoyed mine in London, particularly studying with talented people from so many different places. One of these at Opera School was a magnificent soprano from Malta, Antoinette Miggiani. She possessed a rich and very beautiful voice and had that well-built, hour-glass figure which cartoonists like to draw when caricaturing female opera singers. With great affection we nicknamed her our 'Malteeser', after the chocolate 'with the less fattening centre'. She was graciously long-suffering and took it all in good part. Other students came from Spain, Poland, Hungary, Israel and the larger Commonwealth countries, as well as from all parts of the United Kingdom, so we were a widely international group. Many of these people, including the 'Malteeser', went on to have prominent careers, both in their own countries and internationally, and I am always thrilled when finding recordings they have made and recalling the fascinating times we spent working together.

Chapter 5

The Sound of Music

Not all students at the National Opera School were taking full-time courses. A few already worked professionally in various West End shows or were under some form of contract with an opera company and simply furthering their training on a part-time basis. I hoped soon to be in a similar position. Although opportunities arose for seasonal or understudy work with the Glyndebourne Festival Opera and Sadler's Wells companies, no permanent or full-time contracts came my way and the never-ending consideration of having enough money to survive continued to rule my life.

One of the part-time students at Opera School, mezzo-soprano Marie Lorraine, was playing the role of Sister Berte in Rodgers and Hammerstein's highly successful musical *The Sound of Music* at the Palace Theatre in the West End. The show had been running for well over a year in London by this time, with one change only being made to the original cast. However, a chorus nun was pregnant and about to be involved in her own production, so Marie wondered if I would be interested in auditioning for the vacancy. The management, Williamson Music, had decided not to advertise it in the normal way, as this would have meant spending far too much time listening to hundreds of eager applicants. Instead, a date was set for the auditions and existing cast members were asked to advise anyone they knew who might be suitable. I jumped at the chance, as the pay was very much better than I could earn from my temporary part-time jobs, and although there were eight performances a week (six evenings and two matinees), I would have plenty of hours free to continue studying during the day. I gratefully accepted Marie's suggestion and attended the theatre at the appropriate time.

Despite the vacancy not having been publicly advertised, more than seventy prospective nuns arrived to audition. We were listed alphabetically so, with a surname beginning with B, I was among the first to sing and then had to wait backstage listening to all the others. This turned out to be fortunate as the majority of singers were simply thanked, given the 'Don't call us, we'll call you' line and told they could leave. Only three of us remained at the end of the three-hour process. We each had to sing again, read a few lines from the script and walk humbly and reverently across the stage, looking devout, chaste and nun-like. When at last the decision was made, I was extremely delighted to be the one chosen. I was immediately given the music score and script and told to attend my first rehearsal at 2 pm that afternoon. As luck would have it, or perhaps that's why they chose me, I had no trouble fitting into my predecessor's costumes for we were exactly the same dress size and height and, quite literally, I even wore her shoes. This probably kept the wardrobe staff happy, as they had nothing to replace or alter.

The 1965 film version of *The Sound of Music*, starring Julie Andrews, continues to be shown to this day in cinemas and on television screens around the world. As a result, most people recognise one or more of the songs and many know all the words as well. I certainly thought I was familiar with the music when I auditioned for the show, but my first reading of the score brought some pleasant surprises. During a quick lunch before my afternoon rehearsal, I glanced through it and was immediately impressed by the nuns' ensemble music. This is divided into four and sometimes five parts, much of it sung in Latin and obviously based on traditional church music. All I needed to know now was which line I had to sing.

My sight-reading skills were reasonably good, so the 2 pm run-through didn't present any problems. On my way home afterwards, I could hardly believe my good fortune to be earning a full-time salary as a singer at last and performing pleasant music in a popular show. And yet again, the Palace Theatre was an interesting and historic venue to work in. Richard D'Oyly Carte, of Gilbert and Sullivan opera management fame, had commissioned the theatre to be built in the late 1880s. It opened in 1891 under its first name, the Royal English Opera House. By 1893, the difficulties in finding sufficient productions to keep the theatre in use for its purpose forced it to be sold at a considerable loss. The new owner transformed it into a music hall and renamed it the Palace Theatre of Varieties. This name and use continued until 1927, when it became simply the Palace Theatre. Everything from musicals, ballet and films have played there since, including *The Sound of Music* (2385 performances), right through to more recent times with productions of *Les Miserables*, *Jesus Christ Superstar* and *Cats*. The composer of the last two shows, Andrew Lloyd Webber, bought the theatre in the mid 1980s and is still its owner.

I rehearsed for a week with the company's production and music coaches before going on stage for my first performance. I discovered that we nuns were extremely versatile. Besides our convent duties, we 'moonlighted' as party guests at Captain von Trapp's stately home and seven of us alternated in backing the children vocally behind the scenes during their bigger numbers. In a similar way to the nuns' music, the children's songs are divided into several parts and I covered either Friedrich or Brigitta. I also played the role of the competitor who wins second prize in the contest scene, and has to accept her prize with much curtseying and blowing of kisses to the real theatre audience. In the film version of the show, the second place-getter is a choir singer and appears in Austrian national costume. However, in the original West End show, I played the role of an opera singer, dressed in a rich burgundy-coloured velvet strapless gown with a feather boa-like stole, feathers in my hair and elaborate jewellery. In addition, I enjoyed a swift promotion up the nunnery ranks, for I became first understudy to my friend Marie, as Sister Berte, and second understudy to the Mother Superior, played by the charming retired English opera star, Constance Shacklock. Understudies were required to attend regular rehearsals to ensure we were ready to play any of our cover roles at a moment's notice, so this kept me busier as well.

Soon after joining the show, I found out that when the original auditions for nuns were held before the premiere of the musical on Broadway in New York, and then again for the London opening, Richard Rodgers commented this was the first time in the history of presenting his musicals that he could simply sit back, close his eyes and listen to the quality of the singers' voices, without having to take other attributes such as legs and cleavages into consideration. I don't know how successful I would have been in those respects; luckily, all I had to display on this occasion was my vocal ability.

I spent approximately eighteen months in *The Sound of Music* and loved every minute of it. As an only child and used to my own space, I learned a lot from sharing a dressing room with seven other 'sisters', plus our dresser, and found it most agreeable. We discussed our highs and lows, gave each other presents at Christmas and birthdays, socialised together with our boyfriends or husbands and attended previews of all the new West End shows when this was possible. We were even invited to special occasions by some of our cast; for example, we were among the guests at Liesl's (Susan Passmore) wedding in a magnificent old cathedral, and joined the Mother Abbess (Constance Shacklock) to celebrate her 60th birthday at a lavish party she arranged in her own home, to which she invited the entire cast and many of the stage crew.

At Christmas, the principals gave gifts to the rest of us in the show. I still have an elegant, long white chiffon scarf that was presented to each nun by our Captain Von Trapp, played with great Gallic charm by Paris-born Frenchman, Roger Dann. It is inscribed with his signature and 'Noel, 1962'. Every year during its West End run, Richard Rodgers and Mrs Hammerstein II hosted a no-expense-spared party to celebrate the anniversary of the show's London opening, inviting everyone involved in the production, including the orchestra. One of the parties I attended was held in the Lancaster Room at the Savoy Hotel, for which we each received personal, printed invitations to attend a supper and dance that would take place directly after the evening's performance. As soon as the show was over, we quickly changed into our elegant evening wear and went en masse to the Savoy to dine and dance until dawn the next day. Mrs Hammerstein's involvement was on behalf of her husband, Oscar Hammerstein II, who had died shortly after the opening of *The Sound of Music* on Broadway in 1960. One of the most popular songs from the show, 'Edelweiss', which was added during the preliminary Broadway rehearsals, is said to be the last lyric he ever wrote.

Richard Rodgers came to London approximately every six months to re-rehearse the show. He wanted to ensure standards weren't slipping, and that no un-*Sound of Music* habits (pardon the pun) were creeping in. While we endeavoured to approach each performance as if it were the first, it would have been easy to settle into a familiar routine and simply move into automatic mode. This was never allowed to happen, and the hundreds of people who came back to see the show time and again were assured of a performance that was as fresh and energetic as any they had seen previously. There was only one occasion when I remember the eight of us in our dressing room being 'off'. Because there are some fairly long breaks when the nuns are not on stage, management allowed us to have a small television set in our room, with strict instructions that the sound be kept low enough for us to hear the stage manager's 'on-stage' calls over the Tannoy intercom system. On this particular evening, if my memory is correct, we may have been distracted by watching television reports covering the assassination in Dallas of American president, John F. Kennedy; most people remember where they were when the news of that dreadful event first shocked the world, and I was certainly in *The Sound of Music* at the time. Whatever it was, we missed our call and a sadly depleted nuns' chorus took the stage for that particular entry. Needless to say, we received a severe telling-off and never missed an entrance again during my time in the show.

I continued to undertake singing engagements at Sunday concerts in various centres while I was in *The Sound of Music*, although permission had to be granted by the management. Just before I tried out for this show, my agent sent me to audition for the role of *Carmen* in the opera of the same name, which was due to have one concert performance in Brighton. I was successful in being offered the *Carmen* engagement, but when the contract for *The Sound of Music* came along, I tentatively asked, before signing it, if it would be possible to do the *Carmen* job as well, but permission was refused. Once again, the Brighton opportunity might have led to greater things, but permanent professional singing work was more important to me at that stage.

An unusual experience during this time came about through membership of the British Actors' Equity Association, the theatrical workers union. Until 1981, membership of Equity was compulsory for singers and actors, and some of the stage staff, who worked professionally in theatre or film in the United Kingdom. This inevitably led to the occasional union meeting to discuss and vote on some particular course of action. One of the major scandals in London during the 1960s was the Profumo Affair. John Profumo, Member of Parliament and the Cabinet Minister for War, became involved in a sex scandal which made ongoing headlines and eventually led to his resignation and ultimately that of the Prime Minister, Sir Harold Macmillan. Hoping to cash in on the notoriety of the whole episode, a film company was planning to make a movie about it starring the actual call-girls involved in the scandal, Christine Keeler and Mandy Rice-Davies. Equity immediately stepped in and called a meeting at which members objected to these women appearing in the film on the basis that while they could possibly claim to be working in the 'entertainment business', whatever talents or training they had did not qualify them to join our union, and this made them ineligible to take part in the movie. We voted unanimously to veto the entire production unless Equity members only were employed in every relevant capacity. As a result, the project was cancelled. Twenty-six years later, in 1989, a documentary-type film covering part of the story and entitled *Scandal* was finally released, but still with legitimate actors playing every role. I found it amusing to read in Christine Keeler's autobiography[1] that the gentleman who employed her to work in his cabaret as a topless dancer and hostess refused to employ anyone who was an Equity member. Was this perhaps a case of tit for tat?

Grandma and her bells.

My handsome father in his
Salvation Army uniform.

My mother and I – with Teddy.

Above

The Consul (New Zealand Opera Company 1957). From left: Vincente Major, Mary Langford (back view), Corinne, Mona Ross (at desk) and Terence Finnegan.

Left

Outside my London flat in Notting Hill Gate.

Above

St John's College, Cambridge (UK). A temporary stage for *Dido and Aeneas* was erected in front of the arched door seen in the distance.

Right

'When I am laid in earth' – Dido in the 1960 St John's College production.

My farewell gift from 'Artie' in January 1964.

Ray, aged 21.

Nobody recognised the guest tenor.

Ray with June Trelawney.

On the 1957 *Fra Diavolo* tour in Australia. From left: Pamela Coleman, Jozef Drewniak, Gino Zancanaro, Ramon, Doug Parnell and Madge Stephens.

Left

The Duke of Mantua and Maddalena in *Rigoletto* (New Zealand Opera Company 1964).

[Rehearsal photo: John Ashton]

Below

Maddalena, one of opera's naughty girls.

[Photo: Brian Staniland]

'Questa e Quella'. Ramon (second from right with Kathleen Johnson) in rehearsal for *Rigoletto*.

[John Ashton Collection, Alexander Turnbull Library, Wellington]

NZBC Television production of *L'Heure Espagnole*: Donald Rutherford and Ramon.

New Zealand Opera Quartet. Clockwise: Ramon, Corinne, Lucas Bunt and Kathleen Johnson.

(Photo: John Tudehope)

The Quartet toured in a Rothmans-sponsored station wagon. From left: Ramon, Corinne, Russell Channell (pianist), Kathleen Johnson and Ken Simich (CEO Rothmans).

A school student's drawing of the Quartet.

After more than a year in *The Sound of Music*, I began to realise that I was settling into an extremely comfortable rut. I enjoyed the daily routine of waking and brunching late, meeting other cast colleagues to go to a movie or West End show, or tea-dancing the afternoon away at a Leicester Square cabaret with one of the show's dressers, a tall, blond, gay and extremely handsome Scotsman. When our show finished in the evenings, we moved on to The Establishment Club in Soho, a little further along from the Palace Theatre's stage door in Greek Street, to have supper and dance again, or simply sit back and listen to the rising young comedy star and classically trained pianist, Dudley Moore, playing jazz with his trio until the wee small hours. After all, this was the 'Swinging Sixties' in London, and all work and no play would have made this Jill a very dull girl. My singing lessons were continuing privately with my Guildhall teacher, Joyce Newton, but by now I had finished my studies at the Opera School. So, with the exception of our two matinees and any additional rehearsals, the daylight hours were almost free to do as I wished, and to party after the show well into the night.

While this was all very pleasant, it wasn't advancing my prospects of having an opera career and I was losing sight of my goal. Auditions I'd done for various companies including Sadler's Wells Opera, English Opera Group, Glyndebourne Festival Opera and D'Oyly Carte Opera had not been completely unsuccessful, but apart from the occasional understudy role, no definite contracts had been offered and the message in their letters was that 'there are no vacancies at the moment, however your name is now definitely on our list and we hope that we shall be able to offer you something in the future.' My singing teacher strongly advised me against auditioning for the chorus in any of the major opera houses, as she considered this would limit my chances of eventually being engaged as a principal. She had also been unhappy when I took the nuns' chorus job in *The Sound of Music*, but realised the financial security was necessary to allow me to remain in Britain, and at least I was singing music that wouldn't harm my voice. However, she was worried about the fact that many major Opera Houses are not interested in employing singers as principals if they have a background of working in musicals. This doesn't seem to matter the other way round, for a number of 'retired' opera stars continue their careers in lighter shows. The opera companies I auditioned for advised me to get further experience and increase the operatic roles in my repertoire. Good advice, but how could this be achieved without at least some employment with one of them?

Towards the end of 1963, I received a letter from the New Zealand Opera Company offering me two roles in operas to be presented during their first season for 1964, *Rigoletto* and *The Bartered Bride*, together with the possibility of further work later in the year which would probably include the role of Dorabella in Mozart's *Così fan tutte*. Rehearsals were due to commence on 16 March 1964 so, if I accepted the offer and returned to New Zealand, I needed to move swiftly. The necessary travel arrangements would have to be made and time allowed for the person replacing me in *The Sound of Music* to be selected and rehearsed before I could leave the show. As it turned out, my decision to accept this opportunity and return to New Zealand would lead to many years as a professional singer there and then later again in the United Kingdom. But most importantly, it also led to my meeting the real love of my life and future husband, Ramon Opie.

Chapter 6

Ramon

I left England with mixed feelings. The chance to advance my opera experience at home was wonderful, but life had been good in London, particularly the eighteen months in *The Sound of Music*. My ambition to be fully employed as a singer had been achieved, if not entirely in opera, and the many friends I made there were hard to leave. During my final week in the show, the cast showered me with presents, cards, and entreaties to 'write often'. They also gave me a special *Sound of Music* programme with everyone's signature and messages of affection and good wishes; this remains one of my most treasured possessions. A cartoonist, who worked for a London evening newspaper and was a regular visitor backstage at the Palace Theatre, did an amusing drawing of me for a farewell present. 'Artie' (I don't remember his real name) shows me dressed in my nun's costume with a suitcase beside me, indicating that I am on my way to New Zealand and trying to hitch a ride by showing a bit of leg.

I wept all through my last performance in the show, and it was a desperately sad 'ex-nun' who, at the end of January 1964, caught a train to Liverpool, boarded the Blue Star Shipping Company's container ship *Wellington Star* (cheap and with only 11 other passengers) to begin her journey back to New Zealand.

I arrived home shortly before rehearsals for the New Zealand Opera Company's season of *Rigoletto*, *The Bartered Bride* and *Così fan tutte* were due to start. I'd been memorising my roles of

Maddalena in *Rigoletto* and Ludmilla in *The Bartered Bride* before I left England and during the voyage, so was well prepared and looking forward to meeting and working with the other singers. What I wasn't prepared for was the magnificent voice of the tenor singing the leading role of the Duke of Mantua in *Rigoletto*, Ramon Opie.

Before leaving New Zealand I had heard Ramon sing once, in a Wellington performance of *The Messiah*, and vaguely knew that he'd been working with the New Zealand Opera Company during my absence overseas. I had never seen or heard him in opera. No matter what time of day we rehearsed, be it early in the morning or late at night, Ray sang in full voice; no 'marking' or saving his voice for him. Each time he sang one of his effortless top Cs, the musical director for this season, Georg Tintner, told him to save them for the actual performances – when he'd be paid for them. I discovered that many of the other singers involved in the production were equally in awe of Ray's voice, especially as he was known to party as fervently as he sang. No matter what he'd been up to the previous evening, he happily and easily tossed off high Cs at an early morning rehearsal, while anyone else who'd indulged in a heavy night was transposing his or her music down an octave.

Throughout my five years overseas, I attended dozens of rehearsals and performances at The Royal Opera House Covent Garden, Sadler's Wells and other major European Opera Houses, hearing some of the finest tenors in the world at that time, including Guiseppe di Stefano, Jon Vickers, Franco Corelli, Carlo Bergonzi and Mario del Monaco. Now, back home, I found myself working with a New Zealander who was practically their equal vocally, and it astonished me that such a singer was not also on the international circuit. I learned later that Ray had been offered a rehabilitation scholarship to cover overseas study at the end of World War Two, but he was unable to take this up owing to family commitments. Two other servicemen, bass Inia Te Wiata and tenor Andrew Gold, had accepted these scholarships and both succeeded in highly acclaimed careers. I firmly believe that Ray would have been just as successful, if not more so.

Raymond Fergus Opie was 46 years old when I met him, and in the full flush of his vocal powers. He was born on 9 November 1917 in Winchester, New Zealand, to a baker Arthur William (born 22 July 1874 in Waimate) and his wife, Lilly Agnes (née Gillum, born 27 March 1884 in Winchester), and was the first of their three children. His grandparents, John Opie and Jane Tregonning Collins, were born in Cornwall, England, and immigrated to New Zealand soon after their marriage on 20 August 1866. They travelled on the third pioneer voyage of the Glenmark, which sailed from London on 25 August 1866, arriving at Lyttelton on 17 December. From the family records Ray so avidly researched during the 1970s and '80s, it appears that John and Jane joined the ship at Plymouth, England. The following is taken from a *Lyttelton Times* article dated 21 December 1866:

> The *Glenmark* cast anchor in our harbour on Thursday morning at 3 o'clock after a passage of ninety-six days from the Lizard. She left London on Saturday August 25th, on Tuesday 28th sailed from Gravesend. In the channel she encountered a series of heavy gales from the south-west and succeeded in reaching Plymouth on Thursday, September 6th where she remained within the breakwater till the 13th. Lost sight of the Lizard on the 15th; had light and variable winds to the 15th parallel, losing also the trades. The ship was becalmed several days by incessant heavy rains. On October 20 passed the 20th meridian and commenced running down the longitude under an alternation of gales and strong winds from the north-west; on Sunday November 11 passed the Cape of Good Hope in latitude 43 deg. 41 mins south and experienced nor-westerly winds till off the coast of Tasmania. On December 7 met with light and variable winds from the north; sighted the Snares on December 16th about 10.00am and continued in an easterly direction to get off the land until midday; sighted Akaroa Heads on Wednesday last and Godley Head lighthouse at sundown, arriving at anchorage on Thursday at 3.00am.
>
> The passengers speak in high favour of Captain Wrackmore and his officers and their kindness. One birth occurred on the passage out; on October 14th the wife of Mr Isherwood was safely

> delivered of a son. All the passengers are in the enjoyment of good health.

John and Jane Opie settled first in Waimate, where John found work with the Waimate Roads Board as a road marker. They later moved to Winchester, where he established the butchery and bakery business that would eventually be passed on to his son, Arthur William, Ray's father. John was choirmaster at the St Augustine church in Waimate for many years, and Opie Street in the town is named after him.

Arthur and Agnes married on 13 September 1914 and had three children, Raymond, Doreen and John. On 3 August 1923, owing to Agnes's death from pneumonia in June that year, Ray and his younger brother John were placed in the care of the Salvation Army's Bramwell Booth Boys' Home in Temuka, while their sister went to live with relatives. Although the boys were reasonably cared for as far as their physical and educational needs were concerned, I formed the opinion from Ray's occasional reminiscences of his years at the Home that he was very unhappy there and desperately longed for love and encouragement. One particular childhood memory relating to his father's monthly visits to the Home always upset him. When the visit ended and his Dad had to leave to catch the bus back to Winchester, Ray accompanied him to the stop, said goodbye, then ran after the bus until it was out of sight, after which he miserably returned to the Home. Once there, he got up to some sort of mischief to get attention from someone, even if it was only punishment.

The Bramwell Booth Boys' Home had its own school, known as the Watt-Lowry School, where Ray and John received their early education. Their post-primary schooling was at the Temuka District High School. While records obtained from The Salvation Army Territorial Archives briefly state, 'The only comment about his musical ability was on the admission card – very musical,' orphanage friends and family report that he had an excellent boy-soprano voice and was eager to sing whenever the opportunity occurred. For example, he was part of a group of boys from the Home who regularly sang at local functions and church events, as well as during the Salvation Army's traditional presentation of carols on street corners at Christmas. Some of the concerts, held at halls in Temuka, Geraldine and Winchester, were fund-raising events for the Home, while the back of a truck was the stage on which the young lads sang their carols.

Apart from the occasional short holiday when they stayed with relatives, Ray and John lived at the Boys' Home for over nine years. Ray finished his schooling a few weeks after his fifteenth birthday and left Temuka on 4 January 1933 to live and work on a farm owned by Mr W. Tait at Rangitata Island in Geraldine county. One of his duties was to milk the cows, and he heartily serenaded the herd while working. With remarkable foresight his employer realised that Ray had the makings of a fine singer, and suggested that it might be wise to have proper vocal training. Taking this advice, Ray began singing lessons with Miss Lilian McDonald in Timaru and studied with her for about four years. To attend his weekly lessons he rode a bicycle from the Rangitata Island farm to Timaru and back, a distance of approximately 25 miles there and back, probably singing all the way.

Lilian McDonald was born in Cromwell, but went to Australia to take vocal lessons at the Garcia School of Singing, Sydney, under a teacher whose pupils had included Dame Nellie Melba. Her professional singing career in Australia included concert and opera work, and it is known that she toured with an opera company, possibly the Melba-Williamson Opera Company which travelled throughout Queensland and New South Wales during the 1920s. On her return to New Zealand in 1931, she set up a voice and piano teaching practice in Timaru, where she continued to be actively involved in the music scene over the next fifty years.

Between the 1930s and 1950s, Lilian produced, directed and accompanied several operas as well as coaching the singers in the principal roles, many of whom were her pupils. These productions, together with participation in the various Competition Society festivals throughout the South Island, provided valuable performing experience for the young singers. As early as 1934 she encouraged one of her most gifted pupils, Raymond Opie, then aged 16, to enter the vocal classes at an Ashburton Competition

Society festival, but I have been unable to find out what he sang or where he was placed.

When Ray's younger brother John was also old enough to leave school, he moved to Wellington and took work as a kitchen hand. He eventually encouraged Ray to join him in the capital. Ray arrived there a few months before his 21st birthday and also worked as a kitchen hand and porter at the Salvation Army's private hotel in Cuba Street, the People's Palace (currently the Comfort Hotel). Ray briefly had singing lessons with Lucien Cesaroni, but went on to study far more extensively with Tom Wood, and began entering the men's vocal classes at the Wellington Competition Society's festivals. By a strange quirk of fate, my father assisted backstage at the 1938 WCS festival and was highly impressed with the young tenor's voice. During the 1939, 1940 and 1941 festivals, Ray won the Sacred, Tenor, Special Chappell, Radio and Lieder solos, and was runner-up in the Men's Vocal and Operatic solos, and the English folk song sections.

While Ray's greatest love in life was to sing, he suffered severely from stage fright during those early days, and found competing in the various classes immensely stressful. On several occasions he actually fainted before going on stage, but in his determination to succeed as a singer, he concentrated on overcoming his nervousness. His health problems in later life led surgeons to believe that he may have suffered rheumatic fever at some stage in his youth, resulting in damage to one of his heart valves, and this could have also accounted for the earlier fainting spells.

While working at the People's Palace, Ray met Gladys Elizabeth Averill and they married on 18 April 1940, when Ray was 22 and Gladys 27. They were to have two children, Elizabeth and John. Ray joined the New Zealand Armed Forces in 1942, and over the next three years served at various army camps throughout the North Island including Trentham, Linton, Rotorua and Papakura, before being transferred to the Headquarters of the Army Education and Welfare Service in Auckland. He was considered unfit to serve overseas through having been born with flat feet. However, his Army Education superiors were quick to recognise that Ray's unique singing talent deserved the best tuition available and in 1944 he was awarded a scholarship to assist his further vocal training. This led to nine years study with one of Auckland's finest singing teachers, Dr Kenneth Phillips. Even at this early stage in his career, Ray was singing the tenor solos in church performances of the most popular oratorios, including Stainer's *The Crucifixion* and Handel's *The Messiah*; the latter would become one of his most regularly performed sacred works. A friend who sang in the Kingsland Methodist Church choir remembers that while soloists were not required to attend the choir's rehearsals, other than the final one before the performance, Ray still 'popped in from time to time to help the tenors out,' or simply to sit contentedly at the back of the church and enjoy the music.

With the aid of an inheritance from a relative in South Africa, Ray purchased a house and four acres of land in Maioro Street (previously Munster Road), Avondale and it was here that he was able to do something he enjoyed almost as much as singing. Had he not been gifted as a singer, he would have chosen to work on the land. Many years later, he told me that his ideal life would be to own a farm and raise beef cattle. The Maioro Street property therefore gave him great pleasure and he was soon producing virtually everything his family needed, with a large vegetable garden, two milking cows and poultry. He also grew flowers, in particular irises, gladioli and lilies, for the market.

Soon after his war service finished in 1945, Ray took a full-time clerical job at the Department of Labour in Auckland. He also entered and won the Auckland radio station 1ZB talent quest *Spotlight on Amateurs* and over the next few years continued to win all the relevant classes at the Auckland Competition Society's Festivals, including the Vocal Championship gold medal.

One of Ray's first professional engagements to sing *The Messiah* in Wellington with the Royal Wellington Choral Union on 14 December 1946 almost ruined his future career. At the morning rehearsal before the concert he felt feverish, with a bad headache and dry throat. He thought this might simply be nerves or the onset of a cold or 'flu. Before going on stage that evening, he tried to moisten and soothe his throat with lemon juice and honey, but found this only made him feel worse. Once on stage, he became disorientated and was unable to complete his first solo. The confusion persisted throughout the performance and his voice kept failing him. The critics slated his efforts in their reviews, making various assumptions as to the reason for his difficulties. It transpired however that Ray was in the early stages of mumps, something that only became evident a few days after the performance. With a supporting letter from his doctor, describing the symptoms which occur during the incubation period of the illness, Ray wrote a letter of explanation to the RWCU and enclosed the cheque covering his concert fee.

Immediately after the concert, and before knowing what his problem was, Ray sought the assistance of his previous Wellington teacher, Tom Wood. In an attempt to explain Ray's difficulties, Mr Wood wrote the following letter to the local newspaper, which was published under the heading 'Tenor's ordeal' on 16 December 1946:

> Sir, – I am sure you will grant me the space required to restore the reputation of the Auckland singer, Ramon Opie who passed through a terrifying experience during the performance of *The Messiah* on Saturday night. Tenors of course are rare, and Mr Opie has had a very full year of singing in Auckland. This, combined with his ordinary occupation, has proved to be too much for him and his collapse during 'Evr'y Valley' was the unfortunate result. Mr Opie came to see me after the performance and I considered it wise to advise him to continue with his broadcast from 2YA on Sunday afternoon. He accomplished the task with credit and I am sure all listeners-in wish him a speedy recovery to full health. Mr Opie sang successfully in the Auckland performance of *The Messiah* last year and I know many lovers of the great work would like to see him have the opportunity of singing them in our city at some future performance. I am, etc.
> THOMAS WOOD'

The gossipmongers persisted in airing their views however, and early in January 1947 his current teacher, Dr Phillips, enlisted the aid of Auckland music critic, Arthur Fairburn, who wrote an account of the whole affair that was given nationwide release through the NZ Press Association. This fortunately put an end to the unhappy business and the disastrous effect it could have had on Ray's further professional progress. The RWCU were good enough to return Ray's fee, together with a letter which included these reassuring words: 'The fact that you were unable to sing the solos in *The Messiah* that evening will not prejudice you in any way when the question of soloists comes up for future consideration.' Ray would indeed successfully sing *The Messiah* and other works with them on future occasions.

Over the next few years, while continuing with his singing lessons, working full-time with the Department of Labour and caring for his family and small piece of land, Ray still managed to increase his repertoire by learning and performing an extraordinary number of oratorio works, light operas and general recital programmes. Besides being engaged to sing with various choral societies throughout New Zealand, he was in constant demand as a guest artist for concerts, club 'smokos' or social events, music festivals, special military and business company celebrations, sports, church and Masonic Lodge occasions, weddings and funerals; he even sang at a ceremony celebrating the opening of the Auckland Harbour Bridge in 1959.

There are dozens of stories to be told about these various events, and many of Ray's associate artists have their favourites. Max Cryer tells of a memorable occasion when he was pianist for Ray at a concert in Thames:

> The performers were all front-rank singers, but there was nothing stuffy about them. The audience warmed up very quickly to star soprano June Trelawney who was witty and had no hesitation in singing directly to the men in the audience, much to the glee of their companions. Ray came on stage and his body language immediately indicated that he was 'one of the blokes' and he rapidly sealed that impression by starting with the big ballad 'Because'– always a good crowd pleaser. I had played the piano for Ray many times, and knew that if he was in the mood, he would take the top C at the end, but I had to be ready; if he

> sang the note down rather than up, the piano playing had to fit it. The end of the song came – and Ray unleashed a top C the like of which I don't think Thames had ever heard before. And they heard it for a long time, because the note just kept keeping on – while I made dramatic chords underneath to support the impact of this extraordinary sound. When Ray stopped, there was one of those amazing moments you don't often get in concerts – stunned silence, during which Ray calmly told his audience, 'Could've stayed on that note for a week.' The following burst of applause was deafening – I don't think I heard a silent moment and an equal outbreak of noise like that until years later, when I heard Pavarotti at the Metropolitan Opera in New York. The hall in Thames was not the most elegant to perform in, but that night they heard singing of a very superior quality.

Ray's regular broadcasting work included solo recitals and more than fifteen years as guest artist for a variety of programmes, including the *Just a Song at Twilight* and *Music for You* series. Many of these were accompanied by the Radio 1ZB orchestra conducted by Oswald Cheesman, with either Ossie or Reg Morgan playing keyboards. In 1949, the New Zealand Broadcasting Service engaged Ray to undertake a nationwide tour of radio stations. For those who have noticed spelling changes to his Christian name, these are not typos and the explanation is rather amusing. Early in Ray's broadcasting career, a radio announcer introduced one of the items included in Ray's programme with the words, 'We now hear Raymon Dopie in *A Dream* by Edvard Grieg.' After that aberration, it was speedily decided to drop the Y and the D in Raymond to avoid any further diction lapses by radio announcers and/or concert comperes. This change led to some imaginative publicity in Australia when Ray was on tour there a few years later and the press releases promoted him as the 'exciting new Spanish tenor'.

Also in 1949, Ray sang his first major operatic role, Max in Weber's opera *Der Freischütz*, when it was presented in a concert version by the Auckland Choral Society. The conductor was the Society's extraordinarily gifted musical director, Georg Tintner, who had become Ray's major mentor. Tintner would later state in a letter of reference supporting Ray's application for a New Zealand Government Bursary, that 'I consider his voice is in world class; certainly he has no superior in Australasia.'

Georg Tintner was born in Vienna in 1917 and received the highest forms of musical training there. He began piano lessons at the age of six, was a member of the Vienna Boys Choir from the age of nine to 13 and went on to attend the Vienna State Academy, where he studied conducting under Felix Weingartner and composition under Josef Marx. In 1936, aged 19 and still a student at the Academy, he was engaged by the Volksoper (Vienna's Municipal Opera House) as a part-time assistant conductor and coach; this position became a full-time one after the completion of his studies the following year. When the Nazis seized power in 1938, Tintner fled Austria because he was Jewish and eventually came to New Zealand in 1940, settling in Auckland for several years. To earn a living he set up a poultry farm supplying eggs to the market, but continued to seek employment in his real sphere, the world of music. One of the great misfortunes in New Zealand's musical history is that Georg Tintner's exceptional knowledge and abilities were not appreciated to the extent they should have been, except by a few more enlightened musicians and music critics. It was through one of his few musical appointments in Auckland, as conductor of the Auckland Choral Society from 1947 to 1953, that he first met Ray and, together with Dr Phillips, played a huge part in furthering Ray's career.

I have previously mentioned how the training of a singer's voice can run into difficulties. Ray was distinctly lucky that his vocal teachers recognised his natural vocal technique and did nothing to alter it. Dr Phillips simply worked on the other attributes necessary for an accomplished singer: breathing, diction, phrasing, style, interpretation, repertoire and, above all, *bel canto* or beautiful singing. This probably accounts for the fact that Ray was able to sing very well until the last few months of his life, despite serious heart problems. Unfortunately, there are very few recordings of Ray's work, other than old open-reel tapes and cassettes made privately of radio broadcasts, at home or at parties. The sound quality is poor as they are basically amateur recordings made under bad conditions. However, when listening to one of these, a friend made a remark which for me sums up Ray's innate talent and instinctive ability just to open his mouth and sing superbly. He said, 'Ray sings as if he was taught before he was born.'

One of the major obstacles in Ray's career was the lack of insight by those people who were in a position to help him achieve the international success he would have been vocally capable of. When it became possible for him to consider travelling overseas and continue his training, Ray applied on two occasions for a Government bursary, in 1951 and 1969, but was refused, largely because he was unable to read music and lacked an appropriate musical education. Ask any suitably qualified authority to name the three things that make a great singer, and the answer will always be voice, voice, and voice. I also respect the argument put forward by the renowned conductor and pianist, Andre Previn, who said, when someone criticised a young musician who could play the piano by ear but couldn't read music, 'You talk before you can read.' All the academic qualifications possible will only create a competent musician, not a great one, if they lack that extra special gift in the first place. There is a saying, 'Those who can, do; those who can't, teach.' This is perhaps a little unfair and not entirely true, as many notable performers become fine teachers and generously pass on their wide knowledge and experience. But it must be admitted that this is often only after they have basically retired from their own active careers. I firmly believe that as Ray had a supreme vocal gift, he could have mastered the other skills he lacked with suitable education and support.

While Ray didn't read music, he had a phenomenal ear. He had only to hear the music of a new work played a couple of times, and it was committed to his memory. This also proved a curse, as he found it difficult to change a note value or musical phrase if it was altered or he misheard it in the first place. It was therefore the excellent coaching of Georg Tintner, and later another Auckland Choral Society conductor, Ray Wilson, together with constant assistance from the composer, harpist, teacher and accompanist, Dorothea Franchi, that enabled Ray to quickly master the many difficult oratorio and opera scores he would sing throughout his career.

During the earlier years of his tuition, Dr Phillips was careful to limit Ray's operatic repertoire to only the occasional aria. However, the 1949 *Der Freischütz* concert proved that Ray was ready to sing an entire opera role, and while such opportunities were limited in New Zealand at the time, the situation would improve during the 1950s. His engagements included singing various operatic arias at Promenade and other concerts with the National Orchestra of New Zealand, but it was 1952 before he sang his next full role when the Auckland Operatic Society presented a staged production of Smetana's *The Bartered Bride*, again conducted by Georg Tintner. Ray sang the principal tenor role of Jenik, and his leading lady was a well-loved and popular Auckland soprano, Bette Spiro, who would sing with him on many future occasions.

In 1956, Ray sang the role of Luigi in Puccini's *Il Tabarro*, in one of the Sunday Showcase programmes broadcast on the Wellington radio station 2ZB. The following year, Frank Poore, the musical director and business manager of the Light Opera Club in Auckland, decided to mount a full-scale production of Verdi's *La Traviata*, largely in opposition to the fledgling New Zealand Opera Company. This production was to be a showcase for the young coloratura soprano, Mina Foley, in the role of Violetta, with Ray singing the role of her lover, Alfredo. In the event, Mina was unable to take part in the production owing to a breakdown in her health, and another fine soprano, 18-year-old Mary O'Brien, replaced her. This immensely successful production played to full houses, and the artists involved were virtually a Who's Who of the best singers in Auckland at the time, including Patricia Price, Ian Morton, Noel Mangin, Doreen Harvey, Hazel Millar, Frederick Cox, Maurice Parsons, Jill Evans and Barry Hogan. Three of the opera's leading principals, Ray, Mary O'Brien and Patricia Price, were engaged for a concert tour soon after the *Traviata* season ended. Under the title *Music for the People*, the show travelled as far south as Invercargill.

On 17 October 1953, Georg Tintner conducted his penultimate Auckland Choral Society concert before leaving to settle for a time in Australia and take up full-time employment as Musical Director for the National Opera of Australia. The two works presented at this concert were Beethoven's *Christ on the Mount of Olives* and the first public New Zealand performance of Bruckner's *Mass in F Minor*. A recent biography covering Tintner's life and career, written by his third wife, Tanya Buchdahl Tintner, states that the soloists for this concert were the country's best – soprano Mina Foley, contralto Heather Begg, baritone Ashley Pollock and Ray, and that the *NZ Herald*'s music critic, L. C. M. Saunders wrote:

> But for one man's fervent enthusiasm for one of the 19th century's most neglected composers, Auckland would have missed a choral performance [of Bruckner's *Mass in F minor*] that for an hour touched off a spiritual feeling rarely created in the concert hall. It was not surprising that this was in every way Mr Tintner's night. Both before and after the concert, he received ovations whose warmth indicated the very large audience realised how great a blow will be dealt to Auckland music by his departure at the end of the year.[1]

A recording was made of this concert and the Choral Society presented four open-reel tapes to Tintner as a parting gift. Tanya Buchdahl Tintner writes that three of the tapes 'were among the very few possessions [Tintner] owned at the end of his life.'[2]

Tintner's move to Australia did not finish his association with Ray, however. In 1957, he directed the National Opera of Australia's extensive rural tour of Auber's opera *Fra Diavolo*, and engaged Ray to sing the role of Lorenzo.

When undertaking rural tours, the Australian opera troupe travelled and lived in train carriages, or the Opera Express as they named it. These transported the sets, costumes, wigs and lighting, three stage crew and, of course, the singers and musical director. Tanya Tintner says that the Opera Express carriages were 'coupled to a succession of goods trains, a few kilometres at a time ... and afforded cramped quarters, frayed tempers, limited hot water for showers, disturbed sleep on noisy sidings, wild after-show parties and romances.'[3] On arrival at the town or settlement where the opera was to be played, the carriages were parked in a siding and remained there until the performances were over. The scenery, costumes and lighting were unloaded on to a truck and taken to the appropriate venue where they were set up and the opera performed. Eventually everything, including the personnel, returned to the carriages which were then collected by another goods train and, while the performers tried to sleep, transported to the next centre where the whole process was repeated.

The *Fra Diavolo* tour covered some 5000 miles throughout northern New South Wales and Queensland. It was also to have travelled to southern New South Wales and Victoria, but just before the start of the tour the National Opera of Australia suffered a financial collapse and the existing arrangements, with the exception of the latter part of the tour, were taken over by the Government-funded Elizabethan Theatre Trust.

Ray spent over six months in Australia during this period, hoping to continue his career there on a permanent basis. The Australian Broadcasting Commission engaged him for a number of radio and concert engagements, but these did not provide enough money to live on. He therefore auditioned for and was accepted by an agent who introduced him into the busy entertainment circuit of Australia's large network of Returned Servicemen League clubs where Ray found regular work as a cabaret-type entertainer. Family commitments eventually made it necessary for him to return to New Zealand, and it was not until 1962 that he was again engaged to sing in Australia, as guest artist with the Sydney Symphony and Queensland Symphony Orchestras, and to record several broadcast recitals.

Ray used to tell an amusing story about this second episode in Australia, which came about through the illness of another singer. A prominent international tenor, Thomas L. Thomas, had been engaged for the concert tour but fell ill at the last minute and Ray was chosen to replace him. Immediate arrangements were made for Ray to fly from Auckland to Sydney, where he was to be met by the concert organisers' representatives who would look after his accommodation and other arrangements while he was on tour. I guess these people didn't want to embarrass themselves, or Ray, by holding his name up on a card when he arrived at the airport, and probably assumed a tenor who sang opera would be easily recognisable anyway. Ray was of average height and build, and certainly did not fit the ostentatious or flamboyant image people seem to expect of opera singers. As Max Cryer describes him, Ray was simply an 'endearing Kiwi bloke'. It therefore greatly amused him that he passed all of the people waiting for him without anyone realising who he was, and then had to ask the airport staff to page them advising that he was there. He said he felt like a lost kid looking for his mummy.

In between these two Australian visits, an event took place which deeply upset Ray. His beloved teacher and mentor, Dr Kenneth Phillips, died in 1961. As well as being a fine vocal teacher, Dr Phillips was a composer and had written a beautiful setting of *Ave Maria* which he specifically requested be sung at his funeral by Ray when the time came. The venue chosen for the service was St Mary's Church in Parnell, and as is normal procedure, Ray contacted the organist to arrange a suitable time for rehearsal. When this gentleman saw that the music for the *Ave Maria* had been composed by Dr Phillips rather than one of the more familiar versions by Schubert or Gounod, he told Ray it would not be acceptable because it was not on the list of approved music the Dean allowed to be sung in the church. Bitterly hurt by this, Ray preferred not to sing at St Mary's again.

His first engagement with the New Zealand Opera Company came in 1962 when he sang the role of Cavaradossi in their production of Puccini's *Tosca*, which toured throughout New Zealand. All the leading roles for this season were double-cast, and Ray shared his role with another talented local tenor, Jon Andrew. Alternating in the title role were sopranos Vincente Major and Elisabeth Hellawell, while Italian opera star, Marcello Cortis, was engaged from Italy to direct the opera and sing the role of Scarpia, which he shared with local baritone Graeme Gorton. This was the first time the NZOC had engaged an overseas singer to work with the company, and although Cortis's vocal career was coming to an end, his presence in the cast certainly stimulated the local singers' performances and inspired them to prove they could favourably compare with an international artist. While Ray, Elisabeth and Graeme were not in the opening cast, the *Auckland Star*'s Desmond Mahoney, who reviewed both casts' performances, wrote:

> Not only were the opening principals, Vincente Major, Marcello Cortis and Jon Andrew well matched and balanced, but their alternates, Elisabeth Hellawell, Graeme Gorton and Ramon Opie were if anything superior vocally … on present showing, Mr Opie … will have found the key for making the most of his magnificent natural voice.

A Christchurch reviewer was equally enthusiastic: 'Mr Opie has a tenor voice of thrilling vibrancy and of remarkable power. His Bel Canto is real and the result is a delight to hear.' Even Marcello Cortis himself, a former La Scala Opera House principal, said of Ray, 'If I had a voice like that, I would have been the best tenor in Europe.'

The following year the NZOC's productions included Puccini's *La Bohème*, in which Ray sang the leading role of Rodolfo, again on a nationwide tour. Georg Tintner returned from Australia to conduct this season and an Auckland newspaper article headed 'Tenor and Conductor renewed friendship' began: 'The only singer in the New Zealand Opera Company who responds to the name Caruso is Ramon Opie.' It continues with details of Ray and Georg's previous musical collaborations, and credits Tintner as being the 'man who has done most to advance [Ray's] career.'

Ray also found time during 1963 to be one of the judges for Auckland Radio 1ZB's talent quest *Have a Shot* and to sing as guest artist at numerous private engagements. With the usual December *Messiah* rehearsals and performances, together with his 'real job' during the day and the care of his family and their small piece of land, there would have been little spare time.

Ray resigned from his position with the Labour Department in the early1960s and purchased a small IGA store in Blockhouse Bay. He and his wife managed this together, hoping that having their own business would allow Ray more freedom to continue his ever-expanding singing career. While this worked to some extent, problems arose whenever he had to leave Auckland for an extended opera tour and it was necessary to employ someone to help his wife manage the business in his absence. The singing fees and expenses received for his touring work were often less than the wage Ray had to pay a temporary shop manager and it became obvious that he lost income each time he went away. While he desperately wanted to sing as much as possible, and engagements in Auckland and throughout New Zealand were continually offered, the remuneration was still insufficient to allow him to devote himself entirely to a singing career. This has been and still is the situation for virtually every classical singer in New Zealand who is capable of earning a living in the profession, and the reason why the best and most dedicated of the country's talent has to move overseas. In this earlier part of his career, Ray's total commitment to singing wherever and whenever he could in his homeland, despite always needing to find another source of income to support his family, was a godsend for the country's choral societies, orchestras and the New Zealand Opera Company.

Towards the end of 1963, Ray received a contract to sing the role of the Duke of Mantua in the NZOC's 1964 production of Verdi's *Rigoletto*. An engagement to sing the role of Florestan in a concert version of Beethoven's *Fidelio* presented by the Auckland Choral Society was also offered. He would sing this latter role a number of times in both concert and staged productions in Wellington and Auckland. He finished 1963 on a high note, so to say, when he was engaged by the New Plymouth Bowl of Brooklands Trust as the guest artist for their holiday season concerts.

Chapter 7

The Duke and the naughty girl

The New Zealand Opera Company's first 1964 season, consisting of three operas, began in March and finished at the end of June. While *Così fan tutte* played only in Auckland during that city's annual Arts Festival, *Rigoletto* and *The Bartered Bride* were performed on alternate nights in many other New Zealand centres, including Wellington, Christchurch, Dunedin, Invercargill, Auckland, Hamilton, Gisborne, Napier, Hastings, Palmerston North, Wanganui, New Plymouth and Hawera.

The three-month season opened in Wellington with *Rigoletto*, which played to generally full houses for the rest of the tour. It was directed by John Thompson and designed by Raymond Boyce, with the musical director, Georg Tintner, conducting an augmented New Zealand Broadcasting Corporation Concert Orchestra. The set designer, director and conductor for *The Bartered Bride* were all from overseas. The orchestra toured with the company, so audiences throughout New Zealand heard and saw the complete operas with full orchestral accompaniment.

Mention of the orchestra reminds me of the final dress rehearsal for *Rigoletto* the day before we opened at the Wellington Opera House. The majority of rehearsals for any opera are with piano accompaniment only. The orchestra rehearses separately and the singers only join them for one or maybe more rehearsals, called Sitzproben, before the dress rehearsals in the theatre. The less financial the opera company, the fewer rehearsals there are with orchestra. Taking the cost factor into consideration as well, the orchestra stipulates how many hours it will work, and rehearsals have to fit within that period. Our one and only on-stage dress rehearsal with orchestral accompaniment ran too long, and by the time it came to Maddalena's first entrance in Act Three, the orchestra's session limit had been reached and they left. It was a bit unnerving to sing the opening night of an opera without having previously had a proper orchestral rehearsal on stage. This is where a good conductor can provide much-needed reassurance, and thankfully we had one of the best in Georg Tintner.

The season was a great success and critics were largely enthusiastic. Ray earned good reviews for his work and after the first performance, music critic Russell Bond wrote in Wellington's *Dominion* newspaper: 'To Ramon Opie, however, must go the vocal honours of the evening. His flexible, mellow voice is exactly right for the Duke's insouciant music and he sang with a heart-warmingly fluent ease.'

Reviews in other centres were also good. The Christchurch critic wrote: 'Ramon Opie's voice has a thrilling timbre throughout its large range. He never makes an unsatisfying sound ... he brought artistry and fire to his part ... with the consummate ease of the accomplished artist.' And in Napier: '[Ramon Opie's] ... powerful voice, full throated and rich and admirably true in its tonal quality, filled the theatre.'

Despite Georg Tintner's last few words to me in my dressing room before I went on stage for Act Three, instructing me 'not to sing like a virgin', my reviews for the small role of Maddalena were also good. Russell Bond wrote, 'Best characterisation was the Maddalena of Corinne Bridge,' while Desmond Mahoney in the *Auckland Star* called me 'an altogether perfectly cast Maddalena.' This was echoed by a Christchurch critic: 'Corinne Bridge was a seductive and exciting Maddalena – altogether perfectly cast.'

Opera mezzo-sopranos play many differing roles including maids, mothers, young men ('pants roles', as they are called) and sexy women, for example Carmen, Delilah and Maddalena. This production of *Rigoletto* required Maddalena to be particularly alluring in a seductively designed costume, and the dim stage lighting allowed the audience to use their imagination as to what was perhaps going on up there when the Duke is trying to have his way with her. The dramatic colours of purple and burnt orange were chosen for Maddalena's costume, which had a low-cut bodice and full, heavily fringed and shawl-draped skirt. A slit on one side of the skirt ended at the top of the thigh and my stage movements were carefully directed to ensure that whenever I sat or lay down, the slit faced the audience and the skirt's fabric fell away to reveal the full length of my bare leg. The setting for Act Three is a room at an inn on the outskirts of Mantua. In this production, the room was furnished with a rough-hewn wooden table and Spanish-style carved chairs, a few wine-barrels and several large bales of hay casually stacked at the back, which the Duke used to full advantage during his successful seduction attempt. While this was all very apt for the story of the opera, it led to some embarrassing moments for me at the sponsors' receptions after the performances, from which Ray often rescued me.

A large number of businesses supported the New Zealand Opera Company during the 1960s, including New Zealand Breweries, later Lion Nathan, who were the major sponsors, together with Imperial Chemical Industries, Reid NZ Rubber Mills, Ford Motors, Dunlop NZ, Shell Oil NZ, United Empire Box Company and many others. These sponsors each hosted a particular performance, to which they invited their special guests; wine flowed during the interval and a 'meet the cast' reception was held at a separate venue after the show, with finger food and a great deal more alcohol. As soon as the opera finished and our curtain calls were over, we hurriedly changed out of our costumes, wigs and makeup, and got into our day-clothes to attend the reception. No matter how quickly we did this, the guests had usually imbibed a fair amount by the time we arrived, and during the *Rigoletto* season some of the male guests decided to try their luck with the opera's 'naughty girl'. I was offered several interesting chat-up lines, but the one that has stayed in my memory over the years is, 'Well hello there. My name's Spalding; no doubt you've heard of my balls.' He probably used this line regularly, but not being a sportswoman I had no answer to it. It was at such times, when he could see someone making a nuisance of himself, that Ray came to my rescue.

On another occasion in Dunedin, the reception was held at one of the city's larger hotels. The hotel manager had been drinking heavily and kept insisting that I accompany him to his private rooms, where we could do a little more than admire his 'etchings'. Ray again came to the rescue and after that decided to take on the role of Maddalena's 'minder'.

We did five or six performances of *Rigoletto* in each of the four main cities, with fewer in the other centres. As *Rigoletto* and *The Bartered Bride* played alternately, most of the principals not involved in that particular evening's performance had a free night. My main role was Maddalena, but I was also understudying Dorothy Hitch in her role of Ludmilla in *The Bartered Bride*, and Dorothy was similarly covering me. The company allowed us to do five performances of each other's roles, so this kept Dorothy and me a little busier, and gave us the opportunity to perform the understudy role on stage. Ray had no cover and sang every performance of *Rigoletto*. There was in fact no one else in New Zealand at that time capable of understudying him in this role, and had he been unable to sing for any reason, the company would have been forced to cancel the performance. This very nearly happened in Auckland, when we were performing during the annual Auckland Festival.

Because Maddalena doesn't appear on stage until the third Act of *Rigoletto*, I was permitted to arrive at the theatre later than the rest of the cast, as long as it was before 'Curtain up' at 8 pm. On our last Auckland performance for that season, I arrived at about 7.40 pm and was advised that the director, John Thompson, wanted to see me urgently. Hoping he wasn't unhappy with something in my performance, I went to his office with some misgiving. John's problem turned out to be a major one. He was extremely worried about Ray, who had apparently spent time during the day at a race meeting with friends who were visiting Auckland, and had celebrated rather more than is wise before a performance. On arrival at the theatre Ray requested seats for his friends, but was told that the house was sold out and there was nothing available.

Ray took exception to this and in the best 'primo divo' style, decided that if his friends couldn't see the opera, then he wouldn't sing. Every attempt by John had failed to persuade Ray to change his mind, but he was hoping I might be able to.

Doing some quick thinking, I went to Ray's dressing room and started gathering up his costumes. He was sitting there looking morose, and warily asked what I was up to. I replied that while he wasn't prepared to sing, the rest of us certainly were and there was someone else who could probably take his part. 'There's a young tenor with a very promising voice in the chorus who's been watching your performance each night and singing every word with you,' I told him. 'I'm sure that with help from the rest of us he could get through the opera, so I'll take your costumes down to the men's dressing room and see what can be organised.' It was only bluff of course, but it worked. Ray quickly decided, in fairly colourful language, that this was his 'so-and-so' role and if anyone was going to 'so-and-so- well' sing it, it would be him. He slapped on some makeup, got into his Act One costume and said, 'Point me in the direction of the stage.' The curtain went up a little late, but in his usual incredible fashion, Ray sang as well as ever. By the end of the first Act, he was his normal self again and starting to feel remorseful. The rest of the performance went satisfactorily and there was the usual reception afterwards. Somewhat inauspiciously in this case, however, it was held at the New Zealand Breweries premises in Khyber Pass Road, and Ray took the opportunity to drown his sorrows with the lavish hospitality offered there.

The next day, most of the *Rigoletto* cast travelled by New Zealand Road Services bus to Hamilton for the start of performances there. I was sitting on my own when Ray arrived and asked if he could sit with me. He was wearing a hat and dark glasses and looked very dejected. He spent the first part of the trip apologising for the previous evening's behaviour, and then began pouring out his frustrations regarding the problems touring created for him. While he welcomed every opportunity to sing a major operatic role, he found it depressing having to pay a temporary manager more than he was earning himself in order to keep his Auckland business running. He also found the days and nights difficult when he didn't have to sing and was stuck in a hotel or theatrical digs with nothing much to do other than hang around a bar, play pool or watch television. I commented that apart from his particular financial situation, we were all in much the same position, and suggested that there must be other ways to fill the day which didn't affect the evening performances. This eventually led to a group of us, both singers and orchestra members, regularly getting together throughout the rest of the tour. We hired cars and explored the city or town where we were singing, seeing whatever sights there were to see, visiting museums and art galleries, or just going to the movies. As the cast members came from all parts of New Zealand and we sometimes played in their home towns, we were occasionally invited to their families' homes for a meal or party. Such hospitality was most welcome as it helped combat some of the loneliness that can make one miserable during a long tour.

The first 1964 opera season finished its run in New Plymouth. The vehicle transporting the *Rigoletto* sets, costumes, properties and lighting back to the company's storage facilities in Wellington was due to travel overnight after the last performance, so I took the opportunity to hitch a lift home with the driver. While everything was being loaded into the container, an end-of-show party was held for the cast, and Ray had many of us in tears when he sang the beautiful Act Three tenor aria from *Tosca*, 'E lucevan le stelle', roughly translated as follows:

> The stars shine and the earth smells sweet. A step softly caresses the path and her fragrance enters. I clasp her in my arms. Sweet kisses, lanquid caresses and passion must now be ended. The dawn is breaking and I will die despairing. I, who am so much in love with life.

After the success and enjoyment of the past three months, Ray's sad aria brought us all down to earth. During this time, we'd been paid to work in our real world as singers, which is all we wanted and were best trained to do. Now it was over and once again we faced reality. Our singing careers would be on hold again, and most of us would have to look for temporary work in offices, factories, schools or wherever until the next major singing opportunity came along, if it ever did. Some might never be able to take advantage of such a chance again, if the demands on their lives made it impossible to exist in such a precarious way. It was therefore a tired and dispirited Maddalena who returned to Wellington, wondering what she would do next.

Fortunately for me, a contract from the New Zealand Opera Company arrived soon afterwards, offering the role of Dorabella in a piano-touring production of *Così fan tutte*. This was to be performed throughout the Auckland province and rehearsals were due to start almost immediately. There was also a contract to sing Tisbe, one of the ugly sisters in Rossini's opera *La Cenerentola* or *Cinderella*, to be played in Wellington and Auckland later in the year, so my operatic career was assured for at least the next six months.

But there was a complication of far greater importance facing me at this time. Ray and I had developed into rather more than good friends during the *Rigoletto* season, and he wanted me to consider moving to Auckland. Aware of his marriage, I insisted that he needed to sort out his own affairs first before I could even think about making such a move. He wrote to me almost daily over the next few weeks before I went on tour, and even to my parents, advising them of his feelings for me. The whole period caused a lot of heartache and was extremely difficult for all concerned. There are no easy solutions in such situations and many unhappy endings for some of the people involved. When I finally moved to Auckland there was the usual flurry of gossip, innuendo and unpleasantness which occurs when people a little in the public eye are deemed to have 'fallen from grace'. But that storm had to be weathered and Ray and I managed to do this over the next six years until we were able to marry in 1970. One of the harshest results, however, which Ray only learned about much later, was that a recommendation for him to be awarded a national honour did not go ahead in 1964, 'because of his personal situation'. Justice would be served in 1985 and I believe Ray valued this even more.

Chapter 8

Piano tours

To ensure the entire population of New Zealand was given the opportunity to experience professional opera productions, the New Zealand Opera Company undertook piano tours throughout the country during the 1950s, '60s and early '70s, either before or immediately after an orchestral season in the larger centres. This was in accordance with the founder, Donald Munro's policy of 'taking opera to the people rather than performing just for city audiences.' These tours travelled to as many of the smaller towns and settlements as possible, providing there were passable venues where the company could perform. As the name implies, piano rather than orchestral accompaniment was provided. The following quotation is from a report by Donald Munro covering the work of the New Zealand Opera Company during 1958, which is included in an article written by his son, Dr Doug Munro:

> This year the Opera Company has played in 47 towns throughout New Zealand, to a total of 13,580 people. This excludes the Wellington season where we played for six nights and a matinee to approximately 6,000 people. In all, the Company travelled approximately 4,000 miles. These figures reveal that we are really taking opera to the people and that the people are really taking to opera.

The operas were often 'potted' or shortened, with only the principal roles sung and some of the lesser characters omitted or a singer playing more than one role. For obvious financial and logistical reasons, the large numbers required for a chorus could not be toured. The entire staging and cast usually travelled in a specially adapted New Zealand Road Services bus, with seating left at the front for the singers, stage manager and musical director/accompanist, and the sets, costumes, wigs, props and lighting loaded into the rear where the rest of the seats had been removed. The opera was performed at a different location each night, six nights a week. If a branch of the Community Arts Service existed in the area, it sponsored the visit and its members billeted the cast. Places without a CAS had enthusiastic arts lovers who worked hard to ensure their centres were included as well, and they arranged accommodation for the cast in their own and their friends' homes. The venues were mainly school and community or war memorial halls, with varying types of stage and dressing room facilities. In some places, the enthusiasts even hired or transported their own pianos to the halls when the existing one was really bad or none existed at all. To quote from Dr Doug Munro's article again:

> The condition of some of the country halls in which they performed had to be seen to be believed – but the show went on. In those pre-television days it was one of the few cultural occasions for these small farming communities.

The stage sizes, lack of wings space and limited or no proper dressing rooms created many challenges, so both the sets and singers had to be versatile. Sets were designed to expand or contract, and the furniture and props also had to be adaptable. Besides performing the opera, the singers doubled as stagehands, props' organisers, lighting crew and wigs and costume dressers. These factors led to some interesting and often amusing occurrences during a performance, which the audiences were (usually) happily unaware of. Doors through which one expected to enter or exit would unexpectedly refuse to open, and flowing costumes got caught on all manner of items stored by the locals at the side or back of the stage, often making it difficult to get on to the stage at all. In some places it was even necessary to go outside the hall to make an entrance from the opposite side of the stage, there being no access to cross behind it. That wasn't much fun if it was raining. Rain caused other problems as well. If we were singing in a smaller hall with nothing much above the stage and seating to block out the sound of heavy rain beating down on a corrugated iron roof, the audience could barely hear the performance and the singers had difficulty hearing each other.

Besides the occasional set and stage hiccups, many other unexpected things were likely to happen. During a 1962 piano tour of *Tosca*, Ray again shared the tenor role of Cavaradossi with Jon Andrew. In order to take as little time away from his business as possible, Ray sang at the centres closest to Auckland and returned home directly after the performance, but they covered each other in case one of them became ill. The inevitable happened with Jon losing his voice, and early one afternoon Ray received an urgent summons to travel down to Taumarunui, a distance of approximately 180 miles. He immediately rushed home to pack an overnight bag with everything needed, including his stage makeup, and set off by car.

Stopping only for a quick meal of fish and chips on the way, he arrived in Taumarunui approximately thirty minutes before the performance was due to start. He hurriedly did his makeup and got into costume and was ready in time for his first entrance in Act One. He forgot, however, to powder off his greasepaint makeup before going on stage. After the opening scene and his first big aria, Cavaradossi is joined by his beloved Tosca, and they launch into a passionate love duet. Ardently clasping Tosca in his arms, Ray nestled his cheek against hers while they were singing, but saw to his horror when he drew away that he'd left the imprint of one of his long black greasepaint sideburns on her face. Waiting for a moment when he wasn't singing to warn her, he eventually managed to murmur out of the side of his mouth, 'Don't turn your right cheek to the audience – you're wearing my sideburn.'

The following year *La Bohème* was taken on tour, and a wag in the cast decided to add a little more realism to one of the performances. The floor of the rostrum for the set used in Acts

One and Four was steeply raked, i.e. higher at the back of the stage than the front. These two Acts take place in a rented attic room where the students, or bohemians, live and where the heroine, Mimi, dies of tuberculosis at the end of the opera. During the final Act, Mimi is brought to the room and placed on a bed near the centre of the stage; she and Rodolfo sing of their love for each other and reminisce about happier times until Mimi appears to fall asleep. When Rodolfo's friends tell him that his beloved has in fact died, he throws himself in grief beside the bed and clasps her lifeless body in his arms. On this particular occasion Ray was singing Rodolfo, and the prankster had placed a 'potty' or chamber pot under the bed, well upstage and out of the audience's sight, but as Ray went to embrace Mimi's body, the bed slid further down the raked stage and the 'potty' was slightly exposed. Heads would certainly have rolled had the audience seen this and laughed while poor Mimi was breathing her last.

I was on a later tour of *Madama Butterfly* singing the role of Suzuki, when another unrehearsed incident occurred. Butterfly is a 15-year-old Japanese geisha who has taken the fancy of an American navy lieutenant while his ship is in port, and in order for him to have his way with her, they go through what she believes is a legitimate marriage ceremony. A month after the wedding, her 'husband' returns to the USA and she is left pregnant, but quite certain that he will come back. In Act Two, three years have passed and Butterfly is still waiting, together with her little son – whose name is translated as Trouble when the opera is sung in English. A ship appears in the harbour and, convinced that her 'husband' has returned, Butterfly and her maid Suzuki excitedly gather cherry blossom to decorate the house, then Butterfly puts on her wedding dress, and she, Suzuki and Trouble settle down to await her beloved's arrival. During orchestral seasons of the opera in the larger theatres, two four- or five-year olds played the role of Trouble, rehearsing with us before the season and alternating during it. As it was not possible to take a young Trouble on piano tours, a local child would be quickly rehearsed when we arrived, and we hoped for the best.

Suzuki has to bring Trouble on stage and nurse him during

the 'waiting' scene. The enchanting 'Humming chorus' is softly sung behind the scenes and everything needs to be very quiet and expectant. On this particular occasion, Trouble was in my arms as we knelt beside the moon-shaped shosi, or sliding Japanese window, and while the stage lighting gradually dimmed and the moon rose, we were supposed to fall asleep. Trouble kept wriggling and squirming and I gently whispered to him to close his eyes and pretend to be asleep for just a little while longer. In a loud, high-pitched voice, he protested, 'I can't. I want to go wee-wees.' I had to stay inscrutably in my Japanese character of course, but had visions of a 'wee-wee' soaked kimono before the curtain came down.

In 1965 the New Zealand Opera Company organised a piano tour of two one-act comic operas not previously staged in New Zealand. The first was a little-known American piece by Douglas Moore called *Gallantry*, which the composer aptly describes as a 'soap opera'. It's a parody of the American television programme *Dr Kildare* which was so popular during the 1960s, similar to *Shortland Street* today. The other piece was Ravel's opera about clocks and infidelity, *L'Heure Espagnole*. Ray and I were in the casts for this tour and the season opened at Kingseat, a hospital for mental health patients, situated to the south of Auckland. Billeting arrangements were in the nurses' quarters where we were securely locked in at night. While the hospital had an excellent hall with a reasonably good stage, there were no proper dressing rooms. As soon as we arrived we set up the scenery and lighting, laid out our costumes, props, wigs and makeup in the wings and then went to have a rest and dinner before the evening performance. When I came back later to get ready, I found that my favourite false eyelashes and a few other items from my makeup box were missing. Those eyelashes were my pride and joy and, as they had been purchased in London, I knew they'd be difficult to replace. They consisted of a double row of alternate silver and black hairs, and sparkled glamorously under stage lighting. The items taken were never recovered, but perhaps one of the hospital patients had fun playing with them.

The hall was full for the operas, and the television spoof,

Gallantry, played first. After the scene where an operation is performed, with all the usual slapstick-type antics of using entirely inappropriate surgical instruments to extract sausages and various other unsuitable 'bodily parts' from the wound, Ray, as the patient, had to wake up blearily from his anaesthetic and sing, 'Where am I?' Quite logically, a member of the audience called out, 'In bed, mate.'

To give some idea of the extent of NZOC's piano tours, the *Gallantry* and *L'Heure Espagnole* season covered 2150 miles and played in the following places:

Kingseat (hospital for mental patients)	4 October
Waihi	5 October
Paeroa	6 October
Tauranga	7 October
North Shore (Auckland)	11 October
Cambridge	12 October
Taumarunui	13 October
Taupo	15 October
Tokoroa	16 October
Te Kuiti	18 October
Ardmore (Teachers Training College)	19 October
Warkworth	20 October
Dargaville	21 October
Howick	23 October
Whangarei	26 October
Kaikohe	27 October
Kaeo	28 October
Broadwood	1 November
Thames	3 November
Te Aroha	4 November
Tokanui (hospital for mental patients)	5 November
Te Awamutu	6 November
Te Kauwhata	8 November

We also did a lunchtime performance of *Gallantry* for staff members of Reid New Zealand Rubber Mills in the canteen at their factory in Penrose, Auckland. This company was yet another loyal NZOC sponsor. I remember a further performance of both operas in Wellington's Town Hall Concert Chamber.

The New Zealand Road Services bus driver transporting us during this tour became a good friend and took a keen interest in our work. Although it was not part of his duties, he helped us unload and reload the bus at each venue, and often came to watch the evening performances. Like most Maori New Zealanders, he loved music and said how much he wished he could sing on stage like us. We decided to have some fun one night and give Bob (the driver) an opportunity to make his stage debut, not as a singer of course but in a walk-on role.

As already described above, *Gallantry* is a soap opera. The action takes place in a television studio where the most popular feature programme of the day, a hospital drama, is being produced. Only four characters are involved: the doctor (baritone), patient (tenor), nurse (soprano) and an announcer (mezzo) who extols the virtues of the programme-sponsor's products, Lochinvar soap and Billy Boy wax, during the commercial breaks. Ray, who was playing the patient undergoing an operation, suggested that as people are sometimes sick when coming round from an anaesthetic, we could perhaps contrive some sort of male nurse's costume for Bob, and he could appropriately tend to the patient as Ray recovered. Some might think we were being unprofessional getting up to antics like this, but these tours were hard work and very tiring, so we occasionally needed to amuse ourselves as well. We borrowed a suitable white tunic, trousers and a blue plastic shower cap from one of our billets for Bob, but forgot about providing him with a receptacle for Ray to vomit into. Proving to be a real thespian trooper before he'd even 'trodden the boards', Bob found a bucket backstage and at the right moment walked confidently on stage to tend to his patient. The audience immediately erupted with laughter, in a part where we'd not previously had such a response, and we eventually discovered why. Bob's prop was the bucket normally half-filled with sand and used for stubbing out cigarettes.

He had carefully emptied the sand out, but had either not noticed or didn't think about hiding the large red-lettered NO SMOKING sign printed on one side the bucket, and inadvertently presented this side to the audience.

I played the Announcer in *Gallantry* and had to do the commercials covering the sponsors' products between the hospital scenes, sexily singing such lines as 'The waxy wax that makes you relax,' to promote a floor polish. If the following *NZ Herald* review for the Auckland performance is to be believed, my advertising skills were suitably successful: 'Corinne Bridge was magnificent, alternately seductive, brassy and winsome – all that is required to sell soap and Billy Boy wax.'

One of the funniest events, which could also have proved disastrous, occurred in the little rural settlement of Broadwood. I can't remember the opera we were playing, but I recall that it was a second performance after an opening night at Kingseat Hospital. Broadwood in the 1960s was one of those places where if you blinked when passing through, you'd miss it. A keen group of arts enthusiasts must have lived there, however, as they managed to run a highly successful Community Arts Service which sponsored visits from the New Zealand Ballet, New Zealand Opera Company, New Zealand Players and solo recitalists of all kinds. Performances were held in the Broadwood Memorial Hall, as were most other events in this little farming community. In any one week the hall might be ringing to the sounds of a Mozart opera, a potted Tchaikovsky ballet score or a Shakespeare play, as well as being the venue for a Federated Farmers' meeting, a wedding reception, 21st birthday party, political meeting, a Country Womens' Institute 'Bring and Buy', the Friday night movie or a general 'knees up'. You name it, the Broadwood Hall catered for it.

Like Broadwood itself, the hall was small and consequently the stage was tiny; take five strides across it and you were in the wings again. There were no proper dressing rooms, uncomfortable seating for the audience and worst of all for performers, the only toilet facility was 'front of house'. Whenever we played Broadwood, the women in the cast had to remember to use the 'loo' before the performance, but the men casually said it wasn't a problem as they could just 'nip out the back'. The hall was surrounded on three sides by paddocks containing sheep, cows and, by the look of all the droppings, a great many rabbits as well, while the front entrance faced the main highway.

Usually on a show's opening night, the cast's families and friends send telegrams wishing them luck for the season. As we didn't want to be a nuisance to the staff at Kingseat, it was suggested that any such messages be forwarded to the Broadwood Post Office on the second night instead. This caused quite a stir there, as the post office, together with the telephone exchange and petrol station, was part of the one and only general store. The poor woman trying to operate all these services was soon going frantic as she received telegraphed messages from all parts of New Zealand and then had to close the store while she rushed over to the hall to deliver them. Being 'theatricals', some of the messages we received were a bit risqué and one of them so upset the harried lady that a letter of complaint was sent to the NZOC management after we left. This, again, is another story.

The performance duly started and at the end of the first Act we changed the scenery and lighting in preparation for the second, and the men went outside to relieve themselves before donning their next costumes. What they hadn't bargained for was the fact that country paddocks containing animals are frequently controlled by electric fences. Some very 'shocked' and white-faced men returned backstage, with the deepest baritones suddenly becoming high tenors and the tenors reverting to boy sopranos. Broadwood became forever etched in our memories from then on.

The earlier piano tour of *Così fan tutte* in 1964 went well. The cast included Australian/Italian guest tenor, Gino Zancanaro, who had worked with Ray previously on the *Fra Diavolo* tour in Australia. Two other singers were soprano Kathleen Johnson and baritone Lucas Bunt. Both had sung principal roles in *Rigoletto*, Kathleen as Countess Ceprano and Lucas sharing the Court Jester title role with Graeme Gorton. They were very fine singers and we soon became good friends. In *Così*, Kathleen played Fiordiligi (my sister) and Lucas was Guglielmo (my fiancé). Lucas must have still been in Jester mode as he consistently tried to 'send me up', or make me 'corpse' (laugh) on stage during that tour. I was never quite sure what he'd get up to, but it kept me alert.

As in *Rigoletto*, I was dressed in low-cut period costumes and Lucas took great delight in finding little things to drop down my cleavage as I was about to go on stage. I'm frightened of spiders and he always managed to find something that felt like one, wriggling down my bosom. Inevitably, I decided to get my own back. Lucas's costumes included a pair of pale-blue satin knee-breeches, so one night I filled my little stage make-up sponge with water and just before he went on stage, squeezed it down the front of his pants; he spent the rest of that scene with a gently spreading and darkening blue stain, but good-naturedly accepted that he'd asked for it.

The *Così* tour lasted about five weeks and covered most places from Kaitaia down to Te Kuiti, plus Thames, Paeroa and Morrinsville. As usual, smaller centres were included such as Kaeo, Broadwood, Warkworth, Pukekohe, the Teachers' Training College at Ardmore and a few of Auckland's suburban theatres, including Glen Eden's ghastly, rat-infested Playhouse. This Playhouse has now been magnificently refurbished and I trust it is also rodent-free. We performed at two mental hospitals – Kingseat and Tokanui – and were again billeted in the nurses' quarters and locked in at night. Auckland's Mt Eden Prison was sometimes a venue, but not this time.

Ray was not singing in this particular tour, but kept himself busy in Auckland with concert and broadcasting engagements, including the Ossie Cheesman Singers *Music for You* programmes on both radio and television. He successfully sang the Florestan role in *Fidelio* mentioned previously, in which he was joined by Elisabeth Hellawell singing the title role and Donald McIntyre as Pizarro. In his *Auckland Star* review, Desmond Mahoney said: 'Ramon Opie was perfectly cast as Florestan ... each time he returns to the Auckland stage he reveals greater resource in his singing.'

Later that year, and again with the Auckland Choral Society, he was the tenor soloist in Benjamin Britten's *St Nicholas* and then featured in the usual December round of Messiah performances.

At the end of the *Così* season, I spent some time in Auckland sharing a flat with my friend, Jeanette Trenwith, who had briefly flatted with me in London and was back home in New Zealand from her job in Washington. Rehearsals for the orchestral season of *La Cenerentola* were soon to begin in Wellington, but as several of the cast and the music coach/ repetiteur, Russell Channell, lived in Auckland, we were able to do much of the preliminary work there beforehand. Australian tenor, Gino Zancanaro, stayed on in New Zealand after the *Così* tour to sing the role of Prince Ramiro (Prince Charming), Graeme Gorton played the Prince's valet, Dandini, and Angela Shaw and I were respectively Clorinda and Tisbe, the Ugly Sisters. The opera was mainly staged to bring back home and feature one of New Zealand's finest singers, Heather Begg, in the title role. Heather was at that time enjoying a thriving career at The Royal Opera House in London, but welcomed the opportunity to return to our shores and play this brilliant coloratura-mezzo role.

Heather was a tall and statuesque woman, but to make her look more vulnerable and 'put-upon' by her father and sisters, the costume and set designer, Raymond Boyce cleverly disguised her height with some ingenious costuming both for her and other members of the cast. As Cinderella and the Ugly Sisters were often on stage at the same time, Raymond designed very large and lofty headwear for Angela and me. In Act One of the opera we were dressed in our underwear, with corseted waists, frilly pantaloons, widely hooped petticoats and huge mobcaps, to which we later added voluminous negligées. For the Ball scene I was given a silver wig to wear that was at least 30 cm high and elaborately decorated with feathers and ribbons, while Angela wore a very large turban on top of a ginger-coloured and lavishly coiffured wig. My headwear was quite difficult to sing in but very good for my posture.

Two of the nine performances of *Cenerentola* in Wellington were presented in a similar manner to England's Glyndebourne Festival Opera productions. Act One was performed in the late afternoon, after which there was a long interval when most of the audience moved into a dining area and enjoyed a three-course, silver service dinner with appropriate wines, followed by coffee. One critic mentioned the meal in his review, with the comment that 'sadly the menu did not include pumpkin'. While the diners probably had a pleasant time, I found it tedious having to sit in the dressing room for well over an hour, in full makeup but thankfully out of costume, unable to do much before we continued the opera.

An amusing memory from this production concerns our repetiteur, Russell Channell, who conducted some of the performances when the season's main conductor, Georg Tintner, was not available. The first Act of *Cenerentola* is reasonably long and finishes with the familiar ball scene, which musically is quite difficult because of the speed at which it has to be sung. Our stage set for the ball included an ornamental fountain, placed almost centre stage, with real water gently tinkling throughout the entire scene. The water had an unfortunate effect on Russell, and when he had the conductor's baton, the Act One finale got faster and faster so that as soon as the curtain came down, he could race off to the toilet; the back-stage staff made sure the conductor's exit door was opened immediately they heard the audience's applause.

There was another unexpected incident during one of the Auckland performances of *La Cenerentola*. Graeme Gorton became ill with a sore throat and the possible onset of 'flu, but with no understudy he had to go on. To ensure that what little voice remained could still be heard, he was wired up with a tiny microphone hidden in the elaborate ruffles of his neckwear. As Angela and I had several scenes to sing with him, we were told to project our voices away from his microphone in case it picked us up as well and distorted the balance. In the middle of one of our trios I distinctly heard strange noises, which were certainly not vocal, coming from Graeme's direction. They consisted of a regular series of thumping or booming sounds, and were so disconcerting that a lot of concentration was needed to ignore them and keep singing accurately. We later discovered that Graeme's little microphone was picking up the double bass in a small jazz band playing at the nightclub situated in the lane immediately behind our theatre, the much loved but now demolished His Majesty's. Those sounds were certainly the strangest 'noises off' I've ever experienced during an opera. There was no repeat, however, as Graeme lost his voice completely and was far too ill to go on for the next performance, so the show had to be cancelled.

Chapter 9

Quartets, schools and beauty queens

When one is trying to earn a living in any artistic field in New Zealand, it pays to be versatile and have as many strings to one's bow as possible. It is also necessary to find ways of creating your own opportunities. This is precisely what Kathleen Johnson, Lucas Bunt, Ray and I set about doing after the *Così* tour. Lucas initially came up with the idea of establishing a quartet that would perform 45-minute programmes of the more popular opera selections for students at their schools. Besides an obvious wish to create employment for ourselves when we had no other singing work, or were 'resting' as is said in theatrical circles, we hoped that by introducing opera to secondary school pupils in a relaxed and friendly form, we might arouse their interest in the art and perhaps help to ensure its future in New Zealand, as well as our own.

Finding that Kathleen, Ray and I were willing to give it a try, Lucas approached the District Music Advisor for the Department of Education in Auckland, Colin Pickering, who suggested we put together a programme, contact a few schools in the Auckland area to see if they were interested and if so, carry out an experimental tour. After several brainstorming sessions we came up with a good introductory programme of solos, duets and quartets from a wide range of operas and composers, and sent this to as many post-primary schools in our region as we thought might be interested. Nine schools responded positively, so the New Zealand Opera

Quartet, with our first accompanist, Noreen Pelham, came into being.

Our small initial tour was successful beyond all expectations and the Auckland office of the Department of Education was delighted. The possibility of a wider tour in the Northern Region was then discussed, and Colin Pickering wrote the following letter of recommendation in support, dated 4 June 1965:

> **The NZ Opera Quartet**
> The quartet has just concluded a highly successful experimental tour of Post Primary Schools in the Auckland Metropolitan area. It is experimental in that this is the first occasion on which a vocal group has toured the schools in Auckland and the reception everywhere has been one of delight, enthusiasm and anticipation. Audiences have ranged from 1,500 to 300 students – from F.III to F.IV.
>
> The programme is extremely well chosen, entertainingly presented by the narrator and takes 45 minutes to complete. The selections make an immediate appeal to boys and girls alike and afford a wonderful experience of duet, solo and quartet singing.
>
> This new venture will become a permanent feature of the music scene here in Auckland. I commend highly the tour to other districts.
>
> Colin Pickering, District Music Advisor, Auckland

The response from schools throughout the Northland and Auckland regions was so good that we were encouraged to broaden our horizons and approach every secondary school in New Zealand, both public and private. Again the response was enthusiastic and in 1965 we undertook five- or six-week tours during the remaining terms to most of the secondary schools throughout the country. Over the next few years, the Quartet sang to over 300,000 school students each year and overwhelmingly the young people were attentive and delighted with our programmes.

During the early stages of the Quartet's progress and in the periods when we were not touring the schools, we each had to find other ways of making a living, particularly Lucas who had a wife and three young sons to support. He took a job as a sales representative for the Auckland branch of the cigarette manufacturing company, Rothmans of Pall Mall, and it was not long before he managed to obtain sponsorship for the Quartet through the company's Sports and Cultural Foundation. This enabled us to plan and then complete a further nationwide tour in 1966. Lucas was a persuasive salesman with a friendly and engaging personality, so Rothmans astutely recognised the benefit of allowing him leave to tour from time to time, knowing he'd be promoting their business in the process. While it felt somewhat strange being generously supported by a tobacco company when we were all non-smokers (at this stage anyway), and avoided anyone who did smoke, the Sports and Cultural Foundation's assistance was tremendously important in enabling us to travel as widely as we did.

Before receiving this sponsorship we travelled in Ray's small Hillman car, with a roof-rack added to carry the luggage that couldn't fit in the boot. With four singers and a pianist in the car, the summer journeys were sweaty and uncomfortable. All our tour transportation, accommodation and administration costs had to be met out of the fee we charged the schools for the performances, with hopefully enough funds left to provide each of us with a small wage. When Rothmans became involved, they decided the best way to assist us would be to cover our entire transport costs. They immediately supplied a large station wagon that easily accommodated our luggage, music and us, and eventually some of their products as well. The station wagon was inscribed with large sign declaring:

ROTHMANS SPORTS AND CULTURAL FOUNDATION
NEW ZEALAND OPERA QUARTET
NATIONAL TOUR 1966

A suggestion was made that in addition to the school performances, it might be wise for the Quartet to consider giving evening concerts for adults in some of the places we visited, not only to take full advantage of all the travelling, but to counter any criticism that might be forthcoming regarding tobacco company proceeds sponsoring a project primarily for teenagers. This would greatly increase our workload but it made sense, so we decided to go ahead with public concerts. Apart from requiring acknowledgement of their sponsorship on the cover of the programme for our evening performances and in any advertising or promotional material, Rothmans made no other stipulations regarding their support of our work. They did, however, give us cartons of cigarettes to give away as appropriate, which added enormously to both their popularity and ours. Ray couldn't resist this and took up smoking, which probably contributed to his later health problems.

The 1966 tour covered the entire country and over 7000 miles, from Kaitaia in the north to Tuatapere in the south and all places east and west, wherever there were secondary schools. Our main accompanist for this tour was our good friend, Russell Channell, the New Zealand Opera Company's chief repetiteur and one of the conductors for their orchestral seasons. Russell's many talents included being an excellent concert pianist, so piano solos were included in the evening programmes; while this lightened the Quartet's load a little, it certainly extended his. We often gave three school performances during the day, two in the morning and one in the afternoon, with approximately three or four evening concerts for the general public each week. Some schools met our fee out of their own budgets while others raised the money by requiring students to pay a small amount to attend. The schools that charged for attendance usually ended up with surplus funds which they could use in their own departments to purchase music, instruments or whatever else they needed. We made sure that our programmes were sent to the person in charge of music at each school well before our visit, in the hope they would introduce their classes to a few of the pieces we were going to sing. Many teachers were excellent in this regard and it was pleasing to see the young audiences recognising some of the tunes and even joining in during the performance.

Most schools required compulsory attendance at our concerts, but if the students were anything like me when I was their age, they were probably happy to comply if it meant getting out of one of their normal study periods. Kathleen or I introduced each item, briefly telling the story of the opera and where the particular piece fitted in. While it wasn't possible to tour with costumes and 'props', we included as much movement and action in our performance as possible. The biggest impression we made on the teenagers was the fact that we could produce so much sound without any amplification. They seemed to expect we'd be like pop stars, with microphones and masses of equipment which took hours to set up, and were astonished when all we required on stage were four chairs and a piano and stool for the accompanist. It was our turn to be astonished when, at the end of our performances, the students mobbed us for our autographs as if we were pop stars.

We occasionally struck a school where the audience was initially a bit restive or appeared terribly bored by the whole idea of opera. I found a useful way to get around this was to compare the subject of music to New Zealand's greatest obsession, sport; just because one is a keen rugby, cricket, netball, soccer, hockey or tennis player or fan doesn't mean that the others are rubbish. The same applies to music; one can be a lover of jazz, classical orchestra, chamber music, country, rock, Gilbert and Sullivan light operas or any kind of musical expression, but these are all simply various facets of the world of music. Our particular interest was opera and we wanted to share this with these young people, and at least let them experience it before saying they hated it. There were only two schools I was loath to visit again owing to the behaviour of the audience. Singing at these was like performing in a prison, with hefty male teachers marching up and down the aisles on either side of the students, arms folded across their chests and ready to whack or remove anyone who misbehaved. When one considers we visited approximately 370 schools and only had two difficult ones, we were most fortunate.

Many of the schools made a big event of our visits. The larger ones with their own orchestras took the trouble to learn and play an opera overture for us at the beginning of our concert. Occasionally the school's choir performed for us, or the whole audience sang a song, asking us to join them. Although these tours were extremely tiring, it was exhilarating to see our work being accepted with such enthusiasm and receive requests to come back the following year.

I like to believe the Quartet's tours during the 1960s and early '70s played a small part in creating the following that opera still has in New Zealand, so many years later.

In contrast to the school audiences, the public attendance at the evening concerts was often poor. The newspaper reviews we received were usually flattering, but many mentioned the 'small but appreciative' audiences. There were exceptions, of course, which were largely due to the hard work done by local music lovers promoting us before we arrived. Looking through the many press cuttings my father so avidly collected, it is heart-warming to read reviews like the following:

> Rotorua: 'An unprecedented scene followed the final presentation, the quartet from '*Rigoletto*,' by the NZ Opera Quartet at the Rotorua Concert Chambers last night. Prolonged applause, accompanied by stamping feet, seemed to be the order of the evening.'

> Invercargill: 'Tremendous applause from an audience that almost completely filled the Scottish Hall last night made it plain to the NZ Opera Quartet that their choice of programme and way of presenting it was very much to the liking of Invercargill people.'

> Motueka: 'In the Motueka Memorial Hall last night, four singers and a pianist turned on the best musical performance heard in Motueka since the visit of the … New Zealand Opera Company some months ago.'

> Gisborne: 'Those who availed themselves of the opportunity of hearing a concert given by the NZ Opera Quartet in the War Memorial Hall on Saturday were rewarded with musical entertainment of outstanding quality … They move about with complete freedom in the repertoire and with the confidence that comes from a natural talent for singing and a thorough mastery of the medium. Each member of the quartet is not only a singer of distinction but is a stage personality who is able to establish an intimate relationship with the audience.'

> Inglewood: 'Inglewood charmed by Opera Quartet. Opera stripped of all its trappings could be a very miserable affair. But the Quartet made nothing but delight out of their programme composed of a generous number of the best-loved arias, duets and quartets from opera. There is nothing patronising about their presentation of such a pot-pourri of favourites; with charm and obvious pleasure in their work, the four introduce the excerpts … and then sing them with as much involvement as they would put into a full-scale performance.'

The Rotorua review above reminds me that our concerts there always had the 'House Full' sign out due to the tireless promotional work done by their Public Relations Officer at the time, Ernie Leonard. Ernie had many skills and wholeheartedly devoted his energies towards anything he became involved with. His widely differing interests and activities included music, broadcasting and of all things, wrestling, and it was through this latter medium that he became well known throughout New Zealand as a host of the television sports programme *On the Mat*. As far as we were concerned, however, he was a hugely supportive friend and what's more, he organised fabulous parties after our shows as well.

A friend who looked through some of the New Zealand Opera Quartet's public concert schedules commented that they were 'full on' by any standards, and would probably not be undertaken today. As an example, the following list is our itinerary for one school term during the months of October to December 1966:

Kaikoura	11 October
Rangiora	12 October
Ashburton	13 October
Methven	17 October
Timaru	18 October
Waimate	20 October
Balclutha	1 November
Gore	3 November
Alexandra	5 November
Tuatapere	7 November

Otautau	8 November
Invercargill	9 November
Queenstown	10 November
Cromwell	12 November
Hokitika	14 November
Westport	17 November
Reefton	19 November
Motueka	21 November
Nelson	22 November
Blenheim	23 November
Palmerston North	26 November
Inglewood	28 November
Te Awamutu	29 November
Cambridge	30 November
Rotorua	1 December
Gisborne	3 December

This list covers only the places where public concerts were given in the evening, and it should be noted that the Quartet was performing school concerts at these and other centres during the day throughout the period as well. Looking back now, I guess it can be considered a punishing schedule but we appeared to thrive on it.

Another daunting consideration is that we organised these tours ourselves. After preparing an appropriate programme for schools, we sent it to every secondary school and college in New Zealand and arranged our tour schedules based on their responses. We were then able to contact the appropriate people likely to assist in the organisation of public concerts in some of the areas we'd be visiting, and make the necessary concert hall bookings. The evening concerts needed as much publicity as possible, so besides trying to arrange radio interviews where practicable, we had to prepare and circulate press advertising material and articles, and make ourselves available for photographs and personal interviews soon after we arrived at a particular location.

Amusing memories come flooding back when reading some of the press cuttings from this period and considering the publicity angles used by journalists. Inevitably, Kathleen and I ended up on the Women's Pages and were asked, among other things, about the difficulties of travelling light but needing to have suitable day-wear for the schools and evening dresses for the public concerts. We'd also be asked about the Quartet's accommodation arrangements, and when it was discovered that we mainly shared motels, the next question often concerned food. We tried to keep expenses to a minimum and could rarely afford to eat at restaurants, so we took turns at preparing and cooking most meals ourselves. This sometimes led to requests for our favourite recipes, which would be included in the newspaper articles.

There is one hilarious photograph of Kathleen and me taken for an article in an Invercargill newspaper, where we both look like 'death warmed up' because we were so tired. The item is headed 'Young singers have personality, talent', and goes on to say: 'Two striking young women with a load of personality and talent are bound to captivate Invercargill opera lovers when next week, as members of the New Zealand Opera Quartet, they will present a full and versatile programme.' In spite of the photograph, we had an excellent house for the Invercargill public concert.

While the school performances were not often reviewed, there was one reported in Napier's *Daily Telegraph* which generally summed up our reception throughout New Zealand. Under the heading 'Opera taken to Schools in Napier ... and listeners were pleased', the article included the following:

> Comic sequences from the lighter side of opera brought howls of laughter from 900 voices when the New Zealand Opera Quartet performed at Napier Boys' High School today. The hour-long concert was part of the quartet's tour of New Zealand schools this term – performing to 160 audiences. The four members also sang to pupils of Colenso High School this morning and the Napier Girls' High School on Friday.
>
> The obvious enjoyment of the young Napier audience proved that grand opera had battered down the walls of commercial cacophony – the 'Beatles' and 'Animals' were forgotten; Puccini and Rossini reigned again.

> To 900 boys who had each paid 1s [shilling] for the show, this was a performance out of the box – guaranteeing that the versatile singers will have an enthusiastic audience on any return visit. The singers travelled to Wairoa late today.

We occasionally received fan mail from students, and one clever young artist even produced an excellent cartoon depicting us in full vocal flight. The following letter was received from a pupil at the Wellington Diocesan School for Girls (Nga Tawa) in Marton:

> Dear Miss Bridge,
> I am writing to thank you very much for coming to our school because I enjoyed you all so very much and I want to write and tell you all. Your acting and singing was hilarious and wonderfully done. I wish I could meet you all in real life and if I can, I will see you again in some shows you may be in.
>
> I'm in the fourth form and the rest of the form would all like me to thank you too, so please could you pass on my thanks to the rest of your fantastic group.
>
> When I see people like you I always wish I could be like that, but as I have no singing voice I will just stick to being a plain nurse when I leave school because I love helping others.
>
> I do hope I am not being a nuisance writing like this because I suppose you have 'piles' of letters, but I just wanted to express my thanks and fondest wishes in the near future.
>
> I do hope this letter is not too untidy, anyway thank you very much once again.

Recalling the students' response and our experiences on these tours after more than 40 years brings back snippets of memories, but precise details are often elusive. As mentioned earlier, the two schools where our reception was not so good are firmly etched in my mind, but unfortunately failures do tend to be recalled rather too clearly. One of those schools was very new, and situated in a recently established satellite town with a growing population who came from a diverse range of backgrounds. It is a well-established city now and perhaps some of those bored and unruly students have since become its worthy leaders and citizens. At the top end of the scale were the well-known private and religious schools that welcomed us as honoured visitors and sometimes invited us to stay for a meal with the staff or share tea and biscuits with the prefects.

One of the most pleasant of these was the Queen Victoria College for Maori Girls in Parnell, sadly no longer in existence. We sang there at about 7 pm after the boarding students had finished dinner. It was a warm, gentle summer evening and still daylight after the concert. The prefects took us back to their common room where they served supper and then sang for us. I seem to recall that there was a first-floor balcony facing the area where our car was parked. As we were about to drive away, we heard more singing and looked up to see the girls clustered above, waving and singing their goodbyes. It was a magical evening for us.

Similarly, after a morning concert we gave at a Catholic girls' school in the Wairarapa, the nuns invited us to stay for the midday meal. Their particular Order is one where they take a vow of silence for a large part of the day, but it was amazing how easily they managed to communicate without a word being uttered. There were many smiles and gracious hand gestures conveying their appreciation of our work and offering us hospitality. We were given a tasty lunch, which included home-grown vegetables and herbs, served in a spotlessly clean and simply furnished refectory. We left the convent feeling amply refreshed and at peace with the world.

Because of his Rothmans job, Lucas was unavailable during part of the 1966 school and public concert tour of the South Island. He was replaced by Paul Person, another principal singer with the New Zealand Opera Company. We had worked with Paul previously in *Rigoletto*, and he brought his wife Wendy and eight-week-old baby daughter Linda along with him. They travelled in their own car and lived in a caravan which they towed behind. In 1968, Ray and I also became too busy with opera, radio, television and general concert work to tour for any length of time, so we had to leave the Quartet.

The New Zealand Opera Quartet's life of touring schools

and giving public concerts lasted approximately twelve years. The original members, Ray, Lucas, Kathleen and I, were replaced at various times by sopranos Fay Haddon, Diane Johnson and Irene Tirbutt, mezzo-sopranos Barbara Green, Patricia Price and Marie Therese Laurijssen, tenors Antony Benfell, Silvio Famularo, George Henare, Keith Lewis, John Miley and Gregory Tata, and bass-baritones John Bates and Don Lister. The accompanists also changed from time to time, and those who travelled included Russell Channell, Michael Crowl, Bruce Greenfield, Ian Laird, Noreen Pelham and Jan Preston. Dorothea Franchi and David Harper (Auckland), Mary Anderson (New Plymouth) and Carol McQueen (Whangarei) played for the occasional evening concert given by the original Quartet personnel.

Rothman's sponsorship ceased at the end of 1973, but the New Zealand Chamber Music Federation assisted with funding for the next two years. In 1975, the Quartet became a Quintet but this seems to be the final year of such performances until more recent times. Two young singers whom Ray and I occasionally worked with during the late 1970s and '80s, Susan and John Cameron, eventually formed a highly successful group in 2001 under the title *Operatunity*, which presents lunchtime concerts mainly for senior citizens throughout New Zealand. Before this, they had a schools programme as well, so the idea of our original Quartet has continued.

In addition to the school-touring programme, the New Zealand Opera Quartet was regularly engaged by other organisations. During the years Ray and I were involved, we gave full-length concerts for the Auckland, Devonport and North Shore Festivals, as well as for the British Music Society (NZ) branch in Wanganui and with the local orchestra in New Plymouth. There were lunch-hour recitals in Auckland at the Stars Travel Theatrette and the Art Gallery, and we even provided a cabaret programme for a Whakatane Operatic Society nightclub evening. The following is music critic Desmond Mahoney's review in the *Auckland Star* covering a lunchtime concert we gave during an Auckland Festival season:

> Auckland: Although it has no official connexion with the New Zealand Opera Company, this quartet is carrying out one of the most valuable pioneering efforts in music. Not only are the four excellent singers – and often principals with the Company – but they are also prepared to sing together in schools all over the country and in smaller centres.
>
> Yesterday they sang a programme ranging from Mozart to Menotti, as soloists and in varying combinations, and one was struck by the wealth of talent in this field available in New Zealand – and not all of it used to its full extent.
>
> Each of the singers is a fine soloist and together they made up an excellent programme, presented in a thoroughly easy and professional manner. The continued popularity of opera in Auckland was reflected in the size of the audience, much larger than usual for a lunchtime recital.

Perhaps the most unusual engagement, however, was singing for the Miss Brooklands Festival in New Plymouth. We were asked to select appropriate items to match the floats that would transport the beauty queens as they glided over the lake in front of the Bowl of Brooklands stage. There were five floats in the forms of a Surrey, Butterfly, Fan, Rose and Oyster Shell. Conjuring up all our imagination, we included selections from *Oklahoma* for the Surrey, *Madama Butterfly* for the Butterfly, Gilbert and Sullivan's *Mikado* for the Fan, floral numbers including 'The English Rose' from *Merrie England* for the Rose, and while the Oyster was a bit of a challenge, we simply included a bracket from *The Sound of Music*, and Ray and Lucas sang the ever-popular *Pearl Fishers* duet. During the evening, small firework displays lit up the floats as they ferried the beauty queens across the water, followed by a much grander display at the end of the entire programme. It was certainly a unique experience for four opera singers.

Chapter 10

Wharfies, peacocks and marriage

While a great deal of our time was taken up with the Quartet tours during 1965 and through to the end of 1967, Ray and I were still busy with our own careers which included concerts, broadcasting and television work, and further operas with the New Zealand Opera Company. In 1965, we both sang in the NZOC's piano-tour production of *Gallantry* and *L'Heure Espagnole* mentioned previously, and I sang the role of *Carmen* in a production presented by the Mt Eden Community Operatic Society. The New Zealand Broadcasting Corporation later recorded a televised production of *L'Heure Espagnole* that was shown on WNTV-1. Ray's role of Torquemada in this was his first experience of performing opera on television. Opera singers are used to projecting their performances to audiences in large theatres, with lively facial expressions and dramatic hand and body gestures; television requires everything to be much smaller, as every movement is over-accentuated by a camera that is always 'in your face'. Ray and I found it easier to pre-record the vocal work and then mime the words during filming in the few televised opera performances we did. While accurate miming is not so simple either, we found it less difficult than trying to look reasonably normal when singing with a camera staring at our tonsils.

Later television work included appearances on *Stars on Sunday*, Ossie Cheesman's *Music for You* programmes, Max Cryer's *Town Cryer*, further full-length operas, and concerts for the New Zealand

Broadcasting Corporation in their *Music from the Theatre* series. These programmes were often reviewed in the media and one tends to remember the quirkier comments made. During a *Music from the Theatre* programme, Ray sang a song he performed several hundred times during his career, 'The donkey's serenade'. He was given a Mexican-style costume complete with huge sombrero that almost completely dwarfed him and which, on television, made him look a bit like a mushroom; thankfully they didn't include the donkey. In a *Listener* review following the relay of the programme the costume was mentioned and the reviewer, while praising Ray's singing, added: 'However, he must have felt an ass wearing a hat like that.' Similarly, though fortunately not in a press review, I was apparently not showing my best side in a television programme, for the comment came back, 'Thank God she can sing.'

Between 1965 and 1970, Ray and I were able to earn a living as professional singers for about eight months each year. It was therefore necessary to find temporary jobs to survive the rest of the time. Ray's jobs included working in the New Zealand Breweries factory and as a 'wharfie'. He didn't enjoy either job much owing to the constant strikes and walking off the job if the workers got upset about something. I initially found clerical work through an employment agency which sent me to work at various companies on a temporary basis. My duties included the preparation of debtors' invoices and statements, and the payment of creditors. Among the latter were the employment agency's bills for my services and when I saw that the hourly rate they were charging the company for my work was almost double the amount they were paying me, I decided it would probably be more lucrative to work for the agency itself – a case of 'if you can't beat 'em, join 'em'. An opportunity arose at the agency and they appointed me as one of their personnel recruiters. I quite enjoyed this work, for I not only had to interview prospective jobseekers but also visit the companies to which the agency already supplied staff, as well as new companies, in an attempt to generate more business. My comings and goings when singing engagements came along were accommodated by the agency, so I was fortunate.

A list of our major singing activities is included at the end of this book, but particular engagements stand out for unusual reasons. One of these was a performance of Beethoven's Symphony No. 9 which Ray was engaged to sing with the NZBC Symphony Orchestra in Christchurch. Not having been told otherwise, he sang his first few bars in English at the Friday morning soloists' rehearsal in Christchurch, only to be stopped and advised that the work was to be sung in the original German. He managed to get through the rest of the day's rehearsals, but knew he would need help with accurate German pronunciation before the Saturday night performance, which was also to be broadcast live throughout the country. He rang me in Auckland to see if I had any suggestions.

We had both taken a short period of leave from the New Zealand Opera Quartet because of other engagements, but remembered that they were also currently singing in Christchurch. Lucas Bunt was born in Holland and lived there throughout the World War Two occupation by the Germans, so he was familiar with the German language and would be the ideal person to help. Ray managed to contact Lucas at one of the schools and as soon as he could, Lucas came to the hotel where Ray was staying. They worked steadily through the night, Lucas writing the phonetic pronunciation of the words into Ray's music score and Ray reading them back to him as accurately as possible. Although he was extremely tired, Ray managed to get through both the Saturday morning rehearsal and the evening performance without too many problems, but was greatly relieved when the whole event was over. On his return to Auckland, an Austrian friend, Hilde Burstein, who had listened to the broadcast, rang Ray to congratulate him saying, 'Ramon darling, you ver the only von I could understand.' Thank heavens for Lucas.

An unusual engagement for me was playing the role of Pistache in Cole Porter's *Can Can* in Napier and Hastings. The role certainly wasn't my forte but it was paid work and couldn't be turned down. The final scene in Act One of this show is a fancy-dress ball, and the costume chosen for me was that of a peacock. It consisted of a figure-hugging leotard coloured deep blue and green, with a very long and elaborate tail and a feather-plumed headdress. My legs were fully exposed in dark-blue fishnet tights and I wore exceedingly high-heeled shoes. Pistache has a rather soulful number to sing at the end of this scene and I begged the director and costume designer to give me something to cover me up a little during the item so I wouldn't feel so stupid. They graciously provided a large, blue velvet cloak which hid most of my 'tail' and legs and made me feel a little better. The things one does for one's art.

In 1967, the New Zealand Opera Company's headquarters and rehearsal rooms in Hill Street, Wellington, were vacated owing to a proposed motorway development through the area. To replace this, the company purchased a disused cinema, the Regal Theatre, in the suburb of Karori and converted it into an Opera Centre. The centre included a small theatre where chamber-style productions of opera could be staged, and Beethoven's *Fidelio* was chosen to launch the new conversion. The entire cast was made up of New Zealand singers, with Ray in the vocally demanding role of Florestan and Elisabeth Hellawell in the equally powerful title role. I wasn't singing in this production, but I particularly wanted to see Ray in the staged version of his role and also inspect the company's new home, so I flew down to Wellington for opening night.

Wellington is famous for its perpetually strong winds and there is rarely a day when the air is still. On this occasion it was dramatically living up to its reputation, with a howling southerly preventing all but the largest planes from landing. After my plane had made several attempts to land, the pilot advised he would try once more by actually dropping the plane on to the runway to avoid it being flipped over by the wind – or that's how I interpreted what he said. Seeing me ashen-faced and my white knuckles gripping the sides of my seat, the flight attendant told me to relax and simply go with the movement of the plane; more easily said than done, I'm afraid. Ray had been waiting to meet me but because my arrival was so delayed, he returned to the theatre to prepare for the performance. I eventually arrived there just before his first entrance in Act Two, and was able to enjoy his magnificent singing of what is one of the most challenging of tenor roles. When the short season was over and both Ray and I were back in Auckland, a complete stranger came over to us while we were having a meal in a restaurant one evening and said to me, 'You're a much better colour now than when I last saw you.' With no idea what he was talking about, I asked the gentleman to explain where we'd met. He told me he'd been seated across the aisle from me on that awful flight to Wellington and while feeling sorry for me, he hadn't been too cheerful about it himself. We could laugh it off then, but it was very frightening at the time.

Nineteen sixty-eight was a very busy year for both of us. Ray was engaged as the only soloist in a Christchurch concert of Berlioz's mighty *Requiem*. The choir consisted of 450 voices and was accompanied by almost as many players, including the NZBC Symphony Orchestra, Christchurch Civic Orchestra, Skellerup Woolston Band and the NZBC orchestral trainees. Christchurch's new and beautiful town hall had not been built then and the concert reviewer's only regret was that the venue was a draughty army barracks. He certainly had no problems with Ray's singing:

> As soloist, Ramon Opie once again demonstrated his exceptional vocal technique and grace of delivery, his tenderness of mood and mastery of style. In this work, he evoked passion, fervour and devotion in a beautifully projected voice, true in pitch, even in volume and flexible as a willow branch.

Wow, that kind of review has a very special place in one's scrapbook.

Carl Orff's *Carmina Burana* was presented by the Auckland Choral Society at their first subscription concert in 1969. Ray was the tenor and even sang one of the higher baritone solos. Under the heading 'Mediaeval hippie music was a concert success', Desmond Mahoney wrote in the *Auckland Star*:

> One could only marvel at the manner in which Ramon Opie, in particular, held a cruelly taxing tessitura in full voice in two solos – passages which would have been taken by all but a handful of the world's tenors in falsetto.

The NZOC repeated their production of *Fidelio* in Auckland that year, in a joint season with Mozart's *Il Seraglio* for which they engaged Inia Te Wiata from London to sing his much-performed role of Osmin. I desperately wanted to sing the role of Marzelline in *Fidelio* and after assuring the director, John Thompson, that I was capable of sustaining the higher vocal range needed, I was thrilled to be offered it. I probably worked harder vocally on that role than any other I've performed, as it is written for a soprano, and besides learning and memorising it (the opera was performed in the original German), I needed to develop my vocal technique to cope comfortably with the higher 'tessitura' (range of notes). Apart from my role, the casting was the same as it had been in Wellington. While our houses were not as good as those for *Il Seraglio*, the *Herald*'s music critic, L. C. M. Saunders, stated in his later assessment of music performances throughout the 1960s that *Fidelio* was the 'stand-out' opera performance of the decade. By 1970, however, the NZOC was in financial difficulties, and it was apparent that few or no offers of work could be expected from them in the future. *Fidelio* became the last opera Ray sang for the company while mine was the 'pants' role of Siebel in Gounod's *Faust*.

That production of *Faust* will always hold special memories for me because of an event long hoped for but not entirely expected. Owing to a change in New Zealand's divorce laws in 1970, it was no longer necessary for a couple to have been living apart for a period of seven years before an application could be made to end a marriage legally. Unbeknown to me, Ray had taken the necessary steps to obtain his divorce and was about to be in a position to re-marry. I was in Wellington singing the season of *Faust* when he rang to say that he would be driving down overnight from Auckland and hoped to be with me in time for breakfast. My parents were now living in Auckland, so whenever I was in Wellington I usually stayed with a very long-standing and dear friend, Raymond Hedges. He woke me at 7.30 the next morning to say I had a visitor. It was Ray, of course, and in typically gallant style, he knelt beside the bed and asked me to marry him. He had brought an engagement ring with him, and had made sure it would fit by taking a ring from my jewellery box with him when he chose it. Needless to say I was over the moon and flatly refused to take it off that evening while I performed my young man role, simply covering it with a piece of flesh-coloured sticking plaster.

Earlier in 1970, I had been considering moving back to the United Kingdom if it became impossible to continue my career in New Zealand, and Ray was keen to see if he could get work there as well. He approached a good friend of his, Tom Lusk, a senior executive with the New Zealand Shipping Company, regarding the possibility of us working our way to London as on-board entertainers. Tom rang his counterpart in the Union Steam Ship Company, the general passenger agents in New Zealand for the P and O Lines of Australia, who suggested that we approach that company directly. After much correspondence, Ray finally received a letter dated 3 August 1970 from P and O Australia, offering each of us contracts to work on the *Himalaya* from Auckland to Sydney (which was due to leave New Zealand on 20 November), and then on the *Orcades* from Sydney to Southampton. We were to do cabaret-style spots approximately three nights a week in both first class and tourist class. In return for our work we would be provided with a concession of half the minimum tourist class fare. When Ray first approached the shipping company, it had not been anticipated that we would be getting married before we sailed and two cabins were allocated to us. In the event, no change was made to the accommodation arrangements, so we used one cabin to sleep in and the other as a type of off-stage dressing room.

With a sailing date in November, we were now under pressure to arrange our wedding, finalise the many matters that needed to be attended to in New Zealand before we left and make sure that we had the necessary music, clothes and suitable programmes to perform on the ship.

Ray's first marriage had taken place in a registry office but he desperately wanted our wedding to be in a church. Not all churches were prepared to allow a divorcee to marry in front of the altar at that time, so we were delighted when the Revd Bill Tibbles agreed to marry us in his beautiful old Epsom Presbyterian Church. Ray wanted this particular November to be a really auspicious month in his life, so it included his birthday on the 9th, our wedding on the 14th and our departure for Britain on the 20th.

The wedding was an exceedingly musical occasion. More than seventy-five percent of the guests were either singers or instrumentalists and their singing of the hymns was roof-raising. Some people were surprised when I chose a piece from Verdi's *Requiem* for my exit wedding march, but I was able to reassure them that it was the triumphal and exciting Hosanna section from a work we had both sung and loved. My entry music was the Ode to Joy from Beethoven's Ninth Symphony, and the two pieces performed during the signing of the register were the Intermezzo from Mascagni's opera *Cavelleria Rusticana* and Dr Kenneth Phillip's composition of the *Ave Maria* originally written for Ray, but sung on this occasion by a dear friend from Wellington, Jean Alcock. Some of the music was undoubtedly ambitious for performance on a small church organ, but another friend, Gladys Green, rose magnificently to the challenge, as she would do on many future occasions when playing for us after we later returned to New Zealand.

As if getting married, packing or storing our belongings and organising programmes to sing on the ships were not enough, we also had to arrange the programme for a farewell fund-raising concert to assist us financially. This was sponsored by the Grand Opera Society of Auckland and was scheduled to take place the day after our wedding. It took the form of a *This is Your Life* programme for Ray and included many well-known artists of the day.

The concert was held in the Hotel Intercontinental's sumptuous ballroom with its rich red, velvet-upholstered gilt chairs and exceptionally lavish décor, and those of our friends who had travelled from other parts of the country to attend the wedding were able to join the capacity Auckland audience. The Grand Opera Society of Auckland's newsletter promoting the event read:

> A Farewell Concert will be sponsored on Sunday, 15th November 1970 at 8.00pm at the Intercontinental Ballroom for two old

friends, Corinne Bridge and Ramon Opie, who leave a few short days later for England.

This will be a concert with a difference, as all the artists appearing have played a large part in creating the musical scene in Auckland as we know it and are proud of today.

This unique concert will introduce each artist at the point where they have first been connected with the careers of our friends, Ray and Corinne, in the manner of the English TV programme 'This is your life ....,' and we know it will be an exciting occasion and urge you not to miss it.

Ramon and Corinne have so loyally and so willingly supported us in the past that we are sure you will all wish to enjoy this opportunity of showing your appreciation to them and helping them in a material way in their venture overseas.

The newsletter went on to list the names of the artists who would be appearing. The programme on the night was:

FAREWELL CONCERT
to
CORINNE BRIDGE AND RAMON OPIE

'This is your life ...'

Early years	... Ramon Opie
Competitions	... Betty Spiro, acc. by Max Cryer
Concerts of all kinds in Auckland	... Leo Barnett, acc. by Margaret Barnett
Broadcasting and TV	... Ann Stott, acc. by Eric Bell
Opera in Auckland	... Cyril Kelleway, acc. by Eric Bell
Opera throughout New Zealand and Australia	... Elisabeth Hellawell

INTERVAL

'Rigoletto'	... Corinne Bridge and Ramon Opie
Tours and friends	... Janice Smith and Jack Lunn
'You name it, he's done it ...'	... Silvio de Pra, Accordianist
Schools and Opera Quartets	... Kathleen Johnson, Corinne Bridge, Ramon Opie, Lucas Bunt

Accompanist Dorothea Franchi

Although somewhat jaded after the previous day's celebrations, which continued well into the night, we enjoyed the concert almost as much as the audience appeared to.

Having vacated the rental properties we'd been living in up to this time, we stayed with my parents until sailing date five days later. There was the usual round of farewell get-togethers, and then a large group of friends came to the wharf to see us off. Among these were my godmother and her husband who had come up from Wellington for the wedding and stayed on in Auckland, presumably to wave us farewell as the ship departed. They came aboard to inspect our cabin, and while we were all chatting happily and leaning over the railings to wave to our friends below, I suddenly became aware the ship was moving. I immediately panicked, wondering how on earth we could stop it to let them get off. 'Relax,' they said. 'We're cruising with you until you change ships in Australia.' Not only were Ray and I to have a working honeymoon but, to paraphrase the words of Noel Coward, 'And her [god]mother came too.'

Chapter 11

Travel auditions and Show Boat

While aboard the one-class ship *Himalaya* during the trip to Sydney, we were required to sing every night. It was slightly less busy when we transferred to the tourist and first-class ship *Orcades* where we performed as per contract, that is three nights a week but with a performance in each class. There was a very good band on the *Orcades*, whose leader was a classically trained pianist. We had chosen a mixture of solos and duets from popular shows for the cabaret-type programmes, including *The Sound of Music*, *South Pacific*, *The Merry Widow*, *West Side Story*, *Cabaret*, *My Fair Lady*, and these seemed to go down well. However, the bandleader soon realised our real forte was opera and suggested that we present an early evening classical concert in the main lounge for those passengers who might be interested, with him as our accompanist. He thought that an hour of operatic solos and duets interspersed with him playing piano solos would be suitable, so we decided to try this out. The programme was announced in the ship's daily news bulletin and we thought that perhaps 40 or 50 people might be interested in attending. However, the lounge was comfortably full and the concert was so successful that we had to repeat a similar programme each week for the rest of the voyage. Those performances were full, with people listening and peering in through the lounge windows from the deck as well.

In an earlier chapter I mentioned the sleepwalking problem I had during my childhood. Perhaps it was all the rush and bustle of

Ray telling a joke (probably a rude one) at our wedding reception, with Kathleen Johnson and Lucas Bunt.

Lilac Time (UK), 1973. From left: Susan Maisey, Elton Bennett, Joyce Mandre, Jonathan Courage and Corinne.

Above

In rehearsal for *Madama Butterfly* (New Opera Company, 1975). From left: Malvina Major, Japanese Consul's wife (Wellington) and Corinne.

(Photo: *Evening Post*)

Left

As Goro and Suzuki in *Madama Butterfly* (Northern Opera, 1975).

Opposite above

The Barber of Seville (Perkel Opera, 1978). From left: Maurice Parsons (back view), Corinne and Cyril Kelleway.

Opposite below

Cyril Kelleway and Corinne in *Carmen* (Perkel Opera, 1982).

Above

Auckland Town Hall concert for senior citizens. From left: Max Cryer, Sir Barry Curtis, Lou Clausen, Alice Worsley, Merv Smith, Corinne and Ramon.

(Photo: *Auckland Star*)

Left

Ray and I, a few days before leaving London in 1974.

Opposite above

A couple of cats: Margaret Remi-Kenyon and Corinne.

Opposite below

Sally Sloman and Corinne as the Ugly Sisters in *La Cenerentola* (Perkel Opera, 1985).

Corinne as Flora in *La Traviata* (Perkel Opera, 1980).

The Opie family (Wellington), at a celebration dinner after the QSM awards.

Presentation of cheque for Aotea Centre (1987). From left (standing): Rex Aitchison (ANZ), Neil Jenkins, Dame Catherine Tizard, Donald Trott, Graham Upson (ANZ), Corinne, Robin Hames, Edna Sinclair (Aotea Centre Women's steering committee); (kneeling) Dame Cath's secretary and Rosie Horton (Aotea Centre Women's steering committee).

Left

Worshipful Master, Lodge United Service No. 10 (1988).

Below

Ray arriving in heaven to a great composers' welcome, with Sooty under his arm.

(Cartoon: Susannah MacDonald)

getting married and preparing to leave New Zealand that initiated the problem again when we were at sea. I woke one night to find Ray white-faced and gripping me tightly while I struggled to open the cabin door. He'd been trying to wake me for some time, asking what was wrong and completely mystified by my behaviour. I told him not to worry as I was probably just sleepwalking, and then went contentedly back to my bunk to fall sound asleep again as if nothing had happened. Over the next few nights, Ray made sure the cabin door was locked and the chain securely fastened before we went to bed. His own sleep was fitful while he listened for the chain to rattle and prepared to rescue me if I managed to open the door. His greatest fear was that I'd reach the deck and go over the side. He was soon able to relax, however, as there were no repeat performances of that particular drama.

After visiting all the Australian ports, our ship travelled on to Durban in South Africa, and we spent an enjoyable few hours sightseeing there. The next port of call was Cape Town where our dear friend and colleague, Russell Channell, now lived. Before leaving New Zealand, we had contacted him to advise that our ship would be in port for a day and hoped it might be possible to spend a little time with him. Like us, Russell was among the exodus of musical artists affected by the New Zealand Opera Company's problems, and he now had the position of Associate Conductor / Chorus Master / Repetiteur for the Johannesburg and Cape Town Opera Houses. Delighted to know that we'd be passing through his new home town, Russell suggested that we make full use of the visit by auditioning for the Cape Town Opera House while we were there and he duly went ahead with the arrangements. Our singing was well received and we were assured that if we thought of returning to South Africa there would certainly be work there for us. Ray and I didn't give this much consideration because, while the country itself is stunning, the particular political system at that time was not to our liking and we would have felt extremely uncomfortable performing to segregated audiences. After the auditions, Russell spent the rest of the day showing us the wonderful sights and scenery of Cape Town, including the dramatic Cape peninsula where the wild beauty of the place was breathtaking. Before returning to the ship that evening Ray and I took a trip up Table Mountain; that is to say, I went only halfway as I'm not good with heights but Ray stayed on the cable car right to the top, and reported that the view from there was even more spectacular. It was dusk and the city below sparkled like the diamonds South Africa is particularly famous for. We could see how easy it would be to become spellbound by this country.

From Cape Town we travelled up the west coast of Africa to Dakar (Senegal), and then on to Madeira, Lisbon, Rotterdam and finally Southampton. We celebrated Christmas and New Year's Eve on board ship and then arrived in a cold and grey England on the 1 January 1971.

Before leaving New Zealand we'd arranged accommodation for a few nights at a small bed-and-breakfast hotel near London's Marble Arch. This was just as well, for towards the end of our voyage Ray became extremely unwell with a severe dose of'flu. On arrival in London he simply went to bed and stayed there. With the hotel being so centrally situated, it was relatively easy for me to get him meals from places like the Lyons Corner House or Marks and Spencer's food hall, and appropriate medication from nearby chemist shops. The main problem was coping with his sheets and pyjamas which were soon soaked by his feverish sweating. The room had twin beds so I just kept swapping the sheets around, but dealing with his sodden pyjamas was more difficult. Although I didn't want to leave him alone for too long, we needed to find somewhere more suitable to live where he could be properly cared for. I immediately went flat-hunting and found a small one-roomed bed-sitter in Emperor's Gate, Kensington. We rented this for three weeks while I continued to look for something larger in a less expensive area. New Zealand House was always the first place to check, as their reception area had large notice boards displaying advertisements of all kinds, including those for rental accommodation. As usual, there was plenty of information and I found a fully furnished flat well situated in Wimbledon, with all the necessary facilities close by, so towards the end of January we moved into our first home together since our marriage.

Living in Wimbledon was most convenient. Ray didn't bother

to get a car – we couldn't have afforded it anyway. It was quicker, cheaper and more relaxing to use London's excellent public transport system. For example, if we were going to an opera performance at the Royal Opera House, it took only ten minutes to travel from Wimbledon to Waterloo by British Rail and then another few minutes by Underground direct to Covent Garden. Depending on the traffic, driving there by car would have taken at least an hour and then there was the major difficulty and expense of finding somewhere to park. We became adept at discovering the best and speediest ways to travel wherever we needed to go, including our regular weekend trips out of London to visit places of interest. There were the occasional public transport strikes but these never affected the buses and trains at the same time, so we always had some means of transport to and from our flat.

The next important task was to find work. First, however, I wanted to introduce Ray to my Guildhall singing teacher and ask her advice regarding my own voice. Since meeting Ray I'd been singing out of my correct vocal range rather more than I should have, in the desire to perform some of the well-known soprano/tenor opera duets with him. This had gone reasonably well but I needed my teacher's opinion as to whether my voice required further tuition in the higher register. We made an appointment to see her at her private studio and, while she was impressed with Ray's voice, she was extremely annoyed with me and bluntly advised that I give up any ideas of singing as a soprano and immediately start work on returning my voice to its natural place – as a mezzo. This upset me as I knew it would limit the repertoire that Ray and I could perform together, since there are far fewer duets for the mezzo and tenor voices.

I decided to seek another opinion and requested an audition with a highly acclaimed singing teacher in London, Ruth Packer, who worked with many of the Royal Opera House principals and was known for her careful remedial work with singers who were experiencing vocal changes or difficulties. Ruth was a little gentler than Joyce Newton; having heard me sing, she said, 'I hear a mezzo, I see a mezzo, but let's just work on the middle of the voice and see how it responds.' She was right, of course; after a few months of tuition with Ruth, my voice settled back into its proper place and I've had to be content with being a mezzo, or 'seconda donna', for the rest of my life. Starting work on the voice again meant that it would be unwise for me to audition for any of the major opera companies in the meantime. Ray, however, began exploring every possibility that might provide professional singing employment.

During earlier years in New Zealand, Ray sang at numerous farewell and benefit concerts for other talented artists about to try their luck overseas, including ballet dancer Russell Kerr, pianist/accompanist Susan Smith, singers Cecil Hauxwell (later John Hauvell) and Donald McIntyre, and the two army colleagues from his war-service years, Inia Te Wiata and Andrew Gold. Several of these artists were now enjoying successful international careers and lived in London or nearby. Ray first contacted Inia, whose wife Beryl was most helpful in providing details of appropriate agents to contact regarding theatre or concert work, as well as those who engaged artists for Masonic Lodge functions. Ray was a Mason and regularly sang at Ladies' Night socials and every other type of Masonic Lodge occasion in both New Zealand and Australia, but the engagements in those countries mostly came directly from their programme organisers. In London, things were more formal and such engagements were handled by an agent. While Ray's sights were really set on gaining a contract with an opera company, any professional singing work would be welcome and hopefully lead to bigger things.

Ray also contacted Donald McIntyre who invited us to his Orpington, Kent home for a meal and kindly agreed to add his letter of reference to those Ray already had. With great wisdom, however, Donald pointed out two things which might make it difficult for Ray to be offered a long-term contract with a major opera house: his age – Ray was 53 by this time – and the fact that he had sung most of his opera roles in English, rather than the languages in which they were originally written. It is interesting that Donald was not as harsh as the New Zealand bursary adjudicators had been with regard to Ray's lack of academic musical qualifications, though he admitted that this was a limiting factor. He accepted Ray's innate musical intelligence and the ease with which he memorised difficult works, but recognised this was possible only with the assistance of good accompanists and coaches. His analysis covering Ray's chances of being employed by one of the major opera houses eventually proved to be correct, but only just.

The next three months were deeply frustrating career-wise. We both approached and successfully auditioned for a few agents, but not much work was offered and even some of that was unsuitable. My previous London agent, Norman McCann, sent Ray to audition for a possible part in a forthcoming West End show, but Ray's 'colonial accent' worried the show's producers because dialogue was involved. We sang at occasional Masonic Lodge functions or small concerts but the work was not regular or particularly well paid. Added to this, agents deducted their commission from the fee and so our payment was even less. As I didn't expect to audition for any of the major opera companies until my new teacher felt satisfied that I was ready, I decided to look for an office job to boost our rapidly depleting finances and eventually began part-time work with a charitable agency called Help the Aged. Ray meanwhile sought auditions with the Sadler's Wells Opera Company, Glyndebourne Festival Opera and the Royal Opera House, Covent Garden. While the first two companies advised that they were not holding these until later in the year, he was given an appointment to sing for the Garden on 22 April 1971.

In those days, and possibly even now, a singer's first audition at the Royal Opera House was normally held in the Crush Bar, where patrons have a few drinks and food before the show and in the intervals. While this bar was heavily carpeted and its windows draped with ceiling-to-floor velvet curtains, the acoustics were surprisingly good. If the audition went well, a further date was arranged to sing on the theatre's stage a few months later. Ray sang well at his Crush Bar hearing and was delighted to be asked to sing again on the stage in a fortnight's time. It is always helpful to have friends in the right place when striving for success in any field and

Ray was lucky to have three such people, all New Zealanders who already worked at the Garden, principal singers Donald McIntyre and Heather Begg, and a chorus member, Bill Clothier. Another prominent New Zealander, conductor John Matheson, also worked there and whether by design or accident, he was on Ray's second auditioning panel. These people encouraged Ray with good advice and assured him that they'd 'have a word in the right ears' about his fine voice and previous experience.

The stage audition was held on 6 May and Ray prepared arias from *Der Freischütz*, *La Bohème*, *Turandot* and *Tosca*. The panel chose the *Freischütz* and *Tosca* arias and, in Ray's own words, 'the audition went reasonably well'. Heather Begg and her husband, Johnny King, sneaked into the back of the theatre to hear him and went backstage afterwards to congratulate him. I met them there after work and we adjourned to the famous nearby pub, the Nag's Head, for a few drinks before Heather and Johnny drove us home. On 10 May a letter arrived from the Royal Opera House advising that they had nothing to offer. John Matheson later told Ray that there had been seven people on the auditioning panel, three of whom were in favour of offering him work and four against. The main reasons were, as Donald McIntyre predicted, not Ray's lack of musical qualifications but his age and lack of experience in a range of foreign languages. There had been discussion concerning assistance with the language problem, but it was considered that the amount of time needed to cover this would not be viable or profitable in the long term, given Ray's age.

Needless to say, we were both exceedingly disappointed and Ray even considered auditioning for the Royal Opera House chorus. However, in discussions with Norman Feasey, who was then the Company's senior repetiteur and accompanist for the auditions, Ray concluded that no matter how well he sang, he would not be acceptable in that capacity either, because of the age limit covering chorus singers imposed by the Opera House's musical director at that time, conductor Georg Solti. But Norman Feasey was most impressed with Ray's voice and promised to write letters of recommendation to the BBC and the two largest concert agents in London at the time, Ibbs & Tillett and Inkpen & Williams. Ray regularly kept a diary and his records have been invaluable in pinpointing when various events took place; his diary entry after the conversation with Norman Feasey is a cryptic 'WE WILL SEE!!!'

Earlier in April we both auditioned for a forthcoming West End production of Jerome Kern's *Show Boat*. Inia Te Wiata had been engaged to sing the role of Joe and suggested that if Ray were interested in working in a musical, he should attend the auditions. As I had felt when trying for *The Sound of Music*, the prospect of paid and full-time singing work was appealing, particularly as our finances were getting low. We both auditioned for *Show Boat* at the Theatre Royal in Drury Lane and were recalled to sing again after Easter. The second audition was on 15 April, just before Ray's Covent Garden appointments; I was unsuccessful but Ray was offered a part in the chorus and to understudy the role of Windy. After the disappointing 'nothing to offer' results from the Royal Opera House, Ray decided to accept the *Show Boat* job and immediately joined the British Actors' Equity Association. The usual employment hassles covering non-British-born job applicants were in force at the time, but a special work permit wasn't necessary during Ray's first twelve months in the United Kingdom. The fact that I, as his wife, held both New Zealand and British passports also made things a little easier. All restrictions were eventually waived when Ray was able to produce evidence that both his sets of grandparents had been born in the United Kingdom.

Rehearsals for *Show Boat* began on 21 June 1970 and the show opened at the Adelphi Theatre in the Strand towards the end of July. It was directed and choreographed by Wendy Toye and the cast included the superb Cleo Laine in the role of Julie. Sadly, Inia did not play the role of Joe. He became seriously ill in May and died before *Show Boat* opened. The role was played by a black American opera singer, Thomas Carey, and the two numbers that regularly stole the show each night were his 'Ol' Man River' and Cleo's 'Bill'. *Show Boat* ran for more than two years with the usual eight performances each week and Ray stayed throughout the entire run. Meanwhile, Norman Feasey was as good as his word and Ray received invitations to audition for the larger concert agents and other opera houses. But rather than go through the possibility and disappointment of rejection again, he decided to stay aboard *Show Boat*.

Chapter 12

Tours and tragedy

Ray's working life continued fairly predictably for the next two and a half years with six evening performances and two matinees each week of *Show Boat*, as well as occasionally playing the role of Windy when required during holidays or the illness of the other performer. With most of the daylight hours free he decided to explore his genealogy, or family tree. The reason behind his initial research was simply to establish the dates and locations of his grandparents' births, marriages and other relevant details, so he could supply this information to the British Immigration authorities if it became necessary. Having these details would allow him to continue working in the United Kingdom indefinitely in accordance with the existing rules and regulations. But he became so engrossed in the information he discovered at London's Somerset House, where family records dating back to 1837 were then stored, that he was determined to trace the Opie history back as far as possible. Before 1837, these records were held in libraries and churches situated in the areas where family members had probably been born, so Ray continued his search by correspondence with the appropriate authorities in Cornwall. He was also eager to visit some of the these places and when this became possible during one of his holiday leave periods in 1973, we spent a profitable eight days touring the county with the aid of our good friend, Pam Wilson.

Pam was born in England but loved travelling, and in her

early twenties had enjoyed some of her OE in New Zealand and Australia. She possessed a number of skills, which included being an excellent seamstress. Ray and I met her in 1964 when she took a part-time job as assistant wardrobe mistress for the New Zealand Opera Company's *Rigoletto* and *Bartered Bride* season. This position suited her well as she was able to tour a large part of our country while receiving a small wage and having most of her travel and accommodation expenses paid for. After a year or so down under, she returned to her homeland and we lost touch with her. By an amazing coincidence, however, she was in the audience for the first night of *Show Boat* and couldn't believe her eyes when she saw Ray's rather distinctive name listed in the programme. At the end of the performance she joined the fans at the stage door, eager to see if it really was the Ramon Opie she had known in New Zealand. I was also waiting backstage and there were many hugs, tears and kisses when we all met up again. From then on Pam, Ray and I spent a great deal of time together throughout the rest of our stay in Britain. When Ray mentioned he was thinking of visiting Cornwall, Pam immediately suggested we go in her car, as this would make it easier to visit some of the more remote areas Ray wanted to explore, and she was of course more familiar with the area.

During his research, Ray had fairly definitely established that one of his forebears was the noted Cornish portrait painter, John Opie, RA. John Opie was born in 1761 at St Agnes, near Truro, and we were able to visit his birthplace, named Harmony Cot, which is now maintained as an historic place. The cottage's curator, intrigued to meet an Opie all the way from New Zealand who was probably related to the artist, made sure Ray signed the visitors' book accordingly. John Opie had been something of a child prodigy and came to be known as 'The Cornish Wonder'. He specialised in portrait painting and his works can be found in art galleries, cathedrals and museums throughout Britain and even in the Royal collection at Hampton Court, where there is a portrait of a Mrs Mary Delaney commissioned by King George III. This royal request came when John Opie was only 20 years of age and the painting was completed a few months later in 1782.

Ray also discovered that one of the finest collections of John Opie's work was located at Place House, the ancient seat of the Prideaux Brun family in the coastal town of Padstow. He very much wanted to see this collection, even though in 1973 the house was not open to the public. Having located Place House, and much to my embarrassment, Ray insisted we drive through the extensive grounds to see if the owners would allow us inside to view the paintings. He found a door at the back of the mansion, which was a good deal less imposing than the main front entrance, and rang the bell. The housekeeper answered and Ray, with great self-assurance, gave his name and said he'd come all the way from New Zealand only to find that he was related to 'The Cornish Wonder' and 'Would it be possible to view the John Opie paintings?' The housekeeper told us to wait while she spoke to the daughter of the house as 'the master and mistress are away'.

Having arrived at this stately home at about 9.45 am, we found that the daughter had breakfasted and was now having a bath and getting ready for the rest of the day. I liked to imagine she'd been out for an early morning canter before this as well. If we cared to wait, she'd be delighted to meet us and show us around the house; meanwhile, perhaps the housekeeper 'could make you a cup of tea while you're waiting.' The whole visit was surreal. The daughter proved to be a most elegant, gracious and charming young woman and she happily spent an hour or so telling us the history of her family and their home. We were taken through the house and saw several of the Opie paintings, some of which were quite small and had been completed when the artist was only 16 years old. The Prideaux family had cleverly recognised the humble lad's talent at this young age and initially commissioned him to paint their dogs.

One room that captured my imagination was the magnificent library. It was the size of a small ballroom and contained ancient ceiling-to-floor maps of south-western England dating back to the Elizabethan era. The maps appeared to be painted on canvas and were mounted on long rollers, which allowed them to be pulled up and down like huge window blinds. Place House, built in the late 1500s, stands high on a hilltop site above the town of Padstow, with wide views towards the sea. We were told that throughout its history it was repeatedly used as a lookout point during times of anticipated coastal invasion, beginning with the Spanish Armada in the time of Queen Elizabeth I's reign, right through to possible incursion by German naval forces in World War Two. I guess this is when those huge, precisely detailed maps were used. Besides the many family portraits, impressive furniture and elaborate ornaments that graced the house, we were shown an exquisite female riding habit, complete with a dainty little hat, which had originally been worn by the daughter's great-great-grandmother. She must have been tiny, with the slimmest waist imaginable, as the whole outfit was exceptionally small. Had I been right about the great-great-granddaughter's early morning ride? Having got over my initial embarrassment at invading the family's privacy, I appreciated Ray's audacity which enabled us to spend such a fascinating and unusual morning.

We continued to explore Cornwall and visited graveyards, libraries, churches and, of course, pubs to find out as much as possible about the Opies. Ray was in a perpetual state of excitement, confirming and discovering new links in his family chain, while Pam and I found it all hugely entertaining, especially Ray's Kiwi ingenuity, or just plain cheek, in gaining us access to a variety of places that might hold information. The Cornish cider, or scrumpy as the locals call it, and the freshly baked crusty bread, tasty cheese, chutney and pickled onion lunches we had each day were exceptionally good too.

Back in London, and with Ray happily employed in *Show Boat*, I concentrated on my lessons with Ruth Packer. The voice progressed well, and in April 1972 I auditioned for a production of Gounod's *Faust* being presented by Maidstone Opera. I was offered the role of Marthe, which I had previously sung at the National School of Opera. As most of the principal singers lived in London we rehearsed there, only travelling to Maidstone for the final rehearsals and the June performances. Again making use of the excellent British Rail train service, I commuted throughout the season.

As it was necessary to leave my charity job when I went into rehearsal for *Faust*, I once again looked for part-time work when the season finished, and found a sole-charge office position with a very select silversmiths and jewellers, Victor Crichton Ltd, at 19 Kensington High Street. The shop was never actually open as such; access could only be obtained by ringing the doorbell. The father and son owners of the business had a little button under the counter which they pressed to allow entry, as long as the prospective client looked respectable or familiar. An old-fashioned and highly polished brass bell above the entrance gave a delicate, high-pitched tinkle when the door opened, and this sound, which could clearly be heard in my upstairs office, gave me the sense I was back in a Charles Dickens novel.

The shop was quite small, with dark-stained wood and glass cabinets full of gleaming silverware lining the walls and a little glass-topped counter containing trays of vastly expensive jewellery, both new and second hand. The whole atmosphere was very 'olde worlde'. Only four people worked there: the owners, a general handyman who cleaned and packaged everything, and me doing the secretarial and book-keeping work. The large amount of antique silverware on show was only part of the shop's collection. The most valuable pieces were securely stored in separate vaults away from the shop because the insurance premiums covering them on display would have been prohibitive. I certainly saw how 'the other half lives' during my time there. Lady This and Lady That would come in each day to have their jewellery checked and cleaned; they were all known by name and suitably greeted by the owners. Celebrities from all walks of life made purchases at the shop and the handyman would often ring this Kiwi upstairs to suggest I 'pop down for a minute', as he knew I'd be intrigued by the shop's current client.

The shop offered numerous diversions. On one occasion, a gentleman came in to purchase two identical diamonds for his only daughter who'd just produced twin girls. The diamonds were eventually to be given to the twins on their 21st birthday, when they could each decide how they wished their diamond to be set. In the meantime, I wondered if his daughter might have used them for earrings. My bosses had chosen several large and exquisite diamonds from the casually tissue-paper-wrapped selection brought to the shop by a diamond merchant from Hatton Garden, London's famous diamond centre, and these were shown to the client. He chose two beautiful stones at an astronomical cost. I'd love to know how the twins eventually decided to have the diamonds set 21 years later.

Another absorbing aspect of this business came through items bequeathed to its customers. Sometimes the client simply wanted a particular piece valued, but the most interesting circumstances were when a locked wooden or metal box, for which the key had been lost, was brought in and the client wanted it carefully opened without subsequent damage to either the container or its contents. The unlocked boxes yielded all manner of things: beautiful antique jewellery, ribbon-tied letters, tiny coils of hair or just piles of useless old junk, but whatever the contents, they were always fascinating.

One client had been left a slightly dented and extremely blackened metal jug. He wanted it valued and if it was worth anything he was keen to sell it. On being told it would be preferable for the jug to be properly cleaned and restored before its value could be accurately assessed, the client said he didn't have time for all that and would be happy with a 'best guess'. My boss had an inkling the jug was a piece of Georgian sterling silver but needed to see the hallmarks and other identifying details clearly before he could be sure. He made a rough but very fair estimate of its value and offered to purchase the jug if the client so wished. The surprised and delighted client accepted the offer and went merrily on his way. When the jug was eventually restored to its former glory, it was indeed Georgian silver and worth far more than the original estimate. A little more patience would have been to that client's advantage.

The shop's senior partner had permanent seats in one of the loggia boxes at the Royal Albert Hall. When he discovered I was a singer and loved most forms of classical music, he allowed me to use the seats for any concerts he didn't wish to attend himself. This was wonderful, especially during the annual Promenade concert season. Ray couldn't come with me, of course, being busy with his show in the evenings, but various friends were able to enjoy the 'freebies' offered or I simply went on my own.

During Ray's 1972 holiday break we decided to spend eight days in Austria. We made use of a travel company's package deal tour which included cheap air travel and accommodation, but allowed us the freedom to go our own way as far as the daily optional extras were concerned. We wanted to seek out places of musical interest, of course. The plane left from Gatwick Airport and flew direct to Munich, where we were to be met by a coach that would transport us south to our first destination in Austria. Unfortunately, we travelled at the same time as the 1972 Munich Olympics, when the dreadful massacre of Israeli athletes by Palestinian terrorists occurred. The Israelis had been taken captive and held at gunpoint in a helicopter until it was eventually blown up and all on board killed. Our trip came only two days after this event and although some incoming flights were diverted to Munich's military airport, our plane landed at the same airport where the killings took place. The three helicopters involved in the drama were still on a runway there, two clearly recognisable but the third a completely burnt-out shell. Although arrival procedures in Munich were carried out in a normal manner, our flight back to England at the end of our holiday left from the military airbase, where we were subjected to intense frisking and treated with great suspicion. Men and women were at least sent to separate areas for the examination, but I found the whole experience of being frisked by an extremely large military Frau most unpleasant. Thankfully, we passed muster and were allowed to return to London.

The unnerving start to our holiday did nothing to spoil the trip, however. Our first two days were based in the picturesque township of Seefeld, a ski resort high in the Tyrol Mountains. While the various historic buildings, churches and other sites in this glorious alpine region were fabulous, it's the simpler things that remain in my memory. I fell in love with the charming 'cuckoo clock' chalets which dotted the countryside, their side and front walls completely decorated with multi-coloured, hand-painted murals. The windows were shuttered and each one contained a beautifully carved wooden box full to overflowing with bright red geraniums, while large stones lay on the chalets' shingled roofs to give protection during the long winter snowfalls. As we drove through the lush, green countryside, dreamy-eyed cows lazily raised their heads to gaze at us as our coach passed, but soon lost interest and continued their slow plod over the sunlit fields. Around their necks, hanging from heavy leather straps, were big metal bells which produced dull tolling sounds as they moved.

Travelling on to Salzburg, we had to pinch ourselves to believe we were treading the streets where Mozart walked and could visit his Geburtshaus, or birthplace. Among all manner of family treasures, the house still contained the little clavichord and hammerflüge (fortepiano) on which the three-year-old Wolfgang Amadeus learned to play and compose his first childhood pieces. We watched an abridged version of one of his operas performed by puppets at the Salzburg Marionette Theatre, and at the other end of the scale, visited some of the venues used in the 1965 filming of *The Sound of Music*. These included Count Leopold's palace which became Captain von Trapp's family mansion, the real Nonnberg nunnery, and the church where Maria and Georg's wedding took place. Then it was on to Vienna, that glorious city of music, art and romance, and the birthplace of Franz Schubert and Johann Strauss. We toured as many palaces, cemetery shrines, concert halls and opera houses as we could manage during our brief stay there and indulged ourselves with the delectable cream cakes, pastries and coffee for which Vienna is also famous.

Towards the end of our time in Vienna, we joined the rest of the tour party for an evening of dinner and entertainment at a typical Austrian inn deep in the Wienerwald or Vienna Woods. The tavern was exactly as we'd imagined it would be, warm, welcoming and full of atmosphere. It was furnished with long, rough-hewn wooden tables down the centre of its dining area, the chairs on either side not only beautifully carved but also decorated with traditional hand-painted designs around the little heart-shaped holes in their back rests. Wooden-sided booths, seating up to six people, jutted out from the walls and the plump, rosy-cheeked and full-bosomed Kellnerinnen (cellar maids) skilfully manoeuvred their way between these and the central tables while serving large platters of fattening food. To complete the scene, a small band of players dressed in national costume was enthusiastically oom-pah-pah-ing on a stage in the corner. We settled into a booth and were immediately offered a beer or wine, both of which came in tankards. Ray was quick to notice that if any customer appeared not to have a drink in front of them, the waiters offered the same choice again. Never one to miss an opportunity, he finished his first drink, slipped the tankard under the table and was instantly served again. Convinced he'd died and gone to heaven, Ray gratefully accepted several more helpings of fairly new white wine and even the substantial meal that followed could not prevent his inevitable euphoric inebriation.

The band continuously played local folk tunes and popular medleys throughout the evening, but in his current state Ray decided they should be playing songs from the shows that have made Vienna the operetta capital of the world, such as *The Merry Widow*, *Land of Smiles*, *Gypsy Baron* and the opera *Die Fledermaus*. He weaved his way up to the band leader and suggested that if they could play some of these selections he'd sing along with them. I imagine the band leader wondered what the result would be if he obliged, but perhaps thinking they could probably drown this chap out if he was too bad, he agreed and asked Ray what he'd like to sing. Ray mentioned several well-known numbers including 'Vienna, city of my dreams', 'You are my heart's delight', 'Overhead the moon is beaming' and needless to say, 'Drink, drink, drink' from the ever-popular *Student Prince*. Without more ado, the band and Ray launched forth into their impromptu performance.

When the band leader realised this happily intoxicated customer was indeed a very fine singer, he made full use of the unexpected chance to put on an additional floor show. The inn's guests were delighted and as each song finished they clapped, stamped and roared their approval and called out titles of further old favourites they wanted Ray to sing. He happily obliged but, deciding he needed some help, dragged me up to sing with him as well. When we'd exhausted ourselves, and possibly the band as well, we finally returned to our booth. I was given hugs, kisses and flowers from some of the patrons and even offered money, to which Ray's reaction was, 'I'm doing all the bloody work and you're getting the presents.' Before we left the inn, however, Ray received a hefty bill for the hidden tankards which had been carefully counted and charged for. One might have hoped the innkeeper would have been a bit more generous after all the free entertainment we provided.

On boarding the coach for the journey back to our hotel, the tour guide, who occasionally worked as a ski instructor in New Zealand and particularly liked Kiwis, decided Ray should continue entertaining the group on the way. He summoned him up to the front of the coach and handed him the microphone. By now, however, Ray was past singing and decided he'd rather tell a few 'smoko' jokes. As I was sure his joke repertoire would not go down too well with some of the women on board, I hastily suggested that as we'd be very busy again the next day with more sightseeing and a great deal of walking, it might be wiser for him to have a rest. Ray plodded obediently back down the aisle to our seat, flopped his head on my shoulder and was soon sound asleep.

Late in 1972 I auditioned for a forthcoming production of *Lilac Time* which was to tour throughout England, Wales and Scotland. A well-known producer, Alexander Bridge (no relation), regularly presented operettas such as *The Waltz Dream*, *The Desert Song*, *The Student Prince* and other popular light operas and toured them for several months to what are known as the 'number one' or leading theatres in the United Kingdom, doing eight performances in each centre. Alexander was fortunate in obtaining Britain's 'king of operetta' and matinee idol, John Hanson, to sing the role of Schober in this musical, which is based on the life of Franz Schubert and uses snippets of his music. Having John Hanson in the cast ensured that the show would be successful and play to full houses throughout its 20-week tour. John had previously toured in *Lilac Time*, but this was a new production and he was able to fit it into his busy career. Even while the show was on the road, John rushed backwards and forwards between whatever place we were playing in and London, appearing on television, singing at an All-

Star Celebrity concert at the Royal Albert Hall and recording LPs and BBC *Friday Night is Music Night* programmes.

I was offered the role of Fritzi and rehearsals began on 8 January 1973. For those who may have heard a little about John Hanson's reputation with his leading ladies, I hasten to add that Fritzi is sung by a mezzo and is therefore only a 'seconda donna'! We opened in Hull, Yorkshire on 29 January and I have never been so cold. When I was studying in London during the 1960s my mother sent me a mohair rug as a birthday gift. That rug and the ever-precious hot-water bottle toured with me everywhere throughout my singing career in Britain and kept me from freezing to death on many occasions. I actually wrapped myself in the rug before getting into bed and in this way managed to keep a little warmer between the cold and what often felt like damp sheets on the beds in the various 'digs' I stayed at. I completed the five months tour of *Lilac Time* without getting a cold or 'flu, so my trusty rug and 'hottie bottle' did their job well.

One of the twenty centres *Lilac Time* played in was Swansea in Wales. Ray still had a few days of leave left so he decided to join me there and do some more sight-seeing. We couldn't have been more popular with the people we met in Swansea. We were singers and came from the same country as the All Blacks; what better credentials did we need in this area of excellent male voice choirs and rugby-mad enthusiasts? Ray met me each evening after the show and we adjourned to one of Dylan Thomas's favourite pubs, the Singleton if I remember correctly, for a few drinks and a singalong around the piano; these sessions often continued well into the night and were great fun. Ray also went to two Masonic Lodge meetings in Swansea where he was given a warm welcome and invited to sing. During the day we visited local places of interest, including the beautiful Mumbles and Gower Coast, an area which made us homesick as it is remarkably similar to parts of the New Zealand coastline. The week went all too quickly and we were sad when it came to an end.

Ray was a hopeless cook but had to manage as best he could in my five-month absence from London. However, whenever I was playing in a centre close enough to get back to London on a Sunday, I spent that whole day roasting a couple of chickens and preparing soups and casseroles for him, and storing them in the freezer so there was at least the basis of a few healthy meals available for a short time. One of his favourite sayings was that he 'couldn't boil water without burning it,' so even the food I prepared sometimes ended up as a 'burnt offering' when he tried to do something with it. He could manage breakfast and a sandwich or something on toast at lunchtime, but preparing a main meal was almost beyond him. One tends to eat at strange times working in the theatre anyway, so the occasional takeaway after the evening show kept him going.

Unbeknown to me, however, Ray had been having periodic black-outs. One of these occurred at Charing Cross underground station, where he collapsed and people simply walked over or past him, thinking he was drunk. Luckily, one of the dancers in his show came across him, stayed with him until he recovered and then helped him catch the train home to our flat. I contacted Ray regularly from wherever I was in the country, and on this particular night I telephoned him from Edinburgh at around 11.45 pm but got no reply. I wasn't too concerned, as although it was unusual for him not to be home by that time, his train might have been delayed or he could have been socialising somewhere. I rang again early the next morning and teasingly asked what he'd been up to the previous night. He was forced to tell me about the fainting spell but made light of it, saying he'd probably been a bit hungry and tired after the show. Naturally this was deeply worrying and I said I'd return to London immediately, but he was adamant it wasn't necessary. There was little else I could do from so far away, other than beg him to see a doctor. He didn't, of course. When my show finished at the end of June and I returned to London, Ray seemed perfectly well for the next few months with regular meals and proper care. We even took our trip to Cornwall in the following September and there were no further signs of possible ill-health until the end of October.

Having resigned from my Kensington High Street job when I went into *Lilac Time*, it was once again necessary to find another part-time job and, by a strange coincidence, I found a part-time job in the pathology laboratory of a very upmarket private hospital, the Harley Street Clinic. My duties were simply to type the results of laboratory tests. Being somewhat squeamish like my mother, it was a relief that the little office area I worked in was well away from the business end of the lab, as I certainly wasn't keen to view the various specimens being tested there. However, my curiosity was aroused when I heard one of the technicians make an odd remark about a bag of blood which had come in, presumably for transfusion purposes. The contents of the bag were in two unequal parts with a small amount of red liquid at the bottom and a lot of thick, pale yellow stuff on the top. After commenting that the donor must have eaten fish and chips or Kentucky Fried before giving the blood, the technician explained that the substance at the top was fat. This more than convinced me about the value of a low-fat diet.

Show Boat closed soon after our Cornwall holiday, leaving Ray out of work. As our landlady had returned from overseas and needed her flat back, we were now at another address in Wimbledon which was even closer to the shops and train stations. The new property covered three levels with a lounge, double bedroom, kitchen and bathroom on the second floor and a large attic room on the top floor. The ground floor contained a toilet and two other rooms which were let as offices. To boost our income, Ray and I transformed the attic into a bed-sitter and advertised it both at New Zealand House and on the notice board at the Wimbledon Theatre. We hoped to attract short-stay tenants who were either visiting the United Kingdom from overseas or performing in brief seasons at the theatre. Our first tenants were a charming New Zealand couple from Christchurch, Esther and Mick Tabb, who intended to travel around Europe by campervan but wanted a London base to leave some of their belongings and then stay at when they were in Britain. This suited us, especially as they were happy to pay the full rent whether they were in residence or not. They booked the bed-sitter for eight weeks and we were sorry to see them go when they returned to New Zealand.

The next tenant stayed with us until we eventually left England; this was not what we originally intended but at least the room was occupied. He was a lighting technician at the Wimbledon Theatre and therefore on their permanent staff. We provided simple cooking facilities in the bed-sitter but allowed the tenants to use our kitchen if they wanted to prepare larger meals. Ken Hadfield, the lighting technician, wasn't keen on cooking so we didn't see much of him; in the weeks to come I was to greatly value both his rent money and his presence in the flat.

During October I sang in a short film being made at the Denham Studios in Middlesex. The Anvil Film and Recording Group were making a series of films to introduce opera to young people. Highlights of the appropriate opera, lasting about an hour, provided a brief introduction to the piece and helped to familiarise children with this type of music. The opera I took part in was Verdi's *La Traviata* and we recorded and filmed the two main chorus and principals scenes from Acts One and Three. Denham Studios are well known for the large number of British films they have produced over the years, and once again it provided an interesting venue to work in.

By now my singing teacher considered I was ready to audition for the larger opera houses and agents, so I began preparing the arias I would sing. Arrangements and dates were made and I began to rehearse with a new friend and excellent accompanist, Cilla Stewart. Cilla, also a New Zealander, lived at Clapham Common, only a few railway stops away from Wimbledon, and she invited Ray and me to stay for dinner after one of my late afternoon rehearsals with her. It was a very cold mid-November evening, and when Ray and I were ready to leave at about 11 pm, Cilla and her husband drove us to the station. We waved our goodbyes and started climbing the steps to the appropriate platform. Halfway up, Ray slowed and gradually began to sink to the ground like something simply melting away. I was terrified and tried to keep hold of him in case he fell backwards down the stairs. A passerby came to my assistance and we managed to carry Ray up the remaining stairs to the platform, but he was still in a faint. When he eventually regained consciousness I wanted to find a taxi immediately and take him to hospital, but he insisted we go on to Wimbledon. He said the problem was exactly the same as his previous experiences and he usually recovered well after a good night's sleep. He blamed the cold night air after leaving Cilla's warm and cosy flat and said he'd be fine by the morning. We managed to get home safely, but with Ray's grudging consent I called a taxi the next morning and took him to the doctor.

We later realised how fortunate it was that the doctor instantly recognised Ray's problem. He suspected a faulty heart valve and referred Ray to the local hospital for tests and diagnosis. The hospital confirmed that Ray's aortic valve was malfunctioning and quickly arranged for him to be admitted to St George's Hospital at Hyde Park Corner on 3 December 1973. Ray spent the next eleven days undergoing tests there until a decision was made to transfer him to the National Heart Hospital in Westmoreland Street, conveniently near to my Harley Street workplace. Neither of us knew then just how convenient this move would be, not only for Ray's future health prospects but in allowing me to be close at hand in any emergency.

Chapter 13

Hospitals, teeth and Grim's Dyke

The day after Ray was admitted to the National Heart Hospital he had eight teeth extracted. His doctors wanted to remove all his teeth, but when Ray protested that he would find it extremely difficult to sing with dentures, they reluctantly agreed to extract only those they considered essential to come out. They advised that partial plates would not be an option either, so he would have to put up with a mouth full of gaps. Ray stood firm and said he could cope with fewer of his own teeth far more easily than with false ones.

I visited him soon after this procedure, while he was still asleep. The tears came as I waited for him to wake up; he looked so desolate and lonely lying there, and I suddenly felt defeated by the whole situation and wished we were back home in New Zealand, surrounded by the love and support of family and friends. At this stage, Ray dealt with the whole business far better than I did, and was surprisingly philosophical and positive about everything. Unfortunately, but quite understandably, this would not be the case in the months ahead.

The open heart surgery to replace his aortic valve with a homograft, or human valve, was to take place on 20 December, and although Ray's positive approach to the whole matter persisted, neither of us looked forward to that day. In discussions with his cardiologist, I was told that this type of operation had been pioneered by two highly skilled surgeons, New Zealander Brian

Barrett-Boyes and South African Donald Ross. Mr Ross was at that time the foremost cardiac surgeon in Britain and operated at the National Heart Hospital. But many young doctors specialising in heart surgery also travelled to New Zealand from all parts of the world to study and practise the procedure at Auckland's Green Lane Hospital under Sir Brian's guidance, and one of these would also be involved in Ray's care. In my ignorance, I asked why, if the operation was so expertly performed in New Zealand, we couldn't return home to have it done there. The reply that Ray was far too ill to travel should have been obvious. Ray and I later liked to believe that the New Zealand connection gave his surgeons the added incentive to perform a copybook operation. Mr Ross himself was to be in charge, and there was some comfort in knowing that Ray would have the very best of care at the most prestigious heart hospital in England.

Another worry I discussed with the cardiologist was whether I had been irresponsible in not realising the seriousness of Ray's condition and doing something about it sooner. It was a relief to be told that the problem is hard to diagnose until it reaches a certain stage and the doctor is able to hear the malfunction in the valve as it opens and closes. During Ray's time in hospital, a number of student doctors were brought to his bedside to listen to his heart in an attempt to hear and recognise the appropriate sound. Ray liked to joke about health problems or illnesses which are not directly discernible with the quip, 'No blood, no bloody sympathy.'

My work colleagues at the Harley Street Clinic knew I was worried about my reaction when visiting Ray for the first time after the operation, so they organised ways to help me. The clinic carried out a number of heart operations, and arrangements were made for me to visit patients undergoing such surgery, as long as they were agreeable of course, to see how they were coping. By meeting and seeing strangers with long scars down the middle of their chests and various tubes and monitors placed inside and around them, I should find it easier to deal with seeing someone I loved in the same situation. I managed to visit two patients without feeling too queasy, and was most grateful for this 'rehearsal'.

Ray went into theatre at 8.30 am and his operation took six hours. I was told I could visit him briefly in Intensive Care later that afternoon, so just before the appointed time and to gain a bit of courage, I did something I'd never done before. I went, on my own, to a little pub not far from the hospital and ordered a double brandy. Feeling somewhat more relaxed after this, I headed for the hospital's IC unit. A pleasant nurse immediately took me to Ray's bedside, but she was soon helping me out again and telling me to sit down and put my head between my knees. After that humiliation, I behaved myself and stayed with Ray as long as I was allowed. At this stage he was a great deal brighter and perkier than I was and I wondered if he'd been given some sort of 'happy pills'.

His mood changed significantly after the first two days, however, and he became deeply depressed and weepy. A few things made him smile during the rest of this period in hospital, especially the sight of his surgeon, Donald Ross, carving the turkey for the patients in his ward on Christmas Day. But one thing Ray couldn't do was laugh heartily; the long wound down his chest hurt too much. He progressed reasonably well and was discharged from hospital on 3 January 1974. London was in the grip of a bitterly cold winter that year, so the next problem was to keep him warm. I bought a small second-hand day-bed with an adjustable headrest and put this in our little lounge, which was the easiest room to keep heated all day. Over the next two or three weeks Ray spent most of his waking hours there, covered with blankets and in reasonable comfort.

While we anticipated it would take some time for Ray to recover fully, we began to be concerned when his progress was slow. He tried hard to resume normal everyday living but felt constantly tired and unwell and had difficulty breathing. Neither of us gave any thought to our singing careers and I had cancelled my auditions. Our most important concern was Ray's return to full health. Financially, things were also becoming worrying, so I regretfully left the Harley Street Clinic and found a job with longer hours. Our tenant Ken was still living in the attic, so his payments helped us meet the rent. We'd been paying the usual taxes and National Health Insurance contributions throughout our periods of employment and had managed to build up a reasonable amount of entitlement to free health care. But we were amazed and delighted to learn that Ray's contributions also entitled him to a sickness benefit. All these things made our rather precarious financial position a little more secure.

We had many good friends in London who did everything possible to help us. We were regularly invited for meals and would be picked up and delivered home most willingly. However, both Ray and I were stubbornly independent and accepted assistance only if we felt unable to manage ourselves. Towards the middle of March, we were invited to spend the day with some friends who lived in Hounslow, Middlesex, whom we had met on the Austrian trip. We made our own way there but as Ray became progressively unwell during the day, they drove us back to Wimbledon soon after dinner. Ray's condition continued to deteriorate and I anxiously called an emergency doctor who arrived about 11 pm. After examining Ray, she contacted the National Heart Hospital in an attempt to have him admitted immediately. The hospital requested that this be delayed if possible until early the next morning, when they would send an ambulance to collect him. The emergency doctor wasn't happy about this but advised that as long as Ray stayed in bed and tried to sleep in an upright position, it might be safe to delay his admission. Neither Ray nor I slept much during that night and we were relieved when the ambulance arrived shortly before 6 am. We could have no idea this hospital visit would last for more than three months.

On re-admission to the National Heart Hospital, Ray underwent a series of X-rays and tests and it was discovered he had a serious heart disease caused by an infection called bacteria endocarditis. This disease damages or even destroys heart valves and it had attacked his newly inserted aortic homograft. The bacteria can enter the bloodstream as a result of gum disease, and it was suspected that the removal of Ray's eight teeth before his heart operation might have caused the problem, even though he'd been well covered by antibiotics. We were told this infection occurs only rarely, about one in every 100,000 cases. When it became possible for us to joke about such a serious situation, we decided it was typical of Ray to be the one it happened to as he was a tenor, and really great tenors are said to occur only once in every 500,000 voices, so this was just adding to his exclusivity.

His doctors now had to find ways to kill the bacteria, so for the next two months Ray was on a constant 24-hour intravenous drip of various antibiotics. The type of antibiotic was changed frequently to avoid the bacteria becoming immune to it. He also had to take a lot of other medication, but this cocktail of drugs made Ray bilious and, refusing to eat much of the hospital food offered him, he steadily lost weight. Luckily the wards were equipped with very good kitchens and I was permitted to bring in anything Ray felt he could eat and leave it in their refrigerators. The foods he most fancied were any type of yoghurt, fruit, fresh ham sandwiches and roast chicken. The drugs also made him depressed and he now became a difficult and unhappy patient. He passed the long, boring days reading and wanted every book I could find on English history, particularly the history of London and the River Thames, and of course anything about Cornwall.

It was certain that once the antibiotics had destroyed, or were at least controlling Ray's bacterial infection, another operation would be necessary to replace the damaged valve. Yet again I displayed my ignorance by querying why the diseased valve couldn't be removed immediately and replaced with a healthy one. The answer was obvious: the infection needed to be destroyed first otherwise it would simply transfer to the replacement. Added to this, the cardiologist advised it might not be possible for Ray to receive another human valve owing to the removal of scar tissue, so the next option would be a Starr-Edward plastic valve. He told me this valve can sometimes be slightly noisy and may be heard opening and closing when all is quiet, in bed at night for example. I certainly hoped that the Starr-Edward valve would not be necessary, as I imagined a future of Ray and I lying in bed at nights, listening carefully to be sure it was still working.

Like many hospitals, the National Heart had a small team of non-medical volunteers who regularly visited the wards with trolleys of library books and other items such as newspapers, magazines and toiletries for patients to borrow or purchase. As I planned to visit Ray every day, I offered my services as a ward-hostess and was extremely surprised when the hospital's administration manager asked what office skills I had and did these include typing? It turned out that the hospital's chief engineer needed a part-time secretary for a few weeks and they wondered if I would like to be interviewed for the position. Needless to say, I jumped at the chance, because if they found me suitable, it would allow me to visit Ray more often than during the normal visiting hours and to be closer in an emergency. Ten days after Ray was admitted to hospital, I started my paid employment there, working from 1 pm to 5 pm for the chief engineer, Les Bloomfield. I reduced my hours at the other job, working only during the mornings.

I had no idea hospitals had engineers, but soon learned that my new boss controlled such things as the sterilisation of the operating theatres and provision of the various gases used during operations. One of my duties was to type up the daily schedules of patients' operations and in what particular theatre these would take place; a rotation system covered the theatres that were available, as they underwent stringent sterilisation procedures after a certain number of operations had been performed. The National Heart Hospital had a little museum containing patients' specimens and exhibits from past operations. These included hearts, valves and other relevant parts of the body. One visit to the museum was enough for me but it was certainly interesting. Long after Ray left the hospital and we were back home in New Zealand, Mr Bloomfield wrote to tell us that Ray's diseased homograft valve was still in the museum and a few bacteria remained alive on it for some months after his second operation.

During the many long weeks that Ray was hospitalised, several of our friends and singing colleagues were kind enough to visit him. One of these was a *Lilac Time* friend of mine, Margo Wain, who'd become very fond of Ray. She was singing in a summer season at Brighton, but used her one afternoon off each week to travel up to London and visit him before returning in time for her evening show. Ray received another welcome surprise when he was visited by Kiri Te Kanawa. Kiri and Ray occasionally had sung together in Auckland before she left New Zealand to begin her stellar international career. She had lived in Blockhouse Bay before going overseas and often accompanied her father, Tom, when he made purchases at Ray's IGA store. I met her by chance at New Zealand House while Ray was in hospital and she immediately asked, 'How's my old mate Ray?' I told her of his health problems and where he was. Needless to say, the fact that Kiri spared time to visit him thoroughly delighted Ray, as he well knew how exceedingly busy her life now was.

Not long before Ray returned to hospital, another *Lilac Time* principal, Susan Maisey, contacted me to see if I was interested in being part of a group of five singers performing Gilbert and Sullivan selections at Sir William Gilbert's old home. The house, known as Grim's Dyke, had been built in 1870 and Sir William lived there from 1890 until his death in 1911. His widow remained at the house until she died in 1936, after which Grim's Dyke went through various transformations, including being used as a film and television location. It was converted into a hotel in 1970 and one of the special attractions offered on a Sunday evening was a silver service dinner and appropriate entertainment. This became very popular with tourists, particularly Americans. The programme included five singers, one of them playing the role of Sir William Gilbert, and an accompanist, who was of course Sir Arthur Sullivan. Sir William acted as the evening's host and compère and also sang the 'patter' songs, i.e. the fast ones with dozens of words. The rest of us sang the best-known solos, duets, trios and quartets from their light operas, as well as some of the favourite chorus numbers. As it would have been too difficult to keep changing costumes, we simply dressed appropriately for the Victorian era.

Grim's Dyke had an impressive central staircase leading down to the reception hall of the house. At the beginning of the evening's entertainment Sir William and his four friends swept graciously down the stairs to welcome the dinner guests, who'd been enjoying a sherry or whisky in the lounge, and then everyone moved into the dining room. Sir Arthur was already seated at the piano and enthusiastically played selections from the opera's overtures while the guests were escorted to their tables and given a glass of wine. As Sir William's party, we also settled ourselves at a table and prepared to sing the first item which was usually one of the popular choruses from *HMS Pinafore*, *The Pirates of Penzance* or *The Gondoliers*. Soup was then served and the dinner continued with items between each course. Finally, when the guests were having coffee and a glass of port, we sang 'Dance a Cachucca' from *The Gondoliers* and persuaded a few of them to get up and dance with us. It was fun and I enjoyed singing at yet another interesting venue, on an 'as required' basis, during the next few months.

Chapter 14

'There's no place like home'

Two months after his readmission to the National Heart Hospital, Ray's heart disease, while not completely eradicated, was at a stage where his doctors considered it reasonably safe to perform another valve transplant. They were concerned about his general health and the fact that he'd been on blood-thinning medication, warfarin or 'rat poison' as Ray called it, and warned me these factors would make the second operation more risky. Ray went into the operating theatre at 9 am on 28 May 1974, and while things did not go well, at least he could later boast that he was considered to be a 'miracle man'.

I went to my two jobs as usual and waited to hear from Ray's surgeon, who said he would let me know how things went immediately after the operation. Not having heard from him by 4 pm, I asked my boss, Mr Bloomfield, if he could find out what was happening. He contacted the operating theatre and reluctantly told me that all was not well. A little after 5.30 pm a nurse advised that Ray was still in theatre and it would be wise for me to stay at the hospital. Our good friends, Heather Begg and her husband Johnny King, had invited me to stay with them overnight, as they lived closer to the hospital than Ray and I did, so I telephoned to let them know what the situation was. Heather immediately prepared sandwiches and a thermos of coffee which Johnny brought to the hospital and he stayed with me while I waited. At 7.30 pm we were told that Ray was out of theatre and in Intensive Care but was not yet out of danger, and his surgeon would give me more information as soon as he could. By 9.30 pm, with no contact from either a nurse or the surgeon, I was desperate to know what was happening.

The surgeon finally arrived and apologised for the delay; he'd been called back to the theatre again to carry out an emergency procedure on another patient. He advised that Ray's operation had been particularly difficult, the main problem being bleeding. Despite receiving several blood transfusions, Ray's bleeding could not be controlled and although he was still receiving treatment, the surgeon was not sure he would survive the night. He suggested I go home and try to get some sleep but stay in regular contact with the hospital. In the event of an even more serious change in Ray's condition, they would call me. I left the details of where I was staying and Johnny drove me back to his apartment. During the long and worrying night that followed, he and Heather were wonderfully supportive and did everything they could to keep my spirits up. I rang the hospital every hour until 3 am when I finally managed to get some sleep. My 6 am call resulted in the best possible news: although still very ill Ray was out of immediate danger, the bleeding was under control and I could visit him later in the day. However, it was important to let the hospital staff know my whereabouts at all times over the next few days.

Ray made slow but steady progress during the next two weeks, and on 12 June he was transferred back to St George's Hospital, Hyde Park, for recuperation. In addition to the large amount of medication he was taking, it was suggested he drink a bottle of Mackeson stout each day as this contains a lot of iron and would help build up his strength. This delighted Ray, and it further amused him when he discovered that stout was at one time prescribed for nursing mothers whose breast milk was not as good as it should be owing to weakness after childbirth. I duly took six bottles of stout to the hospital and Ray looked forward to having one each day. He was still being a little difficult with the staff looking after him, and with me too from time to time. So when I arrived the following day and he indignantly informed me that his nurse had given the five remaining bottles of stout to other patients in the ward, I made enquiries as to whether this had really occurred. Ray's account was true, so subsequently I took only one bottle in at a time and he drank it while I was there. During Ray's stay at St George's, he was encouraged to take short daily walks with me. We were allowed to use a small private park near the hospital, where a key was necessary to gain access, and we gradually increased the distance each day as his strength improved. Finally, on 25 June, he came home to Wimbledon.

The difficulties of the past eight months made our decision to return to New Zealand inevitable. We originally planned to travel home by sea, thinking a long, lazy ship cruise would be ideal for Ray, and we even made a preliminary booking. But when the matter was discussed with his doctors, they insisted we travel by air, because appropriate medical assistance would be more quickly obtained if Ray had any health problems en route. We were advised that even to fly home he needed medical clearances from the doctors connected to the airlines we would be travelling with, who would also issue special instructions for Ray's care throughout the journey. A wheelchair was to be provided each time Ray boarded or left the aircraft, and other arrangements, including the provision of oxygen, were to be made for our flights. It was all rather daunting but we went ahead with our plans.

We were due to leave Britain at the end of September 1974 and began the process of finalising the many matters that had to be dealt with before we could depart, such as obtaining tax and National Health Service clearances and 'honourable discharges' from Actors' Equity. While dealing with the health clearances, we were amazed to learn that the weekly financial assistance Ray had been entitled to would run out five days before we left Britain. This sickness benefit, based on Ray's National Health Insurance contributions during the time he was working, had covered hospital costs of well over £30,000 and an allowance of £7 per week during the eight months of his illness. We had the deepest gratitude and only the highest praise for the British public health system.

We spent our last night in London with our Hounslow friends. They took us to the airport the next day and there were floods of tears all round as we made our farewells. Our first flight was with British Airways to Los Angeles, and everything went as planned with the promised assistance provided. Unfortunately the flight with Air New Zealand from Los Angeles to Auckland was another matter. As it had not been possible to check our luggage right through to Auckland when we were at Heathrow, I had to retrieve it and then check in again and obtain boarding passes for the Air New Zealand flight before proceeding through Customs. I found a seat in the airport for Ray and insisted he stay there while I carried out the necessary procedures. It was very hot and there were long distances between the various baggage collection and other areas. Ray bought me a fur coat while we were living in London and the easiest way to get that home was to wear it, so I was 'glowing' profusely as I tried to find my way around. When I finally reached the check-in desk for the boarding passes, I requested that our seats be situated in a non-smoking area of the plane. I was advised there were none left and to take this up with the flight staff once we boarded.

I had difficulty finding Ray again and our names were being called by the time we reached the departure gate. Once aboard the plane I requested the seat change, but was brusquely told to take those allocated as it was not possible to alter them and the matter should have been sorted out before boarding anyway. All the stress Ray and I had gone through over the past year caught up with me and I burst into tears. Ray took over at this point and suggested that the senior flight attendant discuss the matter with us soon after the plane departed. When this gentleman eventually appeared and Ray explained that there should be some information covering our journey which detailed his health problems and the special care we had been told would be provided, records were checked, humble apologies made and new seats allocated. The flight was only half-full anyway until we reached the first brief stopover at Honolulu, so we were allowed to use a whole middle row of seats with the arm rests raised and stretch out fully to get some sleep. I managed to do this but Ray stayed awake for most of the journey. It was a huge relief to arrive back home in Auckland without his experiencing any health difficulties on the way.

We initially stayed with the friend in Epsom where Ray had

lived before we were married. Although we'd arrived home with virtually no money, Ray managed to purchase a small second-hand car on time payment, so at least we had transport. Our first long car journey took us to Opunake, where my parents were now living. On our return to Auckland I started job-hunting, and within a few days had a full-time position at Auckland's Extramural Hospital. My first job was in the medical records section, but I was later transferred to the department which organised the allocation of Meals-on-Wheels and their delivery by volunteer drivers. As I don't drive, it is probably some sort of miracle that there were no disasters during my time planning the delivery routes. But arranging these was rather challenging at times, as a few of the volunteers requested there be no right-hand turns. A map of central Auckland, detailing the area to which our hospital supplied meals, covered an entire wall, and little colour-topped pins marked the site of every meal recipient's home. Each driver delivered about ten meals and, using the map, we carefully planned the route and delivery schedule according to their requests.

However, there was one drawback to my being employed. Ray was not allowed to start work yet, so on his doctor's advice he applied to the Social Welfare Department for a sickness benefit to assist him in the meantime. Because I was earning about $2 a week more than the current rules allowed for working spouses, Ray became ineligible for a benefit and he was only granted a small payment for the six weeks between our arrival back home and the date I started work. Now aged 57, and having lived and worked in New Zealand all his life, apart from about nine months in Australia and the past four years in England, Ray wasn't very impressed with this decision.

The National Heart Hospital in London had referred Ray's case to Green Lane Hospital in Auckland and he was now under their care: he would undergo several less serious operations at Green Lane over the next few years. I started singing again for various clubs and organisations, but there was some tension between Ray and me as to whether his health could withstand the rigours of renewing his career. He desperately wanted to sing, and early in 1975 we were invited to a party where several fellow musicians entertained during the evening. Ray always kept his music-case in the car and was unable to resist any longer. For the first time since his two operations, he sang several songs without any ill effects whatsoever. I bore the brunt of his 'I told you so' and 'You shouldn't have tried to stop me' accusations, but I had simply been trying to protect him from the anguish he would have felt if his voice or his health had let him down. While some of his voice's exciting brilliance had been affected, it was still a wonderful sound and he would continue to sing with much success over the next twenty years.

Chapter 15

Property, pandemonium and Perkel

During our time away from New Zealand, there were several attempts to establish opera ventures to fill the gap left by the demise of the New Zealand Opera Company. An enthusiastic audience for the art had been created during the company's existence and this needed to be sustained if opera was to survive in our country. While a number of the NZOC's principal singers, conductors and directors had taken their skills overseas, there were still people in New Zealand with the necessary expertise to present professional opera, as well as younger singers starting out on their careers who needed the valuable experience of developing their craft by actually performing and working on stage. One of the first companies to attempt to fill the vacuum was the New Opera Company of Wellington.

In 1972, two of our former colleagues from NZOC days, Angela Shaw and Graeme Gorton, established this company, assisted by a group of fellow opera enthusiasts. Their aim was to present full-scale opera performances with professional soloists and amateur choruses that would not only play in Wellington but tour to other centres as well. Their first production was *Così fan tutte*, followed by *La Bohème*, *Don Pasquale*, *La Traviata*, *The Marriage of Figaro* and *The Merry Widow* throughout 1973 and 1974. The February/ March 1975 opera production was *Madama Butterfly*, and I was engaged to sing the role of Suzuki. Other principal singers were Malvina Major in the title role, Antony Benfell as Pinkerton and

Roger Creagh as Sharpless, and the opera played in Wellington, Palmerston North and New Plymouth.

Meanwhile in Auckland, Frank Poore, who had previously been the manager and director of the Light Opera Club, established a company called Northern Opera. This company's first production in 1976 was again *Madama Butterfly* and the programme notes contained the following:

> The reason for forming Northern Opera is that no city the size of Auckland can afford to be without a permanent Opera Company. Auckland is one of the twelve largest cities in the British Commonwealth and, as such, must be recognised for its culture as well as for its other fine amenities. It is not possible to be classed as a cultural centre without a permanent Symphony Orchestra and an Opera Company.

Both Ray and I were engaged for this season, Ray singing the smaller tenor role of Goro and me, yet again, as Suzuki. Other principals included Elisabeth Hellawell in the title role, and Antony Benfell and Roger Creagh as their previous characters. The season ran at a loss, as opera unfortunately often does, and things became a little heated when, at a meeting called shortly after the last performance to discuss the financial situation, the principal singers were asked to accept a reduction in their fees. I asked whether the members of the orchestra would also be accepting less remuneration, but was advised that their situation was different and they would be paid in full. It is always more difficult to argue one's rights as an individual rather than as part of an organisation like an orchestra with its own substantial union backing. In the event however, Ray and I were paid the contracted fees, but the company was short-lived and only mounted two other operas.

At the end of January 1975, Ray took a job selling real estate, which he thought might be a suitable occupation in that he could work at his own pace. He soon found the job frustrating as he spent much of his time driving people to properties they had no real intention of buying; in his words, they were only 'site-seeing'. After six months of this he moved to an office job which he disliked intensely, and finally took a position at the Central Post Office, now the location of the Britomart Train Station, where he worked until he retired in 1982.

Within two months of our return to New Zealand, we rented temporary accommodation in two suburbs, Hillsborough and Mt Albert. One Thursday evening, our Mt Albert flat was broken into and I was severely manhandled by an intruder who had managed to climb in through a small bedroom window. Our unit was the middle one in a group of three, and the man who broke in had stolen some underwear from a neighbour's washing line and used it to muffle the sound of his steel ladder (also 'borrowed') so that it did not scrape against the brick wall of our flat. I had been watching television in the lounge before going to look for something in a spare bedroom, when I was suddenly grabbed from behind and threatened with a sharp object being pushed into my back. We eventually discovered that the weapon was a pair of Ray's gardening secateurs, but obviously I didn't know this at the time. The man had one arm firmly around my throat and kept insisting that if I struggled or made any noise I would be hurt. I couldn't see much of him, as he kept behind me most of the time, but I was later able to tell the police that he was about 5ft 9in tall (175cm), with dark skin and hair, of very thin build, and that a grubby towel covered the lower part of his face. Added to this, his body odour was unpleasantly strong.

I kept asking the man what he wanted and he told me that he and his friends, who would soon be coming to the flat, were going to 'get' my husband. He was under some misapprehension that Ray was having a relationship with a woman, who was either the intruder's wife or sister, at their workplace, which did in fact turn out to be the factory attached to the office where Ray was employed. As a result of this supposed liaison, they were going to 'sort your husband out'. He continually mispronounced our surname and I therefore insisted he had the wrong person and it was all a case of mistaken identity. The man said I was making him angry and dragged me into the main bedroom and forced me on to the bed. He then used one of Ray's neckties to bind my hands tightly behind my back. Pleading with him to leave the flat,

I told him Ray would be home shortly and that as he had not long recovered from two major heart operations, the shock of finding an intruder in the flat and me tied up might be enough to give him a heart attack anyway, irrespective of what this man and his friends had in mind. This appeared to unnerve the intruder and he went to the lounge and made a telephone call. He then came back to the bedroom and because I kept asking him to leave, he became more angry and used further neckties to blindfold and roughly gag me, forcing my teeth to cut into my bottom lip. After wandering around our flat for a short time and stealing a very small amount of money and one of Ray's shirts, he left abruptly through the back door when he heard someone entering at the front. It was Ray, and the first thing he noticed was the bad body odour.

Finding me lying tightly bound in the bedroom certainly shocked him and as soon as he managed to free me, we rang the police. Our explanation of the event must have been somewhat garbled as the call seemed to be interpreted as a 'domestic' and non-urgent. When no one had arrived within 45 minutes, we rang a close friend who was a long serving police officer and fine singing colleague, known in the Force as 'Ace' O'Hara, and he immediately alerted his fellow officers. Within minutes of his call, the police arrived with a dog which they hoped would be able to trace the intruder. However, it was raining and the dog only managed to follow the scent a little way over the back fence and through a neighbour's garden before it was lost.

The press got hold of the incident and a brief article appeared in the *New Zealand Herald* the next morning. Even though I wasn't in much of a state to go to my day job, I arrived a little late at the office and found a reporter and photographer from the evening paper, the *Auckland Star*, waiting there to get a photograph and further details from me. How they found out where I worked I have no idea. Soon after this the police also arrived and asked me to return with them to our flat where they wanted to interview me. During their intense and repetitious questioning about the incident, I began to wonder if they were considering that because Ray and I were singers and had some sort of profile at the time, the whole event might be a publicity stunt. We both had well-advertised concerts to perform the following weekend, and I was about to record and film a televised opera production in Wellington.

The police interview took about three hours, during which I made a remark which has caused constant amusement to my friends ever since. The police asked if I feared being sexually assaulted at any time during the incident. My response was that as my innocence had been lost many years before, I was far more concerned that the intruder's rough arm wrapped tightly around my throat might cause damage to my vocal cords. Whatever they thought of that, the police eventually seemed convinced the whole event had actually taken place, and the usual check for fingerprints was done and 'items of interest' taken away. There was some suspicion that the intruder was a drug addict, because a nearby doctor's surgery had been broken into a few days before my event, but we heard no more. Six months later the police returned the items of evidence.

I managed to sing at the weekend concert and was also contacted to appear on Max Cryer's television programme, *Town Cryer*, the following week, where I was interviewed about the break-in and also sang. I then went to Wellington to record and film Menotti's opera *Amahl and the Night Visitors* for television. Unfortunately, the cut inside my lower lip developed into a cyst which kept catching on my lower teeth whenever I spoke or sang. This was removed at a hospital Accident and Emergency Department and six black sutures were needed to stitch the scar. Singing with a stitched lip wasn't easy, but the *Amahl* sound recording was made separately and I only had to mime during the actual filming. I tried to avoid showing too much of the inside of my mouth, but my bottom lip was still swollen; Amahl's poor old Mum looked as though she'd been in a punch-up.

Although we were renting accommodation, Ray still owned a property in Blockhouse Bay Road and for many years he continued to pay the mortgage. Once various legal matters were sorted out, we moved into that house and remained there for the next twenty years. I would have preferred to have been able to choose a different home together, but our financial position made that impossible. Ray loved this property which, at just under half an acre, gave him the opportunity to grow the flowers, fruit and vegetables he so much enjoyed. Over time we made a number of alterations to the house. Walls were knocked out, the kitchen and bathroom remodelled and carpet and drapes renewed throughout. Much of the reconstruction work was done by our colleague and prominent Auckland singer, tenor Antony Benfell, whose 'real job' was as a builder. I did most of the interior redecoration, painting and curtains, while Ray built a large patio out from the dining room, with attractively shaped tiles underfoot, patterned concrete block walls on all sides, and grapes growing under the opaque Laserlite roof above. This was a real haven in the summer and we had many parties and pleasant hours out there.

With both of us now employed in full-time jobs during the day, our singing had to be limited to evening and weekend engagements or during holiday periods. We regularly sang at the many social and club events held by such organisations as the Travel, Clef, Connoisseurs, Lyceum, Auckland Ladies Luncheon, Orphans and Savage Clubs, Bowling and other Sports Clubs' prize-giving events, the Grand Opera Society, Masonic Lodge meetings, weddings and funerals, all of which kept our vocal cords in practice. They were to get an even better workout when we were asked to join a semi-professional opera company, then known as Perkel Productions.

Two other New Zealand Opera Company principal singers Ray and I had worked with previously, tenor Cyril Kelleway and baritone Paul Person (also our colleague from the New Zealand Opera Quartet days), had been frustrated by the fact that although several experienced opera singers were still available in Auckland, the various companies and ventures that could have employed them, for example the Auckland Opera Trust, had failed, leaving singers without work and nothing for the opera-loving public. Taking matters into their own hands, they formed their own do-it-yourself touring opera company, Perkel Productions, and gathered together a talented group of people to present modest, chamber-type performances in Auckland and throughout the North Island. Using piano accompaniment only, they followed the tradition of the NZOC's piano tours during the 1950s and '60s. Perkel's first operas in 1974 were two of the most familiar and popular in the repertoire, Rossini's *The Barber of Seville* and Mozart's *The Marriage of Figaro*, both of which attracted large audiences. The semi-professional company became extremely popular and was able to present a number of acceptable opera productions over the next sixteen years.

The first Perkel production Ray and I saw was *The Marriage of Figaro*, and we were impressed. Working on a shoestring budget and featuring singers who all had day jobs but rehearsed, performed and toured in their spare time, the opera was appropriately staged. The cast included such excellent performers as the founders, Paul and Cyril, soprano Louise Molloy, who would go on to have her own television programme in New Zealand and continue her career in Australia, and Sally Sloman, another fine soprano. Sally now shares her considerable experience through the opera school she has formed in Auckland, the Opera Factory, which provides a valuable training ground for young singers. The rest of the cast were equally capable and several of them would have certainly been employed in fully professional companies, so high was the standard of their work.

The following year Ray and I were delighted to be asked to join Perkel in their production of *Madama Butterfly*; Ray again sang the role of the marriage-broker, Goro, and as usual I sang Suzuki, a role I have sung in five different productions. The reviews for my performance of this role have been good, and include these:

> Congratulations to Corinne Bridge for a beautiful performance as Suzuki in the recent production of *Madama Butterfly*. Miss Bridge moves faultlessly on stage, she uses her voice well, she enters the role as if it is waiting for her. (Frederic Page, *The Listener*)

> Corinne Bridge's work as Suzuki rouses continuing and increasing admiration. Her voice has the necessary warm and sympathetic quality for the part and her graceful and stylish gestures did much

> to create an authentic and unifed characterisation. (*Christchurch Press*)

Many years later, Cyril Kelleway wrote a book covering the history of the Perkel Opera Company entitled *A Troupe of Strolling Players – the Perkel Opera Story*, to which several of the singers, production team personnel, sponsors and tour organisers contributed thoughts and recollections of their involvement. Here is an extract from my own contribution to the book, in which I talk about the 1975 *Madama Butterfly* season:

> I have good and bad memories of that season. [Suzuki] is one of my favourite roles, not so much from a singing angle as vocally the role is not large, but it is in fact quite a big acting role, as Suzuki is on stage almost as much as Cio Cio San (Madama Butterfly) herself and I revelled in that. During a previous season, I'd been taught parts of the traditional Tea Ceremony by the Japanese Consul's wife (in Wellington) and also how to wear a kimono, use a fan and bow correctly etc., so I always felt I was presenting a reasonably authentic portrayal of the character.
>
> These are the good memories but the bad ones concerned my husband [Ray]. Ray was singing the role of Goro in that season and even though he was desperate to get back into the singing activities he had enjoyed prior to his [heart] operations, there was still a bit of tension between us regarding how much he was well enough to do and would his health stand up to the rigours of a full-time job as well as performances every night during the Auckland season and weekends away touring. Ray had one scare during that period and we ended up at Green Lane Hospital just prior to a performance, but the doctors checked him over and were satisfied that he was well enough to proceed with the evening's activities, so 'on with the show.' I still found myself watching him whenever he was on stage however, and I know I drove him mad with my fussing.

There was yet another amusing occurrence during that season which I mention in *A Troupe of Strolling Players*, but it bears repeating here. The role of Butterfly was double cast and one of the singers, being fairly new to the stage, was highly nervous before her first performance. Most of us suffer some form of nervous tension before performing, but with experience one learns to control and even use this to advantage; this young singer had not yet reached that state. She was made up, wigged and in costume long before the performance was due to start and paced nervously around the dressing room while the rest of us were getting ready.

The opera began and I made my first brief entrance to sing one line before coming off again to await Butterfly's entrance a few minutes later. Standing in the wings with the chorus of geishas, who also make their entry with Butterfly, I suddenly realised she was nowhere to be seen and frantically whispered to one of them to find out 'where the hell she is'. Butterfly sings her first line off stage and, as her cue music was played, I realised someone would have to sing it if she didn't arrive, so in the best musical tradition and at the appropriate moment, I sang it myself. After the number of times I'd sung in the opera, I knew practically everyone's part anyway. Cyril, already on stage and playing the role of her bridegroom-to-be, Lieutenant F.B. Pinkerton, had sudden visions of being married to Butterfly's servant by mistake, rather than the delightful young 15-year-old who'd taken his fancy. Luckily, Butterfly arrived just in time to walk on stage with the rest of the geishas, and the performance continued without any further hitches. She'd apparently been having a 'nervous one' (a visit to the loo), which can be difficult in costume, and hadn't realised it would take so long to rearrange herself.

Writing about costume difficulties reminds me of a comment I made which is quoted in Phyllis Brusey's book covering much of the New Zealand Opera Company's history, *Ring Down the Curtain*. I sang the role of Nancy in their production of Benjamin Britten's opera *Albert Herring*, for which the sets and costumes were created by the company's foremost designer, Raymond Boyce. Raymond was a stickler for authenticity in his designs and everything had to be true to the period the opera was set in. The story of *Albert Herring* concerns a small English village in the late 1800s, where it is traditional each spring to choose one of the local girls to be crowned Queen of the May. Besides being young and attractive, the candidate must also be a virgin. As there were no chaste young ladies in the village that year, the selection committee is relieved to discover that the youthful Albert has the necessary credentials and they decide to have a King of the May instead.

With the opera set in the Victorian era, Raymond was not satisfied to simply dress us in suitable period clothing, but required the women members of the cast to be properly corseted as well. He insisted the costumes would only hang correctly if they were over the proper framework. The fashion towards the end of Queen Victoria's reign demanded a sort of 'pouter-pigeon' look for the ladies, with tiny waists, small bustles and leg-o'-mutton sleeves. We each had our own personal corset made which was shaped at the front rather like a scallop shell. These were heavily boned from the waist upwards, which forced our bosoms to poke up over the top, and laced at the back. As long as the lacings were not tied too tightly, we could just breathe enough to sing. I played one of the 'un-chaste' girls in the village and had a rather sexy little scene to play with my boyfriend Sid. Commenting on the fact that the leg-o'-mutton sleeves required five yards of material each, I said 'These sleeves pose acting problems all of their own. I've a love scene to play and what with these sleeves and the corset ...!'

Everyone involved in the Perkel Opera productions had day jobs and were only free to travel at weekends, so whenever rehearsing and singing in an opera, we spent most of a seven-day week working in one capacity or another. Friday night performances were played in the centres closest to Auckland, such as Warkworth and Wellsford to the north or Hamilton and Morrinsville in the south, which allowed us to leave Auckland mid-afternoon and arrive at the venue in time to 'pack in', i.e. erect the sets and lighting, and then have a quick meal before the show. As had happened during the New Zealand Opera Company days, we were billeted locally with people interested in the arts – or sometimes just with folk kind enough to offer us a bed and a meal. They needed to be fairly longsuffering as we had to 'pack out' after the performances as well. This made us late arriving back at the billets and then we were off again by 8.30 am the following morning to travel to the next venue.

From 1974 to 1990, when Perkel Opera finally evolved into the Auckland Metropolitan Opera Trust, now the National Business Review New Zealand Opera, Ray sang roles in three operas and I sang twelve. We also performed at several Perkel concerts. I became one of the artistic directors for the company and made my debut at directing opera with productions of *The Marriage of Figaro* and *La Bohème*. *The Marriage of Figaro* season was memorable for me, not just because it was the first opera I directed, but also because I had to take over one of the roles at several performances owing to another singer's illness. This was the role of Marcellina, which I first sang with the New Zealand Opera Company in 1958. Among the generally complimentary reviews covering the production, music critic William Dart wrote the following for the *NZ Listener*, under the heading 'A Shaky Marriage':

> Corinne Bridge's production was smoothly mounted but performances varied. Her own as Marcellina was probably the best and her exaggerated playing reminded one of the *commedia dell'arte* origins of the opera. With Donald Trott as a suitably stuffy Bartolo, she provided some of the more stylishly amusing moments of the evening.

Reviews for my direction of the 1983 *La Bohème* were widely different. The *Auckland Star* reviewer, Terry Snow, under the heading 'Mixed standard for Mimi', wrote:

> There are some unexpected let-downs, many musical high spots and the traditional Perkel awkwardness about much of the production which could best be solved by engaging professional help.

But a review in the *Thames Star* by Colin Broadley, headed 'La Bohème – captivating', read as follows:

> Puccini's grand opera *La Bohème* was presented last Friday night to a large and appreciative audience in Thames by Perkel Opera Inc. with such professionalism and sensitivity that it was completely captivating. As a press critic, I seem bereft without at least one point on which to be critical. Finely honed by director Corinne Bridge (remember her as *Carmen*), this very grand opera was to me so flawlessly presented that our Memorial Hall's staging shortcomings were not obtrusively apparent.

Possibly there are greater expectations from critics in the larger cities where professional music and theatre performances are plentiful, compared to those in the smaller centres where such entertainment is rare. But the point made in the *Auckland Star* review about engaging professional help is an interesting one. I'm not entirely sure what the reviewer meant when he wrote that there was often 'awkwardness' about Perkel's productions. If he was referring to the opera direction, the engagement of so-called 'professional help' isn't always the answer. In my own experience many professional theatre directors, who come from a drama rather than opera background and do not have an exceedingly good musical knowledge, find it difficult to cope with the slowness of characters singing words as opposed to speaking them. They also mistakenly think singers can't sing and act at the same time and have us rushing around 'acting' during the periods when we are not singing, but 'parking and barking' when we are singing. There are certainly passages of music in opera which are difficult to sing, and stage movement at those particular moments needs to be tailored to suit. And above all else, the singer must always be able to see the conductor. But opera is mainly about singers, and I would far rather have superb singing first and let my imagination deal with the rest. If, however, the reviewer was referring to the actual staging, this was possibly more to do with the problems of mounting an opera that has to be extensively toured and needs to be versatile enough to fit into many varied venues and on differently sized stages; this seems to me to be the point of the Thames review. However, the Auckland review was constructive rather than destructive and as is apparent, notice was taken.

A singer's greatest fear is catching a cold, 'flu, or getting a sore throat and losing his or her voice. Any other musician, while certainly feeling unwell, can at least place their hands on a keyboard or their bow on an instrument and know they'll still be able to produce sound. One never-to-be-forgotten memory for me is a Friday evening Perkel Opera performance of *Carmen* in Palmerston North, when I had to go on stage but had no voice. On the Wednesday before that weekend, which also included a Saturday performance in Wanganui, there were indications I was getting a cold. My doctor prescribed various types of medication which would supposedly get me through the two performances, including something to dry the phlegm in my throat. We left Auckland fairly early on the Friday morning and travelled as usual in a cold and draughty van, but by lunchtime I knew my voice was going. We telephoned ahead to Palmerston North to arrange an appointment with a throat specialist who could see me immediately on arrival, and might then do something to help me. This doctor examined my throat with great difficulty, as I kept gagging whenever he got near the back of my tongue with his spatula, but pronounced my throat was so dry and raw that it would be totally inadvisable for me to sing or even speak. I was sharing the role with another singer but she was still in Auckland. She was contacted and asked to travel down to Wanganui for the Saturday show, but meanwhile we had to get through this particular performance.

We had already arranged for a small local chorus to join us in Palmerston and luckily they included two mezzo-sopranos who knew the Carmen arias, as did another mezzo in our own company. None of them, however, knew the complete role or the concerted work – that is the duets, trios, quartets and ensembles, so the only option was for me to act the role and speak the dialogue as best I could, while miming the solos which the other mezzos would do their best to sing for me. We managed to get through the opera but I spent the next ten days unable to speak, let alone sing, and was again fearful my vocal cords might have been damaged. As usual, reviews appeared in the local papers and one of them castigated me for ruining the performance; needless to say, I didn't keep that review. The other reviewer, Robert Johnston, did his homework, however, and wrote the following under the heading 'A Night of Triumph for the Perkel Opera Co.':

> ... the company last night were faced with a catastrophe. Corinne Bridge, who plays Carmen ... virtually lost her voice. But like a true trouper, she went on stage and sang softly, transposing the music to the lower register but never being out of tune. ... [She] is such a good actress, a completely convincing Carmen, that enjoyment was not impaired. It was quite a triumph, in the true tradition of the theatre. In the trio in the third Act, facing the audience, it was difficult to realise that someone else was singing the role.

It won't be surprising that this review is still in my scrapbook, and my grateful thanks go to Robert Johnston.

As well as singing and directing, I held the purse strings as Perkel's treasurer for some years and also wrote their newsletters. During the late 1980s when Auckland's opera, concert and convention centre, the Aotea Centre, was being built, Perkel presented two fund-raising seasons to assist the project. I was the production and promotion manager for these and the first opera was Mozart's *The Magic Flute*, where we were joined by another small Auckland opera group, Opera Boutique. This was followed by Gilbert and Sullivan's *The Yeomen of the Guard*, which is that partnership's nearest work to 'grand opera'. With helpful sponsorship from the ANZ bank, Perkel and Opera Boutique were able to donate a total of $36,000 to the Aotea Centre fund-raising committee, and Auckland's mayor at the time, Dame Catherine Tizard, hosted two receptions at which our cheques were presented. Perkel also assisted in an Aotea Centre Open Day, which was organised during the building process to familiarise the Auckland public with the scope of the facility and the type of entertainment that might eventually be provided there. Backstage in the completed centre, which opened in 1990, dressing room 21 bears Perkel's name in silver letters above its door in honour of the company's fund-raising effort.

By forming Perkel Opera, Paul PERson and Cyril KELleway managed to keep grand opera alive in New Zealand and assist in the formation of a fully professional company, NBR New Zealand Opera, which now presents approximately six performances each of two operas a year in Auckland and Wellington. This company has also occasionally taken one lesser-scale production to a few of the smaller centres in the country. But the glory days of the original New Zealand Opera Company have never been repeated. That company provided work and valuable experience, both on stage and off, for (usually) New Zealanders during its eighteen years existence, and toured professional, full-scale, orchestra-accompanied opera throughout the country for many months each year, alternating these seasons with a number of smaller six-week piano tours of abridged or potted operas, playing in even the smallest of rural towns – like Broadwood!

Chapter 16

Public works, television, concerts and fund-raising

By the time Ray and I moved into the Blockhouse Bay home, I had turned 40 and Ray was nearing 60. We had a substantial mortgage on the house which took several years to pay off, so it was important for us both to have reliable full-time employment. With Ray settled at the Central Post Office, I looked for a secure position to add to our stability. In those days, working for a government department was considered a job for life, so when I saw an advertisement for a clerical vacancy in the accounts section of the Ministry of Works and Development, Auckland District Office, it seemed the ideal position. I applied and was successful. It was now 1976, and I continued to work there until the late 1980s when the government of the day restructured the ministry into a State-Owned Enterprise.

On joining the MWD, I was too old to enter the Public Service superannuation scheme, so when the restructuring got underway, I decided to stay with a government department until either reaching retirement age or being made redundant. If the latter occurred, I hoped to receive a full redundancy payment based on my years in the public service. In 1987, a job became vacant at the Department of Internal Affairs and I worked there for a short time before taking a position with the Commerce Department. The inevitable happened in 1992 and the entire Auckland office of that department was closed, making all its employees redundant.

Like my earlier job at the age of 16 with Tip Top, I thoroughly enjoyed my years with the MWD. Eager to be earning as much as possible by the time I reached retirement age, I worked hard to achieve promotion and gained valuable experience in many divisions of the ministry. My duties at various times involved accounts, records and contract management, staff administration and the monitoring and audit of financial grants, working in the Accounts Office, Architectural, Town and Country Planning and Engineering Divisions. The work often took me out of the office as well. During those years the MWD controlled the funds allocated for local authority-subsidised works through the National Roads Board and I became involved in carrying out test checks, or mini-audits, on the various City and Borough Councils' expenditure of these funds. Over 30 local authorities then existed in Auckland, but in 1989 they would also be restructured and dramatically reduced; it has all happened again recently with the formation of the Auckland Super City. Spending three to four weeks at the larger councils and only a few days at the smaller ones, the Auckland MWD's audit team still took over two years to complete an inspection of all the local authorities' NRB-subsidised expenditure on roading works.

In the early 1980s, Michael Lancaster became the Auckland District Commissioner of Works and it was he who reminded me that we had first met in 1952, when we sang in the chorus of our singing teacher Hamilton Dickson's light opera *The Gypsies* in Wellington. Michael's sister, Diana, was also in that production, so it was another example of how people's paths so often cross in this small country of ours.

Ray and I still considered our 'real job' was singing, however, and we took every opportunity that came our way, provided it could be fitted in with our 'day jobs'. The Rothmans Foundation, our supporters during the New Zealand Opera Quartet days, now sponsored lunchtime concerts at the Auckland City Art Gallery and we were engaged to sing individual recitals there.

Ray also became deeply involved with his Masonic Lodge interests and worked his way up through the various Degrees to achieve the position of Master in 1988. Ray first became a Freemason in 1948 and his main Lodge was United Service No 10 (a Blue Lodge), which met in Herne Bay. He was also a member of the Karangahape No 69 Royal Arch Chapter (a Red Lodge), from which he received his Forty Years' Service Jewel. As a result of his masonic work we regularly sang for Lodge Ladies' Nights, Almoner's social functions, special Grand Lodge occasions and individual Masters' events, both in and out of Auckland.

There were still a lot of social-type clubs in Auckland then, and we were regular guest artists on evening or weekend occasions. Most of these have already been mentioned in the previous chapter, but we also helped the fund-raising efforts of various service club organisations such as Rotary, Soroptomist, Zonta, Altrusa, Kiwanis and Lions. Ray particularly liked singing at the Auckland Clef Music Club, which had originally been formed in about 1933 by his singing teacher, Dr Kenneth Phillips, under the title of the Classic Club. Dr Phillips' purpose in creating the club was to provide a venue where his pupils could gain valuable experience by performing in front of an audience, and Ray had sung there many times at the start of his career.

We also entertained at rest homes and retirement villages including the Ranfurly Veterans' Home and Hospital, Hillsborough Heights, and the Masonic Village in Pah Road (now Selwyn Heights Village), so there was plenty to keep us busy.

Ray enjoyed this lighter side of entertaining and was often asked to be Master of Ceremonies on some occasions as well. As noted before, Ray always kept a diary. He chose one small enough to fit into his pocket and wrote the punch-lines of dozens of jokes in the blank pages at the back, so he could use them when compèring. He had a wide repertoire of jokes, some of which were acceptable in mixed company and a great many that weren't. When I was with him, I sat on tenterhooks wondering what he'd come out with next. As happened in Vienna, I tried to censor his yarns before they got out of hand. His nickname for me was 'Charlie' or 'Charlie Girl', and whenever he was about to tell one of his rude stories and could see that I was a bit worried, he'd give me a cheeky grin and say, 'it's just a little one, Charlie.' This kept our friends highly amused, especially when Ray was with us during the Perkel trips; as we travelled home from a weekend's performances,

Ray would start a non-stop session of jokes to which everyone contributed, and by the time we reached Auckland, after a three- or four-hour journey, we'd be hoarse and sore with laughter. This wasn't advisable on the outward journeys, however, as none of us would have been able to sing when we got to the venues.

In 1980, Ray and I took part in two more operas produced for Television New Zealand. Ray played the role of Beppe in Leoncavallo's *Il Pagliacci* and I took the role of Bertha in Rossini's *The Barber of Seville*. I'd previously sung the leading lady, Rosina, in a Perkel Opera production of *Barber*, but this is one of those controversial roles which, although originally written for a coloratura mezzo-soprano, is quite often sung by a soprano, and that was the case on this occasion. Again, both operas were pre-recorded in Wellington, accompanied by the New Zealand Symphony Orchestra, and later filmed at the Avalon Television Studios in Lower Hutt. Ray and I took holiday leave from our day jobs to cover the periods we'd be recording and filming in Wellington, so there was little time left for any type of holiday in 1980. We had also recorded programmes for South Pacific Television's *Stars on Sunday* programme during 1979 (which were shown the following year) but conveniently for us, these were recorded and filmed at the same time in Auckland.

Among the many other concerts we did were those dedicated to raising funds for particular projects. I was a member of Soroptimist International of Auckland, a women's service organisation that 'works through service projects to raise the status of women, advance human rights for all and promote equality, development and peace'. While this group meets monthly for a light meal and to hear a speaker, the major part of their service is devoted to fundraising. Soroptomists work hard to organise and participate in a number of events that raise large sums of money towards whatever project they are sponsoring at the time, but make sure they also enjoy the process of doing so. During my time as a member, and where a musical event was involved, Ray and I invariably sang at or arranged the concert, calling on our friends and associates to help.

One particularly successful concert was held on 27 May

1984 to raise funds for the New Zealand Foundation for the Blind's $1.5 million Talking Books project. Ray and I organised the programme, which included items from the Balkan Folk Orchestra, led by Brian Holden, and the Auckland Boys Choir, conducted by Terence Maskell. The concert was compèred by television newsreader Philip Sherry and Cyril Kelleway, Ray and I sang vocal solos and duets, accompanied by the wonderfully gifted Oswald Cheesman, who also played piano solos. There was a star appearance by the SOROPTIPUSSIES, Priscilla and Tom (actually Soroptimist members – Margaret Remi-Kenyon and me). Music lovers will know that the prolific opera composer, Gioacchino Rossini, wrote a popular duet called 'Duetto buffo di due gatti' or 'Comic duet for two cats'. Margaret was not a singer but she adored cats and, besides working full-time in the travel industry, she also operated a cat sanctuary behind her home. When I told her about the 'Cat duet' and played a recorded version for her, she immediately wanted to perform it and wondered if, with my help, it would be possible. Despite having no real musical background, she was able to hold a line and worked exceedingly hard to learn the duet, with the result that we included it in the programme. At least she had no problem memorising the words: all we had to sing was 'Meow'.

Needless to say, Margaret and I wanted to look the part so we chose our costumes with care. I sang the lower part in the duet so I was the tom cat. Ray's formal dinner suit, complete with tails of course, fitted me, and my outfit was completed with a grey topper sporting little furry ears on either side. Margaret was slim, with good legs, so she became the sexy blonde female cat and wore an extremely short velvet tunic with a fur collar and wide fur cuffs, gold tights and a really long, voluptuous fur tail. Long claws and a gold-mesh, close-fitting hat with large furry ears completed her transformation. Not to be outdone in the tail department, I insisted on having a fur one too, but mine was very small and insignificant beside Margaret's luxuriant effort. However, her tail made a good prop for me to stroke, admire and play with while we performed the duet. With stage makeup to give ourselves catty faces and nice long whiskers, our transformation into cats was complete. Our first performance of the duet at this concert went down so well that we had to repeat it on several other occasions.

Another Soroptimist fundraising project in 1986 was for the Lifeline Counselling Service and the 29 June programme again featured the Balkan Folk Orchestra, together with the Martinis – a group of hand-bell players led by Brian Martin, and four of the Perkel Opera singers – Gillian Trott, Cyril Kelleway, Donald Trott and me. Margaret Barnett, one of our dearest friends, accompanied at the piano and the concert was compèred by another old friend and associate, Les Andrews. No cats appeared this time but a gratifying amount of money was raised.

During this period a Mini-Music Festival, under the auspices of the Auckland Festival Society, was held at the Symphonia Hall in Dominion Road, and included ballet, opera, symphony orchestra, brass band, light opera and musical comedy concerts. Perkel Opera singers were involved in two of the programmes and once again 'cats' appeared. Conductors for this season included Juan Matteucci and Alex Wiltshire. Alex was, and still is, a most versatile young woman who not only played for many of the Perkel Opera seasons but has performed in New Zealand and overseas as a musical director, vocal coach and concert artist, as well as working in television and music theatre. Among her many other achievements these days, she tours as one of the accompanists for the successful entertainment group Operatunity. Alex also sings and it was she who suggested we include the 'Cat duet' in one of the festival concerts, with her as the female puss. This duet is written with piano accompaniment only, but as the Auckland Regional Orchestra was playing for this concert, Alex asked leading percussionist Bruce McKinnon to write a full orchestral arrangement of it for us. Bruce, another highly talented musician and, until recently, Principal of the percussion section with the New Zealand Symphony Orchestra, composed an excellent orchestral adaptation of the duet, which Alex conducted.

When I came on the stage alone to sing the duet, dressed as before in Ray's tails, the audience looked curious as to why there wasn't another cat. Alex, of course, was busy on the podium. The tom cat starts the duet anyway, so I sang my first few lines and then, at the appropriate moment, Alex turned to face the audience and joined in. This caused a ripple of amusement, but more was to follow. Fairly early in the duet there is change of tempo when both the singers and the accompaniment get a bit excited and the cats appear to be on the verge of having a fight. Ray was in the wings listening to us and decided to add a little bit of verisimilitude to our performance. He reasoned that whenever there's a lot of caterwauling going on over the back fence at night, a dog or a number of dogs join in by barking and howling, so Ray duly obliged. The audience burst into laughter, as indeed did the two cats, and it was some time before Alex and I could continue the duet. At the end of our performance, the applause from the audience demanded an encore, so we sang it again – complete with 'noises off.'

Ray had always been a supporter of the National Party, and throughout the 1960s before going overseas and then again on our return at the end of 1974, we regularly sang for local branch fund-raising functions. Someone most dedicated to and involved in this type of work was Harriet Lowry-Bedingham, chairperson of the women's section, College branch. As a young woman, Harriet operated her own business off Pitt Street in Auckland and her accountant was Robert Muldoon. They became firm friends and when Mr Muldoon went into Parliament and ultimately rose to be Prime Minister, Harriet was one of his keenest supporters and hardest-working fund-raisers. She told me she had been the first female member of the Auckland Chamber of Commerce, to which she remained attached for over 50 years. She certainly had many useful business contacts which she utilised to good effect as she never appeared to have any difficulty finding sponsorship for raffles, or goods for her numerous fund-raising activities. It was not only the National Party who benefited from her efforts but many other organisations as well, particularly Birthright which was particularly dear to her heart. To help entertain her guests she regularly asked Ray and me to sing at her soirées.

Harriet was a party girl and found a good companion in Ray, who loved any excuse for a celebration. As a result we spent many happy hours at her home, both entertaining and being entertained, and I recall one very different experience there. The evening was probably a fund-raiser as I know we had our music and an accompanist with us, and towards the end of the evening we were joined by Sir Robert and Lady Thea Muldoon. Everyone was enjoying a few drinks and in his usual 'nothing venture, nothing gain' manner, Ray asked Sir Rob if he would join him in a duet. The Prime Minister said he wasn't much of a singer but he'd 'give it a go,' as long as Ray could supply the words of a song he was familiar with. They went through Ray's music case and came up with 'The sunshine of your smile', which they then proceeded to render, or as Ray preferred to say 'tear apart'. What made this performance so memorable for me was not Sir Rob's actual vocal ability but the fact that he couldn't manage the key in which the song was written, for although it was suitable for Ray's tenor voice it was much too high for the Prime Minister, so he sang everything a very gravelly octave lower. The result was priceless and 'brought the house down'. It didn't inspire Sir Rob to give up his 'day job', unless one takes into consideration his later appearances in *The Rocky Horror Show*. However, I like to recall this good-natured and lighter side of a man who, even after his death, is so constantly vilified.

There were one or two sour notes in our musical and fund-raising activities during these years and strangely enough, these came from singing associates. An example is a comment made by two singers who felt we were making it difficult, and taking work from them and other entertainers, by being happy to sing without a fee if the cause was a worthy one. Their argument was that to be fair to everyone, we should still request a fee but donate it back if we so desired. Perhaps they had a point, but it seems to me that the outcome would be the same anyway.

Chapter 17

Dentures, honours and celebrations

After we returned from the United Kingdom, Ray was under the care of Green Lane Hospital, the specialist heart-care centre in Auckland, for 20 years. During that time he was admitted to this hospital for various procedures, but I think he would agree the most traumatic of these was having his remaining teeth extracted and being fitted with dentures. As stated earlier, he fiercely resisted the removal of all his teeth in London because he was sure he would find it impossible to sing with false ones. Back home in New Zealand, however, there came a time when the Green Lane doctors insisted on it and for once Ray had to do as he was told.

He went through the discomfort some people seem to have when trying to adjust to dentures and found the bottom plate particularly hard to get used to. At home, even when eating, he preferred not to wear either set and in fact rarely wore the bottom one. I lost count of the number of times we left our house to sing at a concert, visit friends, attend a meeting or for any other dozen reasons, when halfway to our destination Ray would say, 'I've forgotten my teeth,' and we'd have to go back to collect them – or at least the top set. This became a standing joke with our friends and the familiar greeting whenever we arrived or met them anywhere was, 'Have you got your teeth, Ray?' He did eventually learn to sing with dentures, and while not having to worry much about the bottom set, because they were rarely in, he was always scared the top set might do something unexpected when he took a high note.

A complete book could be written about the adventures of Ray's teeth, both natural and false.

In November 1985, we individually received letters from Government House advising that it was proposed to submit our names 'to The Queen for the award of The Queen's Service Medal for Community Service (QSM) on the occasion of the New Year.' We were requested to 'inform the writer as soon as possible whether the proposed distinction would be acceptable to us.' We'd heard rumours about someone proposing to nominate us for a New Zealand royal honour and that they had been contacting friends and colleagues for letters of support. However, it certainly wasn't something we were expecting. After Ray became aware that a similar nomination for him had been rejected in the 1960s, he had discounted being considered for an honour again. He was therefore elated when the letters arrived, and on eventually receiving the award, he proudly wore the miniature alongside his World War Two service medals on every suitable occasion. We were both sincerely grateful to those who made it possible, even though I was somewhat overawed by the whole business.

On 1 January 1986, when the New Year's Honours list appeared in the newspapers, the telephone hardly stopped ringing and dozens of cards filled our letterbox for many days afterwards. We'd already been invited to a barbecue that day at the home of my 'cat' partner, Margaret, with her husband and a few other friends. We arrived there, still dazed, to a huge welcome. We'd been approached by several newspapers the previous day, requesting interviews and photographs which also appeared with the list. The main point of interest covering Ray and me was, to quote one report, 'They will be remembered as one of the very few married couples to individually receive Queen's honours at the same time,' to which I think they should have more accurately added 'for the same service.' We knew of two good friends in Whakatane, Herb and Joyce Brabant, who'd also been individually honoured for similar service at the same time, but it is fairly rare.

More excitement came when we received another letter informing us that 'The Queen will hold an Investiture in the Michael Fowler Centre, Wellington at 10.15 am on Friday 28 February

1986 to present insignia to those who recently received awards in Her Honours List.' Her Majesty was to be in New Zealand on a State visit during the February/March period and would carry out the investiture of the New Year's knights and dames and also present her Queen's Service Orders and Medals at the same time. We were allowed to nominate six people each to accompany us at the investiture and they would be sent separate invitations. A further letter came from the Mayor of Wellington with an invitation to attend an official luncheon after the ceremony.

The next few weeks were exceedingly busy. We both needed new outfits, and while I hate wearing a hat, I reasoned that as the Queen herself was presenting the awards it would be best to be correctly attired with hat and gloves. Not every woman wore these accessories at the investiture however, and it was particularly noticeable that few of the official party sitting in the front row of the auditorium, including the Labour Prime Minister's wife and other parliamentary wives, were wearing hats. Perhaps I could have spared myself the expense and discomfort of it all, but at least I'd made an attempt.

Among the many letters, telegrams and cards we received was a diverting poem written by our very dear friend and poet, Lee Dowrick-Grant. Lee and I worked together at the Ministry of Works and Development so were in daily contact. Besides her real genre of serious poetry, Lee could always be relied upon to honour her friends with pertinent verses to cover any special occasion and amuse her work colleagues with insightful and thought-provoking lines about particular work problems or events. We were delighted and humbled to receive the following:

QUITE SUPERB MUSICIANS

It isn't very often
that I scan the Honour's list
becoz the best folks that I know
have usually been missed
and it is very largely filled
by those who are retiring
from well-paid posts

they have held up
while never once perspiring.
This may well be a tribute
to their special kind of strengths
that keep the posts all upright
for the inner circle fence
to keep the sheep within the fold
acknowledged by the Press
or else to know just who they are
we all would have to guess.

But this year they paid tribute to
some lovely friends of ours
who've given freely of their gifts
in many unpaid hours
of bringing song into the hearts
of many people's lives
which helps to keep the world abuzz
and honey in the hives ...
so they did right to honour Ramon
and our Corinne for
they share their riches with us all
so none of us feel poor.

To fill the allotted number of people that could accompany us to the investiture in Wellington, Ray and I were supported by his brother John and several members of John's family, and some very close, long-standing friends of mine. We also took our hard-working, fund-raising enthusiast Harriett Lowry-Bedingham with us from Auckland. She had already been honoured with a Queen's Servicc Medal for her own efforts, but was eager to see this ceremony performed by Her Majesty. Ray's nephew, Collins, arranged accommodation for us at a motor hotel (now a retirement village) in Johnsonville, which lies mid-way between where most of the Opie family live on the Kapiti Coast and the Michael Fowler Centre in the central city. As only Ray and I had been invited to the mayor's luncheon after the awards, we made arrangements for plenty of food and drinks to be available back at our suite, so that our family and friends could return there and enjoy themselves while they waited for us to join them. Naturally this party continued into the wee small hours, but the fun carried on the following evening when Collins had arranged for the entire Wellington Opie contingent, including Ray's nephews, a niece and their respective families, to have dinner with us at the hotel, together with several of my friends. This was another great night, and Ray and I ended up singing a couple of items, *a capella*, for the gathering. Collins sadly passed away at too young an age a few years later, but the memories of everything he did to make the presentation of our awards a special time for us will always be cherished.

Earlier in this chapter, I mentioned Herb and Joyce Brabant. They were very fond of Ray and when I came on the scene, took me to their hearts as well. Their home was in Whakatane, but they made regular visits to Auckland to purchase the bulk provisions they so lavishly served at their many weekend parties. Their house, high on a hill overlooking the sea and township, contained a large walk-in pantry with extensive refrigeration where they stored vast amounts of food and alcohol. Whenever we visited them for a weekend 'do', at which we were usually asked to sing, we spent most of the time in an alcoholic haze as we were not used to such large quantities of 'booze'. We drove down from Auckland after work on a Friday night, making sure to have a substantial meal on the way (or 'blotting paper' as Ray called it), knowing that as soon as we arrived at Herb and Joyce's home they'd sit us down at the kitchen table, produce three bottles of spirits – gin, whisky and vodka – and expect us to keep up with them by drinking well into the night. We fell into bed in the early hours of Saturday morning and after only a few hours sleep, were offered the same hospitality again soon after we got up, not at breakfast, thank heaven, but for morning tea. If we were to entertain their guests later that evening, Ray and I had to take great care that we were actually capable of doing so.

Before Ray and I were married, Herb and Joyce came to Auckland every three months to do their shopping. They arrived fairly early in the morning, parked outside my flat and woke me to suggest that I get hold of Ray, who lived with friends next door, and we join them for a drink in their car. They didn't want to come in as time was short and they needed to be on their way to purchase bulk supplies from various grocery, meat and alcohol providers, but were just 'popping in' to say hello while passing. Herb had a special little case containing compartments for four glasses on either side of a bottle of spirits. There was water somewhere, but I don't remember it being in the case. Unless we were very careful, we could write the rest of that day off as well.

However, among the many other wonderfully generous things they did for their home town was the Ship to Shore Service they voluntarily operated twice daily for more than thirty years. A complete room in their house was dedicated to this purpose, with all the appropriate marine radio communication apparatus required. They had a special call sign and were trained in the use of the International Phonetic Alphabet, together with everything else relating to the work. This was one of the reasons their visits to Auckland were so early and brief, as their periods away from Whakatane had to be fitted in with the set times they operated the transmission service. This valuable work was recognised when they were individually awarded medals in the same honours list.

During one of our weekend visits to them, a radio programme that Ray and I had previously recorded was due to be broadcast, so we took our radio/cassette recorder with us in order to tape it and listen to later. There must have been some sort of Ship to Shore emergency, or our broadcast was on at the same time as their normal transmission service, for all we heard when we tried to replay the recording was the full conversation between Joyce and the master of a vessel out at sea. Obviously their equipment was so highly powered that it completely obliterated our little recorder.

Over the next few years, two other unexpected awards came our way which gave us great pleasure. Ray was awarded a Scroll of Honour from the New Zealand Variety Artists Club 'in recognition of his outstanding contribution to the Entertainment Industry of New Zealand. We acknowledge and salute his dedication and professionalism.' This delighted him, as commendation from one's colleagues always does, especially because it recognised Ray's versatility in using his remarkable talent to sing and entertain in everything from opera, oratorio, concert recitals, television and broadcasting, to lighter social events. Unfortunately, Ray was ill with shingles on the night of the presentation, so I went to accept the award for him. However, he was well again and able to support me when I was honoured on 8 December 1993 with an award from the New Zealand Symphony Orchestra and the Symphony Friends 'for [her] contribution to music in the Auckland Region'.

I was one of several women given awards that particular year, which marked the centennial of universal suffrage in New Zealand and, in particular, Kate Sheppard's involvement with this. Kate Sheppard was a prominent member of the women's suffrage movement in New Zealand and her efforts resulted in this country being the first in the world to give women the vote in 1893. One hundred years later, various organisations decided to honour women from every walk of life that were considered to have made some contribution to the Auckland region. I felt particularly humbled to receive this honour as many of the other women similarly recognised were very prominent and lucky enough to be able to work full-time in their particular professions. Since our return to New Zealand in 1974, it had only been possible for Ray and me to treat our music as a hobby because the greater part of our time needed to be spent earning a living. However, we both tried to use our talents as productively as possible and it was wonderful to have this appreciated.

Chapter 18

'Listen carefully to the stars'

After being made redundant in 1992 at the age of 57, I was suddenly a lady of leisure for the first time in my life and sought out various activities to keep myself occupied. Ray, now in his seventies, was happy in the garden growing and propagating flowers, particularly his favourite lilies, irises and alstroemeria, and spending many hours in the glasshouse and 40-metre long shadehouse he'd built. Another of his great passions was making wine, cider and home brew, the results of which warrant a further book. Suffice it to say that many of our friends have their own hilarious stories to tell about Ray's hospitality, either at our home or theirs. Whatever he was up to, he was always accompanied by a devoted companion, our dearly loved black and white cat, Sooty (of whom more later).

Ray continued to sing at rest homes, retirement villages and on social occasions, besides keeping busy with his Masonic Lodge responsibilities. Sometimes I joined him in these activities, but there was still a lot of day to fill and it couldn't be wasted. I volunteered to work for the Citizens Advice Bureau service and after a six-week training period, joined the Central Auckland branch in Queen Street. I continued to work with the CAB for the next ten years.

While we were not doing much classical concert work now, Ray and I were both members of the Grand Opera Society of Auckland, of which I became president and Ray a committee member. I arranged the monthly programmes for the society, a duty I enjoyed. During the early 1980s, I'd also been involved in singing at concerts to help raise funds for the establishment of the Dame Sister Mary Leo Scholarship, the administration of which was eventually carried out by the Grand Opera Society. There was some concern about the management of the scholarship funds and I was briefly a member of the Trust that was formed to keep proper financial control. Several winners of scholarships through this fund are now engaged in successful singing careers overseas, including Teddy Tahu Rhodes and Jonathan Lemalu.

Also in 1992, a good friend and neighbour suggested I should join a Probus Club. She was a member of the Mt Albert Ladies branch and advised that she'd already put my name on their waiting list. I didn't give much thought to this as there can be delays before a vacancy occurs and I knew very little about Probus anyway. A few months later, however, I received a letter from the local branch of Rotary New Zealand, who assist in the establishment of these clubs, advising that as the three existing Probus Clubs in our area – Pt Chevalier, Mt Albert and Titirangi – had lengthy waiting lists, Avondale was being considered as a mid-point where a new club might be formed. Women whose names appeared on those clubs' lists were therefore invited to attend a meeting at the Avondale Community Centre where the matter would be discussed. The invitation also included a number of questions we were asked to respond to, including the preferred meeting day, time and venue, and if the recipient was willing to serve on the committee. The meeting was duly held and resulted in a unanimous decision to establish the Ladies Probus Club of Avondale. Those attending its inaugural meeting would be considered the foundation members. Without thinking much about it, I had ticked the box indicating that I'd be willing to serve on the committee if an Avondale club was formed, and at the end of this preliminary meeting, the Rotary chairperson came up to me, shook my hand and congratulated me on having been chosen as the foundation president. He also advised that the first meeting would be held in less than a month's time. This was a bit unnerving, but I had plenty of help.

With an excellent foundation committee of hard-working

women, the Ladies Probus Club of Avondale got off to a good start. Several months later, we were approached by Rotary to assist in the establishment of another Probus branch at Blockhouse Bay. I, as the president, together with our secretary and programme organiser, joined the Rotary representatives at a meeting in the Blockhouse Bay Community Centre and again, a new club resulted. Many of the members there knew Ray and me, and when their club's first anniversary was celebrated in 1994 we were invited to entertain. This was a thoroughly enjoyable occasion and our singing went down well. Neither of us knew, however, that this would be the last occasion on which we sang together.

January 1995 brought my 60th birthday, which we celebrated with a party at home. Ray was now 77 and slowing down in his activities, but at that stage I didn't read the signs particularly well. It was only when he started turning down requests to sing that I began to suspect there was something seriously wrong. He hated any fuss and pushed my worries aside when I tried to discuss my concerns with him. A few months later, we discovered a major plumbing leak when the basement that Ray had excavated under our house became flooded. Although I immediately contacted a plumber and made arrangements for the appropriate repairs to be carried out, Ray insisted on doing a large part of the work himself. Yet again I was told not to fuss and the workman I'd called to dig the trench was sent away. The work took a tremendous toll on Ray's health and on my insistence he finally agreed to go to the doctor. We took a taxi to the surgery, despite Ray wanting to drive his car, and the doctor immediately called an ambulance and had him admitted to hospital.

Over the next three weeks the medical staff at Green Lane Hospital debated possible surgery procedures. Ray became weaker while the discussions were taking place and we were both upset when a decision was made some 14 days later to do nothing and send him home. I later came to believe that Ray had been sent home to die there rather than in hospital. He was only home for three days when he became much worse. I called an ambulance which immediately took him back to Green Lane. Over the following week Ray's condition continued to deteriorate, and after his heart arrested on 31 July 1995, he was transferred to the Intensive Care Unit and died in the early hours of the following day.

There are so many things I could write about those three weeks but it is too painful. I continue to believe that had my beloved husband been operated on immediately on admission to hospital, there might have been a chance of recovery. To be fair, I was eventually told that the head surgeon had assessed the possibilities of Ray coming through another operation successfully and, as it was considered doubtful, he was unwilling to approve it. I sought a full clinical report after Ray's death and still wonder about the mention of a bad reaction to one of the drugs he was administered. However, there is little point in speculating, as it simply renews the doubts and unhappiness.

Among the hundreds of tributes for Ray sent to me after he died is the following poem from our dear friend Lee Dowrick:

HEAVENS ABOVE, BUT THEY'RE LUCKY, CORINNE

somewhere   up there
he'll be digging up tree stumps
great big whoppers
and making a deal
with some friendly guy
for a huge heap of fill
and he'll build up a corner
with St Peter's soil
he'll plant it with Alstros
of the rarest kind
for a heavenly splash
of blazing colours
to greet us all
when we arrive
there'll be buckets of broad beans
and burpless cucumbers
gynormous zucchinis
tomatoes and grapes

they'll be piled in the boot
of his airborne chariot
and delivered as gifts
to every cloud
and his guardian angels
will fill the back seat
when he joyfully sups up
the nectar of the gods
he'll tell a rude story
– just a little one, Charlie –
then with lazy ease
sing a note so pure
that the seats upstairs
in the whole grand circle
will be caught in the spell of its magic ...

the plain white petals of honesty
turn to golden coins,
the currency of stars

Lee gave this to me with a little note saying, 'A small bouquet to Ray from Lee to say thank you sweetheart! On clear nights we'll have to listen carefully to the stars ...'

Another treasured tribute was a cartoon drawing by an extremely talented young artist friend of ours, Susannah MacDonald. I mentioned earlier that Ray's totally adoring companion was our cat Sooty. Ray rescued Sooty as a very young kitten after it had been abandoned in downtown Auckland. It managed to find its way to the Central Post Office's loading bay area where the staff became worried it would be run over by one of the mail vans, so Ray was asked to deal with the problem. Ray found the kitten thin and hungry and gave it a drink of milk and the meat out of his lunchtime sandwiches, and over the next two days tried to find someone to give it a home. The kitten had its own ideas, however, and stayed close to its saviour, following Ray everywhere. Finally my soft-hearted husband decided the cat had in fact adopted him and he brought it home to our place.

Sooty was a very friendly little fellow. While he preferred to sleep on my side of the bed at night or cuddle up on my lap in the evenings, he spent most of the daylight hours with Ray, particularly in the garden. When I had a meal ready at lunchtime or dinner, I'd give them both a call from the house and as Ray plodded slowly up from the back of our large garden, he'd be followed by a furry black tail held high in the air like a periscope, which was all I could see of Sooty through the flowers and foliage. He'd been with us for over 14 years when Ray went into hospital, and was unwell with the kidney problem that often affects older cats. During the last hours of Ray's life I stayed at the hospital, renting a room in the nurses' quarters. The veterinary clinic where Sooty went for his general care operated a cattery service, so I left him there while I stayed at the hospital, knowing he'd be well looked after. When I went to collect him soon after Ray passed away, I was told that he was very ill and refusing to eat and the kindest thing would be to put him to sleep. I was unable to cope with this added unhappiness, but agreed that it should be done.

Sooty's story has been included to explain the thoughtful and moving cartoon created by Sue. It shows Ray, with Sooty under his arm, arriving in heaven to a warm welcome from the Angel Gabriel, while the composers of the many works Ray sang during his career add their cheerful greetings as well. There is another angel eagerly scrambling up the ladder to Cloud Ten, possibly to tell the conductor of the heavenly choir that a really good tenor has arrived, or perhaps even to inform the 'Boss' himself. I shed many tears over Sue's drawing, as I did with Lee's poem, but they were tears of delight and gratitude for the aptness of the thoughts behind them and their obvious love of the most important person in my life.

Ray's 'young Sue', as he always called her, also contributed the following memory to a number of tributes prepared for his funeral:

> I have many amusing memories of Ray, but one always stands out. I was a student teacher at the time and Corinne, Ray and I were at a concert. During the interval, Ray introduced me to

> some friends with the quip – she's a teacher now, you've got to call her Sir. I laughed then and X number of years later, I'm still laughing. Ray had a quirky sense of humour which I always found rib-tickling.

I know my darling's ribs would also have been tickled had he seen the imaginative drawing his 'young Sue' created for him.

Chapter 19

Finale

The Prologue to this book covers my reasons for writing it, but there is a little more to add. After Ray died I simply went through the motions of living. With the loss of my mother in 1982 and Dad in 1988, the three people most dear to me were gone, together with the love and encouragement that had moulded the clay of my life and made me the person I am. With no siblings or children of my own, I couldn't immerse myself in the comfort of their activities and families. I was on my own, solo. A few cousins remain that I hardly know or have never met and they mostly live in another country anyway, so apart from the usual Christmas card exchanges, there isn't much contact with them.

There were close friends and associates, of course, and, quite unexpectedly, one of them offered exactly the kind of help I needed. After being made redundant in 1992 and feeling totally disgruntled about it, I decided to be a thorn in the side of the Works and Income Department by making sure I was included in their unemployment statistics, despite the fact that I was not receiving any benefits. To remain on their lists, the department insisted I attend various courses that would assist me to find work; they didn't seem at all interested in my previous employment experience of more than forty years, in many different capacities. One of the few useful things to come out of these courses was an introduction to computers, although it was very basic. I was by far the oldest person attending the courses but it was entertaining.

We were instructed to get 'work experience' by finding ourselves a job for three weeks with an organisation we might wish to be employed by. Thinking back to my enjoyable days of working with the New Zealand Broadcasting Service, I decided to approach the station manager at Auckland's Access Radio, Leona Bresnehan, to see if she could offer me something. Leona had a long and notable career in radio and our paths had occasionally crossed during my singing days. She kindly allowed me to work at the station for the three weeks and gave WINZ a favourable report at the end of it.

Although there was no permanent position available at Access Radio, I continued to relieve at the station for a few days here and there when extra help was needed. Three weeks after Ray died, Leona rang to ask if I would be prepared to work there for four months, as their clerical assistant/receptionist was going on leave and they needed someone to carry out her duties. Because of the emotional state I was in I initially said no, but Leona wisely pointed out the value of having something else to focus on, everyday contact with a vast array of people and a reason to get up each morning. In the end, I took the job and it was exactly what I needed at that time.

There were further advantages to working at Access Radio. The station was situated in the Auckland University of Technology buildings in Wellesley Street and when I worked there, the AUT's catering school was on the floor above. Each morning, the young chefs were taught how to prepare and cook some tasty cordon bleu dish and the finished results were packed into small containers and sold to the other students and staff at lunchtime. I had lost interest in preparing meals for myself at home and was eating very little, but these delicious meals were too tempting to ignore. They were beautifully cooked, nutritious and not too big, so each day I bought whatever was on offer and took it home either to eat that evening or freeze to be eaten later. Earning a salary again was also valuable, as it helped pay another friend to keep my home's half-acre section reasonably tidy. With hindsight, I think Leona's wisdom and kindness saved my sanity during the first few heartbreaking months after Ray's death.

The following March, I went to Wellington for the 1996 International Festival of the Arts. Two of my dearest friends, whom I have known since my teenage years, live there and they and their children have always considered me 'family', as I do them. It was therefore wonderful to spend time with them and again experience the comfort a sense of belonging brings, as well as to attend the many musical events that were on offer during the festival. I met several other old acquaintances during my three weeks there, including singing colleagues and school mates, and came to the conclusion that it would probably be fairly easy to pick up the threads again by returning to live in Wellington. At the end of the trip I came back to Auckland, sold our property and moved to the capital at the beginning of June.

After settling in and completing *The Sound of Music* season mentioned in the Prologue, I looked for other things to keep me busy. I continued my voluntary work with the Citizens Advice Bureau and joined a group of professional singers, Bel Canto, to perform at occasional concerts. Because the members of this group are normally soloists and have the distinctive and definitely loud voices which are not always suitable in choirs, we were known by another amusing name: Can Belto. I had no desire to sing as a soloist, but a colleague from the 1950s, Geoffrey de Latour, with whom I sang in the New Zealand Opera Company's 1958 production of *The Marriage of Figaro*, said it would be a waste not to use the talent I am lucky enough to have. He had a group of singers, most of whom were his pupils, who, to this day, entertain at rest homes, retirement villages and a variety of Wellington's social clubs, and he persuaded me to join them. While it still felt strange to be singing without Ray nearby, it was comforting to see that our music brought pleasure and brightened the long and sometimes difficult days of the people we sang for.

Over the next few years I moved into the newly built house, took overseas holidays and tried to continue my life positively. Then I began writing, and many things changed after my first throwaway attempt to produce a story. I will always be grateful to the publisher who accepted those initial, casually written lines as, without her being aware of it, she created the opportunity for me to 'move on' and find something that gave me pleasure again. The process of recalling and writing about cvcnts and experiences shared with those I loved has allowed me to continue my life in contentment and to accept the fact that one finally has to 'let go'. While their journeys are over, mine carries on a little longer and is enhanced by keeping their memories close to me in the best possible way.

My life has been surrounded by singing. Even before I was born and while I was young, it was the voices of my parents and relatives. As I grew older I sang, and singing became my profession, leading me to Ray and his exciting and wonderful voice. Although I was barely conscious of it, Ray said I continually sang around the house, something he would tell his audiences before performing the following song, dedicating it to me. The song is a simple ballad with music written by Eric Coates and words by Royden Barrie.

I HEARD YOU SINGING

I heard you singing when the dawn was grey
And silver dew on every blossom lay;
And though the rising sun too soon
Drank up the dew,
I thought I heard you singing
All the long day through.

I heard you singing in the silent hour
When evening came with sleep for bird and flower;
A song like happy murmuring
Of woodland streams,
I thought I heard you singing
Down the vale of dreams.

Beloved, when the last call echoes clear,
And I must part from all that is so dear,
I shall not fear the valley
That before me lies,
If I may hear you singing
As I close my eyes.

(Courtesy: Chappell's Music)

I rarely sing these days, around the house or anywhere else. At my age it's time to leave that to the younger ones anyway. The vocal cords get a brief workout at community singalongs or, regrettably, when I attend an increasing number of funerals and join in the hymns. With a bit of regular practice the voice wouldn't be too bad, but it certainly doesn't meet the standards I once achieved, so whether through conceit, nerves or selfishness, I prefer not to sing. Music continues to fill my life, however, and it always will. With my particular love of opera, the weekly radio broadcasts, occasional live performances and many excellent films and DVDs available provide the fulfilment I need.

For those who don't like opera or have never been to one, I can only quote one of Ray's regular comments after he sang a particular song. It was a favourite in his popular music repertoire, written by Irving Berlin and included in the film *White Christmas*, starring Bing Crosby and Danny Kaye. Perhaps rather appropriately for this country of ours, it is called 'Count your blessings instead of sheep'. At the end of the song, as the last notes of the accompaniment were played, he'd give his audience a beaming smile and say 'Try it sometime.'

Notes

Chapter 1

1 National Library, Papers Past, *Evening Post*, 16 May 1927.
2 Peter Downes and Peter Harcourt, *Voices in the Air: Radio Broadcasting in New Zealand*, Methuen/Radio NZ.
3 *Ibid.*
4 National Library, Papers Past, *Evening Post*, 22 May 1939.
5 See Chapter 4, pages 58–59.
6 Food quantities:

Fat	4 to 5ozs per month
Suet	2 ozs per month
Eggs	1 per month
Tea	2 ozs per month
Milk	1 pint a day for three people
Bacon	1 rasher per week
Tinned salmon	36 points
Dry Biscuits	8 points per lb
Tinned pears	4 points per tin
Tinned sardines	4 points per tin

Clothing, linen etc. was also rationed – a total of 24 points per person in the family entitled to a ration book:

Pyjamas	9 points
Shoes	8 points
Overcoat	10 points
Man's shirt	5 points
Handkerchief	1 point
Wool	1 point per oz

Chapter 4

1 *Singers of Today* by Donald Brook (London, 1949).

Chapter 5

1 *The Truth at Last: My story* by Christine Keeler with Douglas Thompson (Sidgwick & Jackson, 2001).

Chapter 6

1 *Out of Time – The vexed life of Georg Tintner* by Tanya Buchdahl Tintner (University of Western Australia Publishing, 2011).
2 *Ibid.*
3 *Ibid.*

Appendices

Symbols and abbreviations

acc	accompanist/accompanied by
ACS	Auckland Choral Society
ALSO	Alex Lindsay String Orchestra
ASO	Auckland Symphonia Orchestra
ASP	Auckland String Players
b	bass
bb	bass baritone
bar	baritone
c	contralto
cond	conductor
dir	director
incl	including
LO	Lindsay Orchestra
md	musical director
ms	mezzo-soprano
Nat. O	National Orchestra of New Zealand
NPCS	New Plymouth Choral Society
NZBC	New Zealand Broadcasting Corporation
NZBCSO	New Zealand Broadcasting Corporation Symphony Orchestra
NZBS	New Zealand Broadcasting Service
NZOC	New Zealand Opera Company
NZSO	New Zealand Symphony Orchestra
OC	Orpheus Choir
PC	Phoenix Choir
RWCS	Royal Wellington Choral Society
SOA	Symphonia of Auckland
s	soprano
t	tenor

Appendix 1

Ramon Opie

Complete opera repertoire

Auber	*Fra Diavolo* (Lorenzo)
Beethoven	*Fidelio* (Florestan)
Leoncavallo	*Pagliacci* (Beppe)
Moore	*Gallantry* (Donald)
Puccini	*Il Tabarro* (Luigi)
	La Bohème (Rodolfo)
	Madama Butterfly (Pinkerton and Goro)
	Tosca (Cavaradossi)
Ravel	*L'Heure Espagnole* (Torquemada)
Johann Strauss	*Die Fledermaus* (Eisenstein) (excerpts)
Smetana	*The Bartered Bride* (Jenik)
Verdi	*La Traviata* (Alfredo)
	Rigoletto (Duke of Mantua)
Weber	*Der Freischütz* (Max)

Light operas, operetta and musicals

S Coleridge-Taylor	*A Tale of Old Japan*
	The Song of Hiawatha
German	*Merrie England*
Gilbert and Sullivan	*Iolanthe*
	HMS Pinafore
	The Gondoliers
	The Mikado
Kern	*Show Boat*
Lehár	*Gypsy Love*
	The Merry Widow
Romberg	*The Desert Song*
Sullivan/German	*The Emerald Isle*

Oratorios, Masses And Symphonies

Bach	*St Matthew Passion*
	Cantata No. 137 – 'Lobe den Herren'

Beethoven	*Christ on the Mount of Olives*
	Missa Solemnis
	Symphony No. 9 in D Minor (Choral)
Berlioz	*Requiem*
Britten	*St Nicholas*
Bruckner	*Mass No. 3 in F Minor*
Handel	*Judas Maccabeus*
	Samson
	Dettingen Te Deum
	The Messiah
Haydn	*The Creation*
	The Seasons
Mendelsshon	*Elijah*
	St Paul
Orff	*Carmina Burana*
Verdi	*Requiem Mass*

Major Performances (and associated artists where known)

1944

The Messiah (Handel) NPCS.

1945

The Messiah (Handel) ACS; Mary Negus (s); Mary Pratt (c); Raymond Opie (t); Ken Macauley (bar) ASP, Colin Muston (cond).

HMS Pinafore (Gilbert and Sullivan) Ex-Services Operatic Society; *Sir Joseph Porter* Laurence Southwick (bar); *Captain Corcoran* Cliff Firth (bar); *Ralph Rackstraw* Raymond Opie (t); *Dick Deadeye* Gil Cornwall (b); *Josephine* Valerie Isbister (s); *Little Buttercup* Florence Hickson (c); with orch, J A Blitz (cond); J C Reid (dir).

Iolanthe (Gilbert and Sullivan) Combined Services Operatic Club; *Phyllis* Valerie Isbister (s); *Strephon* Alfred Whitworth (t); *Iolanthe* Valerie Henly (ms); *Fairy Queen* Florence Hickson (c); *Lord Chancellor* Richard Stevenson (bar); *Earl Tolloller* Raymond Opie (t); *Earl Mountararat* Gil Cornwall (bar); J A Blitz (cond); J C Reid (dir).

1946

The Messiah (Handel) RWCS, in conjunction with the NPCS: Peggy Knibb (s) (Australia); Christina Young (c); Raymond Opie (t); Stewart Harvey (bar).

1947

Gypsy Love (Lehár) Ex-Services Operatic Society.

The Messiah (Handel) NPCS; Claire Ward (Australia) (s); Margaret Edwards (c); Ramon Opie (t); Fred C Cooper (b); with orch, R Laurie Cooper (cond).

The Messiah (Handel) Beresford Street Congrational Church; Ada Lynn (s); Helen Kersey (c); Ramon Opie (t); Stewart Harvey (bb); Geo. E Wilson (cond).

A Tale of Old Japan (Coleridge-Taylor) NPCS; Mrs Seth Harris (s); Marjorie Ure (c); Ramon Opie (t); Len H Kerr (b); R Laurie Cooper (cond).

1948

Hiawatha (Coleridge-Taylor) NPCS.

The Creation (Haydn) ACS: Lesley Daikin (s); Ramon Opie (t); Ashley Pollock (b); 1YA Studio Orchestra, Georg Tintner (cond).

Gypsy Love (Lehár) Ex-Services Operatic Society: Cast included Ramon Opie; Valerie Isbister; Phil Holland; Joyce Martin; Pamela Henley; Lindsay Hall (cond); John Reid (dir).

Merrie England (German) Hamilton Civic Orchestra and Choir.

The Messiah (Handel) ACS; Myra Sawyer (s); Etta Bernand (c) (Australia); Ramon Opie (t); Stewart Harvey (bb); 1YA Studio Orchestra, Georg Tintner (cond).

1949

Der Freischütz (Weber) ACS; *Agathe* Verlaine Henry (s); *Aennchen* Lesley Daikin (s), *Max* Ramon Opie (t); *Caspar* Ashley Pollock (b); *Cuno* John Gillett (b); *Prince Ottakar* Ernest Briggs (bar); *Kilian* Lawrence Pountney (t); *Zamial and Narrator* John Gordon (spoken); 1YA Studio Orchestra, Georg Tintner (cond).

The Gondoliers (Gilbert and Sullivan) Auckland Amateur Operatic Society.

1950

The Emerald Isle (Sullivan/German) New Plymouth Choral Society; Helen Fountain (s); Mabel Roper (c); Ramon Opie (t); Len Kerr (bar).

Dunedin Music Festival – Nat. O concerts: soloists Linda Parker (s) (Australia) and Ramon Opie (t). (Ramon's arias included excerpts from Act 2 of Wagner's *Lohengrin* and Weber's *Der Freischütz*.)

The Messiah (Handel) Mt Albert and Kingsland Methodist Churches; Constance Manning (s); Nell Leather (c); Ramon Opie (t); John Wentworth (b); W Simpson, organist; R Leather (cond).

1951

The Seasons (Haydn) ACS; Phyllis Maunder (s); Ramon Opie (t); James Hoskins (bar); ASP, George Tintner (cond).

The Messiah (Handel) Te Awamutu Choral Society; Joan Bryant (s); Merlyn Heerdegen (c); Ramon Opie (t); Leo Dove (b); Albert Bryant (cond).

1952

St Paul (Mendelssohn) ACS?

The Bartered Bride (Smetana) Auckland Operatic Society; *Marenka* Betty Spiro (s); *Jenik* Ramon Opie (t); *Kecal* James Hoskin (bb); *Vasek* Ronald Spence (t); *Krusina* Ronald Gregory (bar); *Ludmilla* Heather Begg or Lydia Stow (ms); *Hata* Nola Machin (c); Georg Tintner (cond).

The Desert Song (Romberg) Ex-Services Operatic Society.

The Messiah (Handel) ACS; Olga Burton (s); Beatrice Jones (c); Ramon Opie (t); Lloyd Spears (b); ASP, Georg Tintner (cond).

1953

Merrie England (German) for NZBS to commemorate coronation of Queen Elizabeth II. Soloists included Olga Burton, Constance Manning, Beatrice Jones, Ramon Opie and Stewart Harvey; Auckland Choral Group; Stewart Harvey (cond); Bernard Beeby (dir).

Dettingen Te Deum (Handel) – Festival Coronation Concert ACS; Dorothy Hopkins (s); Heather Begg (c); Ramon Opie (t); Stewart Harvey (bar); with the Dorian Singers, ASP, Harry Luscombe (cond).

Mass in F Minor (Bruckner) and ***Christ on the Mount of Olives*** (Beethoven) ACS; Mina Foley (s); Heather Begg (c); Ramon Opie (t); Ashley Pollock (b); Specially assembled orch, George Tintner (cond).

The Messiah (Handel) ACS; Edith Black (s); Beatrice Jones (c); Ramon Opie (t); James Hoskins (b); ASP, Trevor Sparling (cond).

The Messiah (Handel) – Whangarei.

1954

Samson (Handel) ACS; Beatrice Webb (s); Beatrice Jones (c); Ramon Opie (t); Ashley Pollock (b); ASP, Trevor Sparling (cond).

1955

Promenade Concerts Nat. O – Auckland; soloist Ramon Opie (t).

1956

Judas Maccabeus (Handel) ACS?

Il Tabarro (Puccini) Nat.O; Vincente Major (s); Bertha Rawlinson (c); Ramon Opie (t); Robin Gordon (t)?; Donald Munro (bar); Laszlo Rogatsy (bar). James Roberston (cond).

Australian Broadcasting Commission concert – Queensland: soloist Ramon Opie.

1957
(In Australia for six months)
Fra Diavolo (Auber) National Opera of Australia; *Fra Diavolo* Walter Rychtowski/Gino Zancanaro (t); *Lorenzo* Ramon Opie/Harry Quick (t); *Zerlina* Madge Stephens/Rosalind Keene (s); *Matteo* - Douglas Parnell (b); *Lord Allcash* Antony Fenech (t); *Lady Allcash* Ailene Fischer/Pamela Coleman (ms); *Giacomo* John Pooley (b); *Beppo* Joseph Drewniak (t); with Brian Johnson, Herbert Cox, Brian de Fouesnel, Jeanette King, Jean Reeve and Desmond Patterson. Georg Tintner (md/piano); Simon Montague (dir).

Afternoon Recital (Australian Broadcasting Commission) – Sydney Town Hall: Margaret Moore (s); Ramon Opie (t); Vivien Tuck (piano); Michael Dyer (organ); NSW Police Choir; Geoffrey Parsons (accompanist).

The Messiah (Handel) RWCS; Robin Bell (s); Alice Graham (c); Ramon Opie (t); Martin Wilson (b); ALSO, Laurence C Scott (cond).

The Messiah (Handel) ACS; Mary O'Brien (s); Mary Pratt (c); Ramon Opie (t); Donald McIntyre (b). ASP, Ray Wilson (cond).

1958
Merrie England (German).

1959
La Traviata (Verdi) Auckland Light Opera Society; *Violetta* Mary O'Brien; *Alfredo* Ramon Opie; *Germont* Noel Mangin; *Flora* Jill Evans or Patricia Price; with Frederick Cox (t), John Michael (t); Doreen Harvey (s), Hazel Millar (s), Maurice Parsons, Barry Hogan and Ian Morton (b); with orch, Frank Poore (cond); Ronald Montague (dir).

1960
St Matthew Passion (Bach) ACS; Rosemary Rogatsy (s); Valda McCracken (c); Noel Signal (t); Ramon Opie (t); Peter Evans (bar); Laurence Barker (bar); Donald McGregor (b). ASP, Ray Wilson (cond).

The Emerald Isle (Sullivan/German) NPCS: soloists Helen Fountain; Mabel Roper; Ramon Opie; Len Kerr.

Elijah (Mendelssohn) ACS; Verlaine Henry (s); Mary Pratt (c); Ramon Opie (t); Peter Evans (b); Charles Naylor (b); ASP, Ray Wilson (cond).

The Messiah (Handel) Kingsland Methodist Church:

1961
Elijah (Mendelssohn) Auckland.

Tosca (Puccini) NZOC; *Tosca* Vincente Major or Elisabeth Hellawell (s); *Cavaradossi* Jon Andrew or Ramon Opie (t); *Scarpia* Marcello Cortis or Graeme Gorton (bar); with orch, John Hopkins (cond) Marcello Cortis (dir); (4 months NZ tour with orchestra)

The Messiah (Handel) Kingsland Methodist Church.

1962

Australia tour, as guest artist with Sydney Symphony Orchestra and Queensland Symphony Orchestras.

Tosca (Puccini) (see cast for 1961) – Piano tour (Ramon Opie sang 10 performances in Kingseat, Pukekohe, Epsom, Takapuna, Tokoroa, Taumaranui, Te Kuiti, Tokanui, Paeroa and Hamilton).

1963

La Bohème (Puccini) NZOC; *Mimi* Maria di Gerlando (USA)/Mary O'Brien (s); *Rodolfo* Robert Williams (USA)/Ramon Opie (t); *Marcello* Ronald Maconaghie/Graeme Gorton (bar); *Musetta* Valerie Morgan/ Lynne Cantlon; *Colline* Ian Morton/Neil Warren Smith (Australia) (b); *Schaunard* Paul Person/Grant Dickson; with orch, Georg Tintner (cond); John Thompson (dir). (Three months tour with orchestra to Wellington, Christchurch, Dunedin, Invercargill, Nelson, Auckland, Hamilton, Gisborne, Napier, Hastings, Masterton, Palmerston North, Hawera, Wanganui and New Plymouth).

Missa Solemnis (Beethoven); ACS; Mary O'Brien (s); Patricia Price (c); Ramon Opie (t); Charles Naylor (b); SOA, Ray Wilson (cond).

The Messiah (Handel) ACS; Elisabeth Hellawell (s); Hannah Tatana (c); Ramon Opie (t); Maurice Taylor (bar); ASP; Ray Wilson (cond). (Two performances - Auckland Town Hall)

The Messiah (Handel) ACS; Further televised performance from the Auckland Baptist Tabernacle. Soloists as above.

The Messiah (Handel) Kingsland Methodist Church; Ann Stott (s); Margaret Taylor (c); Ramon Opie (t); John Parker (b); Ross Lewis, organist; Arthur Reid (cond).

1964

Rigoletto (Verdi) NZOC; *Rigoletto* Graeme Gorton/Lucas Bunt (bar); *Gilda* Angela Shaw/Maurine London (USA) (s); *Duke of Mantua* Ramon Opie (t); *Sparafucile* Grant Dickson/Neil Warren Smith (Australia)/Ronald Gray (b); *Maddalena* Corinne Bridge/Dorothy Hitch (ms); *Monterone* Grant Dickson/Donald Smith (b); *Marullo* Paul Person/Lucas Bunt (bar); *Borsa* John Poole/Boyd Gavin (t); *Countess Ceprano* Kathleen Johnson (s); *Count Ceprano* Ronald Gray/Nelson Wattie (b); *Giovanna* Jean Williams/Colleen Dawe (ms); *Page* Betty Shanks (ms); *Usher* Maxwell Jarman (bar); The Concert Orchestra of the NZBC; Georg Tintner (cond); John Thompson (dir).

Fidelio (Beethoven) ACS: Concert performance; *Leonora* Elisabeth Hellawell (s); *Marzelline* Beryl Dalley (s); *Florestan* Ramon Opie (t); *Don Pizarro* Leo Barnett (b); *Rocco* Grant Dickson (b); *Jacquino* Michael McGifford (t); *Don Fernando* Roger Creagh (bar); Sydney Musgrove, Narrator; SOA, Ray Wilson (cond).

St Nicholas (Britten) ACS; Ramon Opie (t); SOA, Ray Wilson (cond).

The Messiah (Handel) ACS; Angela Shaw (s); Hannah Tatana (c); Ramon Opie (t); Grant Dickson (b); SOA, Ray Wilson (cond).

1965

The Creation (Haydn) Cantabile Singers and combined church choirs from Tauranga and Te Puke; Beatrice Webster (s); Lindsay Marchant (s); Carlton Kerr; Ramon Opie (t); Barry Mora (bar); with orch, Ray Wilson (cond).

L'Heure Espagnole (Ravel) NZOC; *Concepcion* Elisabeth Hellawell (s); *Torquemada* Ramon Opie (t); *Gonzalve* Robin Gordon; *Ramiro* Don Rutherford; *Don Inigo Gomez* Graeme Gorton (bar); Piano tour – Russell Channell (md/piano).

Gallantry (Moore) NZOC; *Announcer* Corinne Bridge (ms); *Dr Gregg* Graeme Gorton (bar); *Lola* Angela Shaw (s); *Donald* Ramon Opie (t); Piano tour – Russell Channell (md/piano).

St Matthew Passion (Bach) Wellington Harmonic Society; Elisabeth Hellawell (s); Heather Begg (c); Robin Dumbell (t); Ramon Opie (t); Charles Naylor (b); Grant Dickson (bb); ALSO; Dobbs Franks (cond).

NZ Opera Quartet – First tour Auckland district.

1966

L'Heure Espagnole (Ravel); (see cast for 1965) Recorded for NZBC Television 7 – 13 February.

NZ Opera Quartet – Nationwide tour 28 February – 7 April, 13 June – 2 August, 10 October – 4 December.

Madama Butterfly (Puccini) NZBC; *Cio Cio San* Vincente Major (s); *Lt. B F Pinkerton* Ramon Opie (t); *Sharpless* Grant Dickson (bar); *Suzuki* Corinne Bridge (ms); *Goro* Bruce Chandler (t); *Bonze* and *Prince Yamadori* John Parker (b); *Kate Pinkerton* Peggy Roberts (s); NZBCSO, Juan Matteucci (cond), live broadcast.

NZBC Little Symphony Orchestra tour (early October) to Tauranga, Tokoroa Arts Festival and Te Puke; guest artists - Ramon Opie (t) and Corinne Bridge (ms); Ossie Cheesman (cond).

The Messiah (Handel) NZBC (Wellington); Molly McGurk (Australia) (s); Corinne Bridge (ms); Ramon Opie (t); Brian Hansford (Australia) (b); The Orpheus Choir; NZBCSO, Malcolm Rickard (cond).

1967

NZ Opera Quartet – Nationwide tour 10 February – 5 May, 25 May – 7 July.

St Matthew Passion (Bach) Wellington Harmonic Society; Elisabeth Hellawell (s); Heather Begg (c); Ramon Opie (t); Robin Dumbell (t); Grant Dickson (b); Charles Naylor (b); ALSO, Dobbs Franks (USA) (cond).

The Merry Widow (Lehár) Auckland Light Opera Society; *Hanna Glawari* Angela Shaw (s); *Valencienne* Barbara Hamilton (s); *Camille* Ramon Opie (t); *Prince Danilo* Graeme Gorton (bar); *Baron Zeta* Ernest Stanley (bar); with orch, Frank Poore (cond); David Stevens (dir).

Symphony No. 9 in D Minor (Choral) (Beethoven): Elisabeth Hellawell (s); Heather Begg (c); Ramon Opie (t); Charles Naylor (b); Christchurch Harmonic Society; NZBC, Juan Matteucci (cond).

NZ Opera Quartet – Secondary Schools, Auckland Festival Lunchtime concerts, New Plymouth Bowl of Brooklands Festival; British Music Society (NZ) Inc. Wanganui branch concert, Whakatane Operatic Society (Inc) night club evening.

1968

Requiem (Berlioz) NZBC; Ramon Opie (t); Christchurch Harmonic Society Choir; Royal Musical Society Choir; NZBCSO; Christchurch Civic Orchestra; Skellerup Woolston Brass Band, Juan Matteucci (cond).

Fidelio (Beethoven) Auckland Festival Concert performance: *Leonora* Elisabeth Hellawell (s); *Marzelline* Emily Mair (s); *Florestan* Ramon Opie (t); *Don Pizarro* Donald McIntyre (b); *Rocco* Grant Dickson (b); *Jacquino* Noel Signal (t); *Don Fernando* Lucas Bunt (bar); Sydney Musgrove – Narrator; ACS; NZBCSO, Ray Wilson (cond).

Fidelio (Beethoven) NZOC staged season in Wellington: *Leonora* Elisabeth Hellawell (s); *Marzelline* Emily Mair (s); *Florestan* Ramon Opie (t); *Don Pizarro* Paul Neal (b); *Rocco* Grant Dickson (b); *Jacquino* Ken Casey (t); *Don Fernando* Michael Kingsford (bar); ALSO (augmented), Juan Matteucci (cond); John Thompson (dir).

Die Fledermaus (J. Strauss) (Act 2) Christchurch Harmonic Chorale; Elisabeth Hellawell (s); Anthea Moller (c); Ramon Opie (t); Grant Dickson (bb); Christchurch Civic Orchestra; William Hawkey (cond).

The Messiah (Handel) ACS; Elisabeth Hellawell (s); Laurette Gibb (c); Ramon Opie (t); Grant Dickson (b); Symphonia of Auckland, William Power (cond).

1969
Fidelio (Beethoven) NZOC staged season in Auckland: *Leonora* Elisabeth Hellawell (s); *Marzelline* Corinne Bridge (ms); *Florestan* Ramon Opie (t); *Don Pizarro* Paul Neal (b); *Rocco* Grant Dickson (b); *Jacquino* Ken Casey (t); *Don Fernando* Michael Kingsford (bar); Symphonia of Auckland, Ray Wilson (cond).

Carmina Burana (Orff) ACS; Anne Rasmussen (s); Ramon Opie (t); Thomas Hanna (bar); Ray Wilson (cond); Symphonia of Auckland.

Requiem Mass (Verdi) (Auckland) NZBC; Rosemary Gordon (s); Maureen Forrester (Canada) (c); Ramon Opie (t); Charles Naylor (b); Juan Matteucci (cond); NZBC Symphony Orchestra.

The Seasons (Haydn) (Autumn section) ACS; Anne Rasmussen (s); Ramon Opie (t); Thomas Hanna (bar); Ray Wilson (cond); Symphonia of Auckland.

Requiem Mass (Verdi) (Wellington) NZBC; artists and orchestra as for Auckland performance above.

Music from Rome and *Music from Vienna* (Opera excerpts) Symphonia of Auckland; Corinne Bridge (ms); Ramon Opie (t); Juan Matteucci (cond).

Recital – Tauranga Festival Corinne Bridge (ms); Ramon Opie (t); Susan Smith (acc).

1970
Requiem Mass (Verdi) The Royal Christchurch Musical Society; Rosemary Gordon (s); Lauris Elms (Australia) (c); Ramon Opie (t); Charles Naylor (b); NZBCSO, Robert Field-Dodgson (cond).

Missa Solemnis (Beethoven) SOA; Mary O'Brien (s); Patricia Price (c): Ramon Opie (t); Charles Naylor (b); ACS, Ray Wilson (cond).

Music from the Theatre – TV One NZBCSO; Corinne Bridge (ms); Ramon Opie (t).

Cantata 137 'Lobe den Herren' (Bach) ACS; Carol Jones (s); Patricia Price (ms); Ramon Opie (t); Charles Naylor (b); SOA; Ray Wilson (cond).

1971–74 (United Kingdom)
Show Boat (Jerome Kern) Adelphi Theatre, London: *Magnolia* Lorna Dallas; *Ravenal* Andre Jobin; *Julie* Cleo Laine; *Joe* Thomas Carey; *Frank* Kenneth Nelson; *Ellie* Jan Hunt; *Captain Andy* Derek Royle; *Parthy* Pearl Hackney; *Queenie* Ena Cabayo; *Windy* Len Mabey/Ramon Opie; with orch, Ray Cook (md); Wendy Toye (dir) (909 performances).

1975

Madama Butterfly (Puccini) Perkel Productions; *Cio Cio San* Louise Molloy/Heather Pascual (s); *Pinkerton* Cyril Kelleway (t); *Sharpless* Paul Person/Brian McKay (bar); *Suzuki* Corinne Bridge (ms); *Goro* Ramon Opie (t); *Kate Pinkerton* Gillian Kendrick (ms); Ingrid Wahlberg (piano); Paul Person (dir). Played Whangaparaoa, Morrinsville, Westlake Girls High School, Southwell School, Hamilton, Te Puke, Maungatoroto, Dargaville, Auckland – Centennial Theatre (7 performances), Cambridge, Taumarunui, Glen Eden Playhouse.

1976

Madama Butterfly (Puccini) Northern Opera; *Cio Cio San* Elisabeth Hellawell/Louise Molloy (s); *Pinkerton*Anthony Benfell (t); *Sharpless* Roger Creagh (bb); *Suzuki* Corinne Bridge (ms); *Goro* Ramon Opie (t); with orch, Juan Matteucci (cond); Bruce Woods (dir).

1978

The Messiah (Handel) Pakuranga Choral Society; Carol Jones (s); Corinne Bridge (ms); Ramon Opie (t); Malcolm Smith (b); Geoffrey Skerrett (organ); Hal Marryatt (cond).

1979

Pagliacci (Leoncavallo) TV One; NZSO; *Canio* Anthony Benfell (t); *Nedda* Heather Pascual (s); *Tonio* Timothy Hawley (bb); *Beppe* Ramon Opie (t); *Silvio* Lyall Kennaway (bar); Mischi Inoue (cond); Peter Coates (dir).

1987

The Messiah (Handel) Hibiscus Coast Choral Society; Jennifer Kirker and Pamela Hodson (s); Beverley Hickson and Lorna Donald (c); Ramon Opie (t); Richard Weston (b); David James (cond).

The Messiah (Handel) RWCS; Marjorie Rowley (s); Corinne Bridge (c); Dixon Tizard (t); Charles Naylor (b); with orchestra, Harry Brusey (cond).

1955

The Bartered Bride (Smetana) Opera-Technique; *Marenka* Maureen O'Donaghue (s); *Jenik* Lionel Bailey (t) *Vasek* Ian Telford (t); *Kecal* Grant Tilly (bb); *Micha* Martin Prescott (bar); *Hata* Corinne Bridge (c); *Krusina* Graham Cooper (bar), *Ludmilla* Marlene Reader (ms); *Esmeralda* Betty Shanks (ms); with orchestra, Harry Botham (cond).

The Sorcerer (Gilbert and Sullivan) Wellington Gilbert and Sullivan Society; *Aline* Rosemary McKeefry (s); *Alexis* Norris Smith (t); *Dr Daly* George Morrison (b); *Sir Marmaduke Pointdextre* Ian McNeilage (bar); *John Wellington Wells* Raymond Hedges (bar); *Lady Sangazure* Corinne Bridge (c); *Mrs Partlett* Jean Alcock (s); *Constance* Nancy Alexander (s); *Notary* George Thomsen (bar); with piano, Raymond Hedges (dir).

The Emerald Isle (Sullivan and German) *Terence O'Brien* Clifford Dowling (t); *Pat Murphy* Thomas Hanna (bar); *Molly O'Grady* Corinne Bridge (c); *Earl of Newtown KP* Max Borra (b); *Countess of Newtown* Merline Coffey (s); *Dr Fiddle DD* Ernest Henry (bar); *Professor Bunn* Louis Doyle (t); *Lady Rosie* Elaine Sutton (s); *Susan* Lenore Spencer (s); *An Old Man* William Arnold (bar); ALSO, Hamilton Dickson (cond).

The Messiah (Handel) Lower Hutt Methodist Church; Muriel Hitchings (s); Corinne Bridge (c); Reg. Saunders (t); John Dellow (b); Ray Nelson (organist); E A Surtees (cond).

1956

Blossom Time (Schubert/Clutsam) NZBS; *Schubert* sung by Robin Gordon (t), spoken by Alan Jarvis; *Mayrhofer* sung by Thomas Hanna (bar), spoken by Tim Elliott; *Schwindt* sung by John Dellow (b), spoken by Peter Varley; *Vicki* sung by Daphne Ellwood (s), spoken by Wendy Gibb; *Count Rudi* sung by Peter Nisbet (bar),spoken by William Austin; *Lulu* sung by Rae Gibbons (c), spoken by Angela Shafto; *Elsa* sung by Claire Newman (s), spoken by Stephanie Cuming; *Wimpassinger* sung by Martin Wilson (bar), spoken by Selwyn Toogood; *The Archduchess* sung by Corinne Bridge (c), spoken by Jessica Weddell; *Countess Frangipani* sung by Joan Vause (s), spoken by Davina Whitehouse; with orchestra, Harry Brusey (cond); Bernard Beeby (producer).

Merrie England (German) OC, for opening of Lower Hutt Little Theatre; Jean Bassett (s); Corinne Bridge (c); Clifford Dowling (t); Thomas Hanna (bar); ALSO, Malcolm Rickard (cond).

Hansel and Gretel (Humperdinck) NZBS; *Hansel* Edna Boyd Wilson (s); *Gretel* Marjorie Rowley; *The Witch* Bertha Rawlinson (c); *Gertrude*

Raewyn Lamb (s); *Peter* Lazlo Rogatsy(b); *Sandman* Corinne Bridge (c); *Dew Fairy* Sybil Phillips (s); Nat. O; James Robertson (cond).

1957

The Messiah (Handel) OC, for opening of Lower Hutt Town Hall; Sybil Phillips (s); Corinne Bridge (c); Robin Gordon (t); Martin Wilson (bar); ALSO; Malcolm Rickard (cond).

Eugene Onegin (Tchaikovsky) NZBS; *Tatiana* Sybil Phillips (s); *Olga* Corinne Bridge (c); *Lensky* Robin Gordon; *Onegin* Ninian Walden (bar); PC, Nat. O, James Robertson (cond).

General Gore (Hamilton Dickson) *General Gore* Max Borra (b); *Major Algernon* Alex Veysey (bar); *Madam Gore* Corinne Bridge (c); *Joan Gore* Loretta Dickson (s); *John* Peter Roberts (t); *Dawn* Daphne Ellwood (s); *Maud* Doreen Ellery (ms); *Michael* William Arnold (b); *Landlord* Louis Doyle (t); ALSO, Hamilton Dickson (cond).

The Consul (Menotti) NZOC; *John Sorel* Donald Munro (bar); *Magda Sorel* Vincente Major (s); *The Mother* Alice Graham (c); *The Seretary* Mona Ross (ms); *Mr Kofner* Martin Wilson (bar); *The Foreign Woman* Beryl Dalley (s); *Anna Gomez* Mary Langford (s); *Vera Boronel* Corinne Bridge (c); *The Magician* Terence Finnegan; with Antony Vercoe (bb); Anthony Larsen (bar); Corbett Woodall and Brian Adams; Nat. O, James Robertson (cond); Richard Campion (dir).

The Messiah (Handel) Masterton Choral Society; Sybil Phillips (s); Corinne Bridge (c); Robin Gordon (t); Martin Wilson (bar); ALSO, L R Cameron (cond).

1958

Come Ye Sons of Art (Purcell) Nat.O; Sybil Phillips (s); Corinne Bridge (c); Molly Atkinson (c); Donald Munro (bar); PC; John Hopkins (cond).

A Child of our Time (Tippett) NZ premiere Nat. O: Sybil Phillips (s); Corinne Bridge (c); Leslie Andrews (t); Donald Munro (bar); PC; John Hopkins (cond).

Le Nozze di Figaro (Mozart) NZOC; *Figaro* Geoffrey de Latour (bar); *Susanna* Beryl Dalley (s); *Bartolo* Frank Malthus (bb); *Marcellina* Corinne Bridge (c); *Cherubino* Honor McKellar (ms); *Count Almaviva* Donald Munro (bar); Don *Basilio* Terence Finnegan (t); *Countess Almaviva* Marie Robinson (s); *Barbarina* Kathleen Johnson (s); *Don Curzio* Newton Goodson (t); Nat. O, John Hopkins (cond); Frank Pontin (dir).

Merrie England (German) Daphne Ellwood (s); Corinne Bridge (c); John Thompson (t); John Dellow (bar); Nelson Civic Choir, George E Wilkinson (cond).

1959 (United Kingdom)
Studying at the Guildhall School of Music and Drama.

1960 (UK)
Orfeo ed Euridice (Gluck) Guildhall School of Music and Drama; *Orfeo* Corinne Bridge/Julia Meadows (ms); *Euridice* Mary Murphy (s); *Amor* Phyllis Glavin/Petals Calcutt (s); with orch, Roger Clynes (cond).

Dido and Aeneas (Purcell) Cambridge Arts Theatre Club; *Dido* Corinne Bridge (ms); *Belinda* Jacqueline Rayner; *Sorceress* Isabel Faulkner (c); *Aeneas* Michael Rippon (bar); Cambridge University String Orch, Richard Steinitz (cond); Camille Prior (dir).

1961(UK)
Cantata No. 12 (Bach) London Music Society; Corinne Bridge (c); Donald Storer (t); with orch, Alan Reddish (cond).

Hugh the Drover (Vaughan Williams) Guildhall School of Music and Drama; *Hugh* Robert Bateman/Edgar Thomas (t); *Mary* Sylvia Gray/Mary Bass (s); *John* Russell Smith (bb): *Aunt Jane* Ruth Little/ Corinne Bridge (ms); *William* Ramon Remedios (t); *Robert* Thomas Lawlor (bar); *Sergeant* and *Cheap Jack* Robert Bateman (bar); with orch, Lawrence Leonard (cond); Sumner Austin (dir).

Five Mystical Songs (Vaughan Williams) St Clement's near Eastcheap: Corinne Bridge (ms); with piano, Andrew Pearson (cond).

Serenade to Music (Vaughan Willams) Henry Wood Birthday Concert – Royal Albert Hall: Patricia Brigenshaw (s); Lorna Elias (s); Lorna Haywood (s); Angela Jenkins (s); Corinne Bridge (ms); Jean Evans (c); Margaret Lamb (ms); Margaret Price (ms); Michael Clarke (t); James Lewington (t); Edgar Thomas (t); Kenneth Woolam (t); Robin Fairhurst (bar); Michael Rippon (bar); Geoffrey Shaw (b); Russell Smith (bb); with orch, Sir Malcolm Sargent (cond).

The Messiah (Handel) Thurrock Choral Union, Stanford-Le-Hope; Pamela Smith (s); Corinne Bridge (c); James Lewington (t); Robin Fairhurst (b): with orch, Ronald Stansfield (cond).

1962– 63 (UK)
The Tales of Hoffmann (Offenbach) National School of Opera; *Hoffmann* Dennis Brandt (t); *Olympia* Jenny Hill/Sheila Amit (s); *Antonia* Pauline Tinsley (s); *Giulietta* Antoinette Miggiani/Hanula Rzoska (s); *Nicklaus* Sally Langford/Joy Domzalski (ms); *Antonia's Mother* Corinne Bridge (ms); *Evil Genius* Bryan Drake/MichaelMaurel (bb); with orch, James Loughran (cond); Colin Graham (dir).

The Messiah (Handel) Maidenhead New Town Hall Festival; Pamela Smith (s); Corinne Bridge (ms); James Lewington (t); Brian Harper (b); with orch, Leonard Piercey (con).

Three Mystical Songs (Ronald Tremaine) (First London performance) NZ Music Society 10th anniversary, Wigmore Hall; Corinne Bridge (ms); The Harvey Phillips String Orchestra, Ashley Lawrence (cond).

Requiem Mass (Verdi) Guildhall School of Music and Drama concert at Guildhall of London; Corinne Bridge (ms); Ramon Remedios (t); with orch, Sir David Willcocks (cond).

BBC Variety Playhouse (8 December 1962) *Singers:* Elizabeth Rust, Rae Woodland, The George Mitchell Singers; *First Broadcast:* Corinne Bridge, William E Bailey; *Trumpet:* Clifford Haines; *Comedy:* Hattie Jacques, Leslie Crowther, Ronnie Barker; *Guest Star:* Dennis Price; *Playhouse Theatre:* Stephen Murray, Sheila Grant and Lewis Stringer; BBC Revue Orchestra, Vic Oliver (cond).

BBC Variety Playhouse (4 May 1963) *Singers:* Ava June, Corinne Bridge, Edward Byles, Peter Glossop; *First Broadcast:* Margaret Taylor; *Comedy:* June Whitfield, Leslie Crowther, Ronnie Barker; *Guest Star:* Sir Donald Wolfit; *Playhouse Theatre:* Rosalind Iden; BBC Revue Orchestra, Vic Oliver (cond).

The Sound of Music (Rodgers and Hammerstein) Palace Theatre, West End, London; *Maria* Jean Bayliss; *Georg* Roger Dann; *Mother Abbess* Constance Shacklock (Corinne Bridge – understudy); *Max* Harold Kasket; *Elsa Schraeder* Eunice Gayson: *Sister Berte* Maria Lorraine (Corinne Bridge – understudy); *Sister Margaretta* Olive Gilbert; *Sister Sophia* Diana Dove; *Herr Zeller* Peter Swanwick; *Franz* Jay Denyer; *Frau Schmidt* Diana Beaumont; *Liesl* Susan Passmore; *Rolf* Nicholas Bennett; with orch, Alan Ward (cond); Jerome Whyte and Joe Layton (dir) (approx. 600 performances).

1964

Rigoletto (Verdi) NZOC; *Rigoletto* Graeme Gorton/Lucas Bunt (bar); *Gilda* Angela Shaw/Maurine London (USA) (s); *Duke of Mantua* Ramon Opie (t); *Sparafucile* Grant Dickson/Neil Warren Smith (Australia)/Ronald Gray (b); *Maddalena* Corinne Bridge/Dorothy Hitch (ms); *Monterone* Grant Dickson/Donald Smith (b); *Marullo* Paul Person/Lucas Bunt (bar); *Borsa* John Poole/Boyd Gavin (t); *Countess Ceprano* Kathleen Johnson (s); *Count Ceprano* Ronald Gray/Nelson Wattie (b); *Giovanna* Jean Williams/Colleen Dawe (ms); *Page* Betty Shanks (ms); *Usher* Maxwell Jarman (bar); Concert Orchestra of the NZBC, Georg Tintner (cond); John Thompson (dir)
(played from 2 to 4 performances each in Wellington, Christchurch, Dunedin, Auckland, Hamilton, Napier, Hastings, Palmerston North and New Plymouth).

The Bartered Bride (Smetana) NZOC; *Marenka* Elisabeth Hellawell/ Rosemary Rogatsy (s); *Jenik* Peter Baillie/Ronald McLeod (t); *Kecal* Neil Warren Smith (Aust.)/Grant Dickson (b); *Vasek* John Poole (t); *Ludmilla* Dorothy Hitch/Corinne Bridge (ms); *Hata* Colleen Dawe/ Lily Latisheva (c); *Krusina* Paul Person (bar); *Micha* Ronald Gray/Grant Dickson (b); *Esmeralda* Ann Gordon (s); *Manager* Basil Cudby/Silvio Famularo (t); *Indian* Boyd Gavin (t); Concert Orchestra of the NZBC, Georg Tintner/Edouard Fischer (cond); Stephan Beinl (dir) (played from 2 to 4 performances each in Wellington, Christchurch, Dunedin, Invercargill, Auckland, Hamilton, Gisborne, Hastings, Palmerston North, Wanganui, Hawera and New Plymouth).

Così fan tutte (Mozart) NZOC; *Fiordiligi* Kathleen Johnson/Janice Smith (s); *Dorabella* Corinne Bridge (ms)/Angela Shaw (s); *Don Alfonso* Grant Dickson/Ronald Gray (b); *Ferrando* John Poole/Gino Zancanaro (t); *Guglielmo* Don Rutherford/Lucas Bunt (bar); *Despina* Ann Gordon/ Beryl Dalley (s); Russell Channell (md/piano); John Thompson (dir).

La Cenerentola (Rossini) NZOC; *Angelina (Cinderella)* Heather Begg (c); *Clorinda* Angela Shaw (s); *Tisbe* Corinne Bridge (ms); *Don Ramiro (Prince)* Gino Zancanaro (t); *Dandini* Graeme Gorton (bar); *Don Magnifico* Grant Dickson (b); *Alidoro* Ronald Gray (b); Concert Orchestra of the NZBC, Georg Tintner/Russell Channell (cond); John Thompson (dir).

1965

Four Pioneer Portraits (1949) (Dorothea Franchi) Auckland Festival lunchtime concert; Corinne Bridge (ms); Dorothea Franchi (piano).

Carmen (Bizet) Mt Eden Community Operatic Society; *Carmen* Corinne Bridge (ms); *Micaela* Lyn McBeth (s); *Don Jose* Boyd Gavin (t); *Escamillo* Lawrence Barker (bar); *Frasquita* Paulette Moran (s); *Mercedes* Elsie Bulger (ms); *Le Dancaire* Alistair Meldrum (t); *Le Remendado* Graham Boyle (bar); *Zuniga* Neville McMillan (b); *Morales* Richard Hall (bar); *Lillas Pastia* John Reece (b); with orch, Ulric Burstein (cond); Gwyneth Allen (dir).

Gallantry (Moore) NZOC; *Announcer* Corinne Bridge (ms); *Dr Gregg* Graeme Gorton (bar); *Lola* Angela Shaw (s); *Donald* Ramon Opie (t); Piano tour – Russell Channell (md/piano).

Mass in G (Schubert) Auckland Harmonic Society; Gillian Redstone (s); Corinne Bridge (ms); Lawrence Barker (b): Janet Sanson (organist); Ulric Burstein (cond).

NZ Opera Quartet – First tour Auckland district.

1966

Albert Herring (Britten) NZOC; *Albert Herring* Peter Baillie (t); *Lady Billows* Elisabeth Hellawell (s); *Florence Pike* Heather Begg (c); *Nancy* Corinne Bridge (ms); *Sid* Don Rutherford (bar); *Miss Wordsworth* Angela Shaw (s); *Vicar* Neale Patterson (bar); *Superintendant Budd* Grant Dickson (b); *Mayor* Boyd Gavin (t); *Mrs Herring* Bertha Rawlinson (c); NZ Opera Orchestra, Laszlo Heltay (cond); John Tasker (dir).

NZ Opera Quartet – Nationwide tour 28 February – 7 April, 13 June – 2 August, 10 October – 4 December.

Madama Butterfly (Puccini) NZBC; *Cio Cio San* Vincente Major (s); *Pinkerton* Ramon Opie (t); *Sharpless* Grant Dickson (bar); *Suzuki* Corinne Bridge (ms); *Goro* Bruce Chandler (t); *Bonze* and *Prince Yamadori* John Parker (b); *Kate Pinkerton* Peggy Roberts (s); NZBCSO, Juan Matteucci (cond), live broadcast.

NZBC Little Symphony Orchestra tour (early October) to Tauranga, Tokoroa Arts Festival and Te Puke; guest artists – Ramon Opie (t) and Corinne Bridge (ms); Ossie Cheesman (cond).

Elijah (Mendelssohn) OC; Heather Taylor (s); Corinne Bridge (ms); George Metcalfe (t); Charles Naylor (b); LSO, Malcolm Rickard (cond).

The Messiah (Handel) NZBCSO (Wellington); Molly McGurk (Australia) (s); Corinne Bridge (ms); Ramon Opie (t); Brian Hansford (Australia) (bb); The Orpheus Choir; NZBCSO, Malcolm Rickard (cond).

1967

NZ Opera Quartet – Nationwide tour 10 February – 5 May, 25 May – 7 July.

Madama Butterfly (Puccini) NZOC; *Cio Cio San* Kiang Hwa/Elisabeth Hellawell (s); *Pinkerton* Nicola Filacuridi/Noel Signal (t); *Sharpless* Paul Neal (bar); *Suzuki* Corinne Bridge (ms); *Goro* George Henare (t); *Kate Pinkerton* Arianthe Garland (s); with orch, Juan Matteuci (cond); John Thompson (dir) (three months tour throughout NZ).

Can Can (Cole Porter) Hastings Musical Comedy Company; *La Mome Pistache* Corinne Bridge; *Judge Aristide Forestiere* Haldane Scougall; *Claudine* Judith Cater; *Boris* Gooch Parahi; with orch, Cedric White (md); Laurie Swindell (dir).

Carmen (Bizet) – concert version: highlights Gisborne Choral Society Inc; *Carmen* Corinne Bridge (ms); *Don Jose* Revell Rice (t); *Micaela* Mary Quinn (s); *Escamillo* Maurice Taylor (b); *Zuniga* Cliff Anderson (b); Concert Orchestra, Wilfred Kohn (cond).

Mass in B Minor (Bach) ACS; Rosemary Gordon (s); Corinne Bridge (ms); Maurice Larsen (t); Maurice Taylor (b); SOA, Ray Wilson (cond).

The Messiah (Handel) ACS; Rosemary Gordon (s); Corinne Bridge (ms); Maurice Larsen (t); Maurice Taylor (b); SOA, Ray Wilson (cond).

NZ Opera Quartet – Secondary Schools, Auckland Festival lunchtime concerts, New Plymouth Bowl of Brooklands Festival; British Music Society (NZ) Inc Wanganui branch concert, Whakatane Operatic Society (Inc) night club evening.

1968

The Sound of Music (Rodgers and Hammerstein) The Light Opera Club (Inc), His Majesty's Theatre, Auckland; *Maria* Jean Bayliss (from West End production, London); *Captain von Trapp* Paul Person; *Mother Abbess* Corinne Bridge; *Max* Donald Hope-Evans; *Elsa Schraeder* Barbara Keene; *Sister Berte* Desma Hudson; *Sister Margaretta* Maureen Chappell; *Sister Sophia* Esther Clements; *Herr Zeller* Con O'Leary; *Franz* William Mitchelhill; *Frau Schmidt* Mina Frater; *Liesl* Marie Yalland; *Rolf* Roger Fowler; with orch, Frank Poore (cond); David Stevens (dir); Doreen Yalland (choreographer).

Symphony No. 2 (Mahler) Wellington; Elisabeth Hellawell (s); Corinne Bridge (ms); OC; NZBCSO, John Hopkins (cond).

Mass in F Minor (Bruckner) ACS; Anne Rasmussen (s); Corinne Bridge (ms); Maurice Larsen (t); Fanie Johnson (b); SOA, Ray Wilson (cond).

Mass in E Flat (Schubert) NZBCSO; Alison Maloney (s); Corinne Bridge (ms); George Metcalfe (t); Richard Greager (t); Grant Dickson (b); Royal Christchurch Musical Society, John Hopkins (cond).

Stabat Mater (Pergolesi) Kathleen Johnson (s); Corinne Bridge (ms); Roger Harris String Orchestra, Roger Harris (cond).

Hansel and Gretel (Humperdinck) NZOC; *Hansel* Corinne Bridge (ms); *Gretel* Anne Rasmussen (s); *Peter* Paul Neal; *Gertrude* Elisabeth Hellawell (s); *The Witch* Dorothy Hitch (ms); *Dew Fairy* Margaret Burnett (s); SOA, Juan Matteuci (cond); John Thompson (dir).

1969

Fidelio (Beethoven) NZOC staged season in Auckland: *Leonora* Elisabeth Hellawell (s); *Marzelline* Corinne Bridge (ms); *Florestan* Ramon Opie (t); *Don Pizarro* Paul Neal (b); *Rocco* Grant Dickson (b); *Jacquino* Ken Casey (t); *Don Fernando* Michael Kingsford (bar); Symphonia of Auckland, Ray Wilson (cond); John Thompson (dir).

Mass in B Minor (Bach) OC; April Cantelo (UK) (s); Corinne Bridge (ms); George Metcalfe (t); Charles Naylor (b); LO and players from NZBCSO, John Hopkins (cond).

An Edith Sitwell Song Cycle (1964) (Carr) Corinne Bridge (ms); Janetta McStay (piano); Ronald Webb (oboe).

Music from Rome and ***Music from Vienna*** (Opera excerpts); Corinne Bridge (s); Ramon Opie (t); Symphonia of Auckland, Juan Matteucci (cond).

Recital – Tauranga Festival Corinne Bridge (s); Ramon Opie (t); Susan Smith (acc).

1970

The Gondoliers (Gilbert and Sullivan) The Light Opera Club (Inc); *Gianetta* Sunny Morete (s); *Tessa* Corinne Bridge (ms); *Marco Palmieri* Cyril Kelleway (t); *Guiseppe Palmieri* Robert O'Hara (bb); *Duke of Plaza Toro* Ronald Miller (bar); *Duchess of Plaza Toro* Anne Hodgetts (c); *Casilda* Ann Stott (s); *Luiz* Anthony Benfell (t); *Don Alhambra* Roger Knights (bb); with orch, Gordon Cole (cond); Phyllis Mackney (dir).

Faust (Gounod) NZOC; *Faust* Peter Baillie (t); *Mephistopheles* Grant Dickson (b); *Marguerite* Mildred Allan (USA) (s); *Valentin* Barry Mora (bar); *Siebel* Corinne Bridge (ms); *Marthe* Dorothy Hitch (ms); NZBCSO, Gerald Krug (Australia) (cond); Tom Brown (Australia) (dir).

Music from the Theatre – TV One NZBCSO; Corinne Bridge (ms); Ramon Opie (t).

1971–74 (United Kingdom)

Faust (Gounod) Maidstone Opera; *Faust* Neville Williams (t); *Mephistopheles* Gerwyn Morgan (b): *Marguerite* Rosalind Abraham (s); *Valentin* Robert Bateman (bar); *Siebel* Carolyn Maia (ms); *Marthe* Corinne Bridge (ms); *Wagner* Mark Lufton (bar); with orch, Bela de Csillery (cond); Gerwyn Morgan (dir).

Lilac Time (Schubert/Berte) West End Artists Ltd; *Baron von Schober* John Hanson (bar); *Schubert* Meston Reid (t); *Mitzi* Joyce Mandre (s); *Litzi* Susan Maisey (s); *Fritzi* Corinne Bridge (ms); *Otto Zell* Alexander Bridge (bar); *Adelina Taliani* Olga Saunders (ms); with orch, Derek Taverner (md); Alexander Bridge (dir) (played 8 performances each in Hull, Wimbledon, Eastbourne, Swindon, Southsea, Birmingham, Bristol, Nottingham, Wolverhampton, Sunderland, Lytham St Annes, Bournemouth, Edinburgh, Manchester, Norwich, Swansea, Aberdeen, Glasgow, Bradford, Cardiff – 160 performances).

La Traviata (Verdi) Film of highlights – Denham Studios, Middlesex.

1975

Madama Butterfly (Puccini) Perkel Opera; *Cio Cio San* Louise Molloy/ Heather Pascual (s); *Pinkerton* Cyril Kelleway (t); *Sharpless* Paul Person/ Brian McKay (bar); *Suzuki* Corinne Bridge (ms); *Goro* Ramon Opie (t); *Kate Pinkerton* Gillian Kendrick (ms); Ingrid Wahlberg (piano); Paul Person (dir).

1976

Missa Solemnis (Beethoven) ACS; Elisabeth Hellawell (s); Corinne Bridge (ms); Anthony Benfell (t); Charles Naylor (b); SOA, Ray Wilson (cond).

Madama Butterfly (Puccini) New Opera Company; *Cio Cio San* Malvina Major (s); *Pinkerton* Anthony Benfell (t); *Sharpless* Roger Creagh (bb); *Suzuki* Corinne Bridge (ms); *Goro* Edward Driscoll (t); *Kate Pinkerton* Fay Haddon (s); Wellington Regional Orchestra, William Southgate (cond); John Thompson (dir).

Symphony No. 2 (Mahler) Christchurch, Wellington and Auckland; Angela Shaw (s) – Christchurch and Auckland performances; Elisabeth Hellawell (s) – Wellington performance; Corinne Bridge (ms) all performances; NZSO, Franz Paul Decker (cond).

Cavelleria Rusticana (Mascagni) Perkel Opera; *Santuzza* Phyllis Thorburn (s); *Turridu* Everett Thorburn (t); *Alfio* Paul Person (bar); *Lola* Shirley Kauter (ms); *Mamma Lucia* Corinne Bridge (ms); Ingrid Wahlberg (piano); Paul Person (dir).

Amahl and the Night Visitors (Menotti) TV One production; *Amahl* John Robinson (boy soprano); *Mother* Corinne Bridge (ms); *Balthazar* Roger Wilson (b); *Kaspar* Anthony Benfell (t); *Melchior* Roger Creagh (bb); *Page* Timothy Hawley (bar); Wellington Regional Orchestra and members of the NZSO, William Southgate (cond); Terry Bryan (producer).

Mass in G (Schubert) NZSO concerts in Christchurch and Dunedin.

1977

Lilac Time (Schubert/Berte) Perkel Opera; *Lilli* Sally Sloman (s); *Tilli* Dorothy Paykel (s); *Willi* Corinne Bridge (ms); *Schubert* Cyril Kelleway (t); *Schober* Graham Buxton (bar); *Marini* Margaret Metcalfe (ms); Jennifer Goldsmith (piano); Maureen Kerr (dir) (piano tour and Auckland season).

1978

Eugene Onegin (Tchaikovsky) Perkel Opera; *Onegin* Paul Person/David Skinner (bar): *Tatiana* Patricia House/Gillian Trott (s); *Olga* Anne Van der Sluis/Anne Young (c); *Larina* Elaine Dow (s)/Corinne Bridge (ms); *Filipyevna* Lynne Anderson/ Anne Hayden (ms); *Lenski* Cyil Kelleway/

Malcolm Campbell (t); *Prince Gremin* John Parker/Maurice Parsons (b); *Captain Zaretski* Graham Allan/Michael Kyle (bar); *Monsieur Triquet* Victor de la Varis (t); Alexandra Wiltshire (md and piano); Donald Hope-Evans (dir) (North Island piano tour and Auckland season).

Il Trovatore (Verdi) Perkel Opera; *Leonora* Elaine Dow/Leonie Symes (s); *Count di Luna* Salvatore Gagliardi/Robert O'Hara (bb); *Azucena* Corinne Bridge/Lindsay Mika (ms); *Manrico* Cyril Kelleway (t); *Ferrando* Graham Allan/Maurice Parsons (bar); *Ruiz* Terence Finnegan (t); *Inez* Anne Hayden (ms); Alexandra Wiltshire (md and piano); Alan de Malmanche (dir) (North Island piano tour and Auckland season).

Il Barbiere di Siviglia (Rossini) Perkel Opera; *Rosina* Corinne Bridge (ms)/Patricia House (s); *Count Almaviva* Cyril Kelleway/Terence Finnegan (t); *Figaro* David Skinner/Lyle Kennaway (bar); *Don Bartolo* Brian McKay/Malcolm Smith (b); *Berta* Anne Hayden/Lindsay Mika (ms); Joy Crabtree/Frances Wilson (piano); Paul Person (dir) (North Island piano tour and Auckland season).

The Messiah (Handel) Pakuranga Choral Society; Carol Jones (s); Corinne Bridge (ms); Ramon Opie (t); Malcolm Smith (b); Geoffrey Skerrett (organ); Hal Marryatt (cond).

1979

Quattro Vespri Sacri (Verdi) and ***King David*** (Honegger) ACS; Corinne Bridge (ms) (Verdi soloist); Maureen Carney (s); Corinne Bridge (ms); Kenneth Cornish (t); Raymond Hawthorne (narrator); *The Witch of Endor* Elizabeth McRae; SOA, Ray Wilson (cond).

The Consul (Menotti) Perkel Opera; *Magda Sorel* Patricia House (s); *John Sorel* Paul Person (bar); *Secretary* Corinne Bridge (ms); *The Mother* Linda Shearer (c); *Magician* Jon Zealando (t); *Mr Koffner* Neville McMillan (b); *The Foreign Woman* Shirley Kauter (ms); *Anna Gomez* Elaine Dow (s); *Vera Boronel* Lindsay Mika (ms); *Assan* Gregory Patel (t); Christine Cuming (piano); Paul Person (dir).

1980

The Marriage of Figaro (Mozart) Perkel Opera; *Figaro* David Skinner (bar); *Susanna* Patricia Aldersley/Sally Sloman (s); *Count Almaviva* Paul Person (bar); *Countess Almaviva* Patricia House/Elaine Dow (s); *Cherubino* Shirley Kauter/GillianKendrick (ms); *Dr Bartolo* Donald Trott (b); *Don Basilio* Cyril Kelleway/John Stanley (t); *Marcellina* Margot Lloyd/Corinne Bridge (ms); *Antonio* Gregory Patel (t)/Stephen Rosser (bar); *Don Curzio* John Stanley/Cyril Kelleway (t); *Barbarina* Bernadette Horne/ Frith Trezevant (s); Christine Cuming/Rosemary Stuart (piano); Corinne Bridge (dir) (North Island piano tour and Auckland season).

Mass in F Minor (Bruckner) ACS; Wendy Dixon (s); Corinne Bridge (ms); Kenneth Cornish (t); Roger Wilson (b); SOA, Georg Tintner (cond).

La Traviata (Verdi) Perkel Opera; *Violetta* Margaret Dixon-McIver/ Sally Sloman(s); *Alfredo* Malcolm Campbell/Cyril Kelleway (t); *Germont* David Griffiths/PaulPerson (bar); *Flora* Corinne Bridge/ Margot Lloyd (ms); *Annina* Elizabeth Stride/Christine Tresider (s); *Baron Douphol* Dennis Clarke(bb); *Dr Grenvil* Stephen Rosser (bar); (Christine Cuming (piano), Paul Person (dir) (North Island piano tour and Auckland season).

Serenade to Music (Vaughan Williams) ACS (125th anniversary season); Wendy Dixon, Elisabeth Hellawall, Heather MacDonald, Heather Taylor (s); Lynne Anderson, Corinne Bridge, Barbara Lynch, Colleen Roche (ms/c); Anthony Benfell, Kenneth Cornish, Paul Hogg, Maurice Larsen (t); Peter Hind, John Parker, Paul Person, David Skinner (bar/b); Special Symphony Orchestra, Ray Wilson (cond).

1981

Mass in D Minor 'Nelson' (Haydn) NZSO – Napier concert; Gillian Trott (s); Corinne Bridge (ms); Kenneth Cornish (t); Martin Thomas (bar); Napier Civic Choir, Albert Rosen (cond).

Madama Butterfly (Puccini) Perkel Opera; *Cio Cio San* Sally Sloman/ Doreen Donnell (s); *Pinkerton* Cyril Kelleway/John Stanley (t); *Sharpless* Dennis Clarke/David Skinner (bar); *Suzuki* Corinne Bridge/Margot Lloyd (ms); Lynn Daniell (piano), Paul Person (dir) (North Island piano tour and Auckland season).

1982

Carmen (Bizet) Perkel Opera; *Carmen* Corinne Bridge/Margot Lloyd (ms); *Don Jose* Cyril Kelleway/John Stanley (t); *Escamillo* David Skinner/Derek Miller (bar); *Morales* Martin Thomas (bar)/Gregory Patel (t); *Zuniga* John Bates/Donald Trott (b); *Frasquita* Maureen Carney/Fay Hadon (s); *Mercedes* Shirley Kauter/Susan Hirst (ms); *El Dancairo* Martin Thomas/Dennis Clarke (bar); *El Remendado* Gregory Patel/Peter Frazer (t); *Lillas Pastia* John Gray/Earl Wood (b); with small orch, Paul Person (cond); Paul Person (dir) (North Island piano tour and Auckland season).

Il Barbiere di Siviglia (Rossini) TV One; *Rosina* Frances Green (s); *Count Almaviva* Frank Carter (t); *Figaro* Tim Hawley (bar); *Don Bartolo* Geoffrey de Latour (b); *Don Basilio* Grant Dickson (b); *Berta* Corinne Bridge (ms); *Fiorello* Roger Wilson (b); NZSO; Peter Coates (producer).

Symphony No. 9 in D Minor (Choral) (Beethoven) ACS; Wendy Dixon (s); Corinne Bridge (ms); Anthony Benfell (t); Grant Dickson (b); Auckland Regional Orchestra, Ray Wilson (cond).

1983

La Bohème (Puccini) Perkel Opera; *Mimi* Patricia House/Gillian Trott (s); *Rodolfo* Cyril Kelleway/John Stanley (t); *Marcello* Derek Millar/ David Skinner (bar); *Colline* Roger Knights (b); *Schaunard* Dennis Clarke (bar); *Musetta* Fay Haddon (s); *Alcindoro* Donald Trott/Earl Wood (b); Joy Crabtree/David Vine (piano); Corinne Bridge (dir) (North Island piano tour and Auckland season).

1985

La Cenerentola (Rossini): Perkel Opera; *Angelina (Cinderella)* Yuko Takahashi (c); *Clorinda* Sally Sloman (s); *Tisbe* Corinne Bridge/Linda Shearer (ms); *Don Ramiro (Prince)* Allan Marter (t); *Dandini* David Skinner (bar); *Don Magnifico* Eric Badcock (b); *Alidoro* Donald Trott (b); with orch in Auckland, cond. Michael McLellan and Wellington cond. Peter Walls; Lynne Daniell (piano on tour); Alma Woods (dir). (North Island piano tour and Auckland and Wellington seasons)

1986

Te Deum in C (Bruckner) ACS; Wendy Dixon (s); Corinne Bridge (ms); Anthony Benfell (t); Eric Badcock (b); APO, Ray Wilson (cond).

Eugene Onegin (Tchaikovsky) Perkel Opera; *Onegin* David Skinner (bar); *Tatiana* Gillian Trott/Patricia House (s); *Olga* Anne Van der Sluis (c); *Larina* Beverley Anderson (ms); *Filipyevna* Corinne Bridge (ms); *Lenski* John Stanley/Malcolm Campbell (t); *Prince Gremin* Donald Trott (b); *Captain Zaretski* Earl Wood (b); *Monsieur Triquet* Cyril Kelleway/ Marshall Watt (t); with orch, Mark Hodgkinson (md and cond) Auckland season; Joy Crabtree/Dianne Harvey (piano on tour); Paul Person (dir) (North Island piano tour and Auckland season).

1996

The Sound of Music (Rodgers and Hammerstein) Pan Pacific Productions – Wellington season; *Maria* Sarah Lineham; *Captain von Trapp* Ray Woolf; *Mother Abbess* Corinne Bridge; *Max* Lloyd Scott; *Elsa Schraeder* Vivienne Labone; *Sister Berte* Nan Sanders; *Sister Margaretta* Joanne Hodgson; *Sister Sophia* Lesley Graham; *Herr Zeller* Shaun McKean; *Franz* Peter Nelson; *Frau Schmidt* Joan Foster; *Liesl* Angela Gibbs/Erika Takacs; *Rolf* Jolyon Ludbrook; Wellington Sinfonia, Frank Dew (md); Pat Snoxell (dir); Bonita Edwards (choreographer).

Bibliography

Brusey, Phyllis, *Ring Down the Curtain*, C. Rex Monigatti Publishing, 1973.

Clarke, Dennis and Kelleway, Cyril, *A Troupe of Strolling Players*, Cyril Kelleway, 2004.

Jensen, Owen, *NZBC Symphony Orchestra*, A.H. and A.W. Reed, 1966.

Noffke, Elizabeth, *Ramon Opie QSM: Distinguished New Zealand tenor*, Polygraphia, 2011.

Simpson, Adrienne, *Hallelujahs and History: Auckland Choral 1855–2005*, Auckland Choral, 2005.

Simpson, Adrienne, *Opera's Farthest Frontier: A history of professional opera in New Zealand*, Reed, 1996.

Thomson, Alister, *The New Zealand Roll of Honour: 150 years 1845–1995*, Alister Thomson, 1998.

Tintner, Tanya Buchdahl, *Out of Time: The vexed life of Georg Tintner*, University of Western Australia Publishing, 2011.

Tonks, Joy, *The New Zealand Symphony Orchestra: The first forty years*, Exisle, 1996.

Index